Easy Freelance Graphics for Windows

Sue Plumley

Easy Freelance Graphics for Windows

Library of Congress Catalog No.: 94-65892

ISBN: 1-56529-768-7

96 95 94 6 5 4 3 2 1

Interpretation of the printing code: the rightmost double-digit number is the year of the book's printing; the rightmost single-digit number, the number of the book's printing. For example, a printing code of 94-1 shows that the first printing of the book occurred in 1994.

Screen reproductions in this book were created with Collage Plus from Inner Media, Inc., Hollis, NH.

Publisher: David P. Ewing

Associate Publisher: Corinne Walls

Publishing Director: Lisa A. Bucki

Managing Editor: Anne Owen

Product Marketing Manager: Greg Wiegand

Credits

Acquisitions Editors
Thomas F. Godfrey III
Nancy Stevenson

Product Directors
Lisa D. Wagner
Steven M. Schafer

Production Editors
Pamela Wampler
Heather Kaufman

Technical Editor
Robert L. Weberg

Book Designer
Amy Peppler-Adams

Cover Designer
Jay Corpus

Production Team
Angela D. Bannan
Claudia Bell
Anne Dickerson
Bob LaRoche
Jay Lesandrini
Beth Lewis
Andrea Marcum
Linda Quigley
Sandra Stevenson
Michael Thomas
Donna Winter
Robert Wolf
Lillian Yates

Indexer
Michael Hughes

Composed in *Stone Serif* and *MCPdigital* by Que Corporation

About the Author

Sue Plumley owns Humble Opinions, a consulting firm that offers training in popular software programs and system connectivity. In addition, Sue is the author of several Que books, including *Windows 3.1 SureSteps*, *Crystal Clear DOS*, and *Crystal Clear Word*. She is also a contributing author to *Using WordPerfect 6 for DOS*, *Using OS/2 2.1*, Special Edition, and *Using Microsoft Office*.

Acknowledgments

I would like to express my appreciation to the people at Que who made this book possible. They are a talented and dedicated group of professionals, as well as friendly and delightful. Thanks to Tom Godfrey and Nancy Stevenson in Acquisitions for their ongoing quest to "keep me busy"; keep up the good work. Thanks to Steve Schafer and Lisa Wagner for their expertise and guidance. I also want to thank Pamela Wampler and Heather Kaufman for their attention to detail and encouragement in the editing of this book. And thanks to the tech editor, Robert Weberg, for his suggestions and comments.

As always, I want to express my sincerest thanks to my husband Carlos and to my family—Geneva, Carlos, and Bessie—for their patience, support, and understanding.

Trademark Acknowledgments

Contents at a Glance

Contents

Part III: Formatting Styles 70

Part IV: Creating an Organization Chart 86

Part V: Creating a Table 98

Part VI: Creating a Chart 116

Part VII: Viewing and Editing the Presentation 138

Part VIII: Creating a Screen Show 154

Part IX: Sample Slides 170

Part X: Glossary 184

Index 194

Introduction

What You Can Do with Freelance Graphics

Freelance Graphics is an amazing presentation software program. Using Freelance, you can create a professional display of important information—including graphics, charts, and tables—that illustrates or highlights your company's product or service. Freelance provides many backgrounds, preformatted page layouts, and symbols and images that make it easy to quickly produce an attractive presentation. When you are ready to use the presentation, you can print it to a color printer. The printed presentation, complete with color illustrations, can enhance your verbal presentation. Additionally, you can display your presentation on-screen for clients and customers to view.

Specifically, you can use Freelance to perform these functions:

- *Choose from many background colors and designs.* Freelance includes over fifty background designs from which you can choose to enhance your presentation. Each background, or SmartMaster set, provides color, graphics, and an exciting design that provides a setting for your information. You can choose city skylines, forests, or mountains; or you can choose specific symbols. For example, you can use symbols to represent the medical community, Japan, or an oil refinery. Finally, you can choose nonspecific designs using colors, graphic lines, boxes, blocks, and so on.

- *Use various page layouts.* When producing a presentation, you may have many different kinds of information to present and you may need various page layouts to accommodate the data. Freelance supplies 11 page layouts fully equipped with matching styles of fonts, indents, graphics, and so on. You can choose from various page layouts, including a Title page; Bulleted List; 2-Column bullets; 1, 2, or 4 Charts to a page; Table; and so on.

- *Enter text with ease.* Freelance supplies easy-to-use "Click here..." text boxes that contain preformatted styles. When you click, a text box appears in which you type. After typing the text, you can easily edit, delete, or add to the text. Additionally, you can create your own text boxes in which you can enter and format text.

- *Add symbols from Freelance's symbol library.* Freelance includes over fifty symbol documents, each containing sometimes as many as fifty or sixty symbols. You can add such symbols as computers, state outlines, vehicles, people, food, and more. Symbols and images add pizzazz to a presentation.

- *Format type and paragraphs.* Freelance provides preformatted styles that look professional and attractive. However, you can change typefaces, type size, alignment, and other type attributes to enhance and personalize your presentation.

- *Check your spelling.* Freelance includes a spelling checker that reads your presentation and reports any misspelled words and words not found in the Lotus dictionary.

- *Create an organization chart.* You can quickly produce an organization chart in Freelance by choosing the Organization chart page layout and letting Freelance guide you step-by-step. Choose a style of chart from a Chart Gallery, and then add or delete entries, promote or demote entries, format the text, and even change chart types at any time.

- *Add a table to your presentation.* Using Freelance's easy step-by-step "Click here" technique, you choose a table style from the Table Gallery and then adjust the number of columns and rows to suit your data. You can adjust the text attributes, cell backgrounds and borders, and even resize columns and rows.

- *Create a chart to illustrate your data.* Freelance provides an extensive Chart Gallery from which you choose a chart type, including bar, stacked bar, line, pie, area, scatter, or three-dimensional chart types. You can enter the data directly into a worksheet provided by Freelance or import data from another application. After the data creation, you can modify the chart by changing the chart style, altering axis labels and legends, and adding titles and notes.

- *Change the look of the presentation.* After you complete the pages of your presentation, you can change the order in which the pages display, choose a different SmartMaster set for a background, change background colors, and more.

- *Write and print your speaker notes.* Freelance offers a handy feature called Speaker Notes. With this feature, you can create note cards with important information you need to remember during your presentation. When your notes are completed, print them for later use.

- *Print your presentation.* You can print your presentation to a black-and-white or a color printer to create impressive pages you can organize in a notebook, for example. Additionally, you can print to transparencies if you want to use your presentation on an overhead projector.

- *Create a screen show to display on your computer.* Freelance offers many effects for creating a screen show with your presentation. You can choose page order, transition effects, how long each page displays, and whether the show displays automatically or manually. An impressive screen show just may sell that service or product for you.

Task Sections

The Task sections include numbered steps that tell you how to accomplish certain tasks, such as saving a presentation, creating a chart, or checking the spelling of a presentation. The numbered steps walk you through a specific example so that you can learn the task by actually doing it.

Big Screen

At the beginning of each task is a large screen that shows how the computer screen will look after you complete the procedure that follows in that task. Sometimes the screen shot shows a feature discussed in that task, however, such as a shortcut menu.

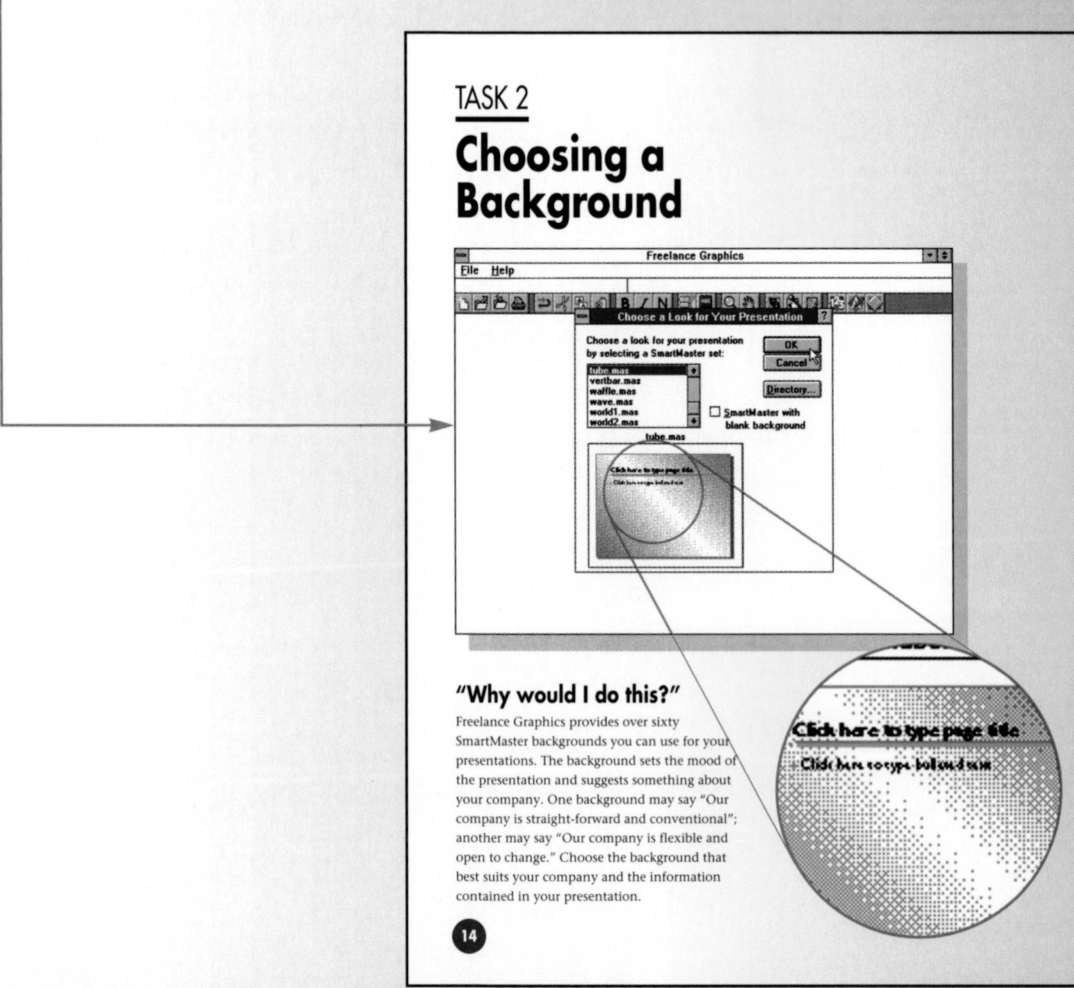

TASK 2

Choosing a Background

"Why would I do this?"

Freelance Graphics provides over sixty SmartMaster backgrounds you can use for your presentations. The background sets the mood of the presentation and suggests something about your company. One background may say "Our company is straight-forward and conventional"; another may say "Our company is flexible and open to change." Choose the background that best suits your company and the information contained in your presentation.

14

Step-by-Step Screens

Each task includes a screen shot for each step of a procedure. The screen shot shows how the computer screen looks at each step in the process.

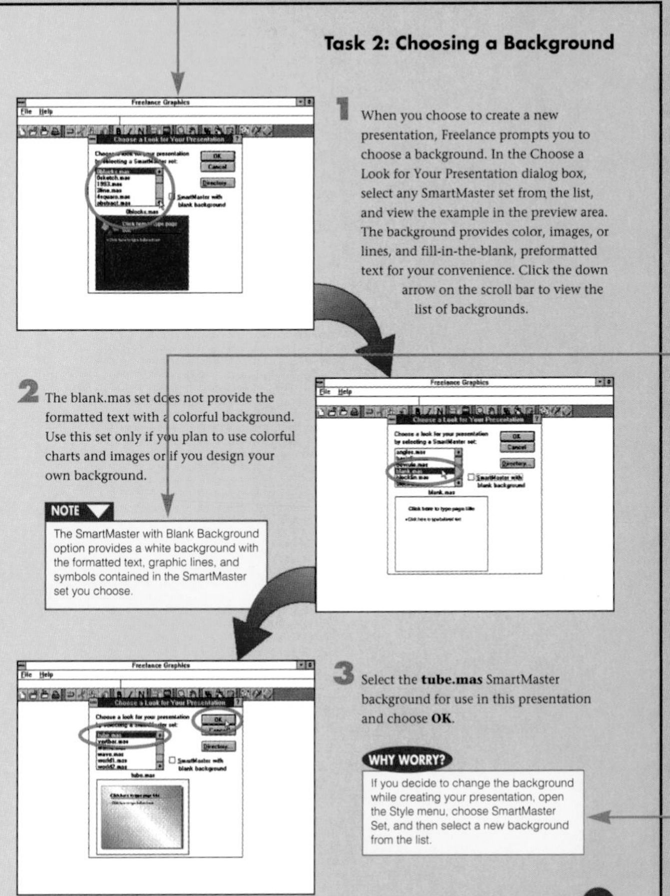

Task 2: Choosing a Background

1 When you choose to create a new presentation, Freelance prompts you to choose a background. In the Choose a Look for Your Presentation dialog box, select any SmartMaster set from the list, and view the example in the preview area. The background provides color, images, or lines, and fill-in-the-blank, preformatted text for your convenience. Click the down arrow on the scroll bar to view the list of backgrounds.

2 The blank.mas set does not provide the formatted text with a colorful background. Use this set only if you plan to use colorful charts and images or if you design your own background.

NOTE

The SmartMaster with Blank Background option provides a white background with the formatted text, graphic lines, and symbols contained in the SmartMaster set you choose.

3 Select the **tube.mas** SmartMaster background for use in this presentation and choose **OK**.

WHY WORRY?

If you decide to change the background while creating your presentation, open the Style menu, choose SmartMaster Set, and then select a new background from the list.

15

Notes

Many tasks include other short notes that tell you a little more about certain procedures. These notes define terms, explain other options, refer you to other sections when applicable, and so on.

Why Worry? Notes

You may find that you performed a task, such as changing a font, that you didn't want to do after all. The Why Worry? notes tell you how to undo certain procedures or get out of a situation, such as displaying a Help screen or offering a method of performing a task not covered.

Freelance Graphics - [Untitled1]
File Edit View Page Style Text Chart Arrange Tools Window Help
No Selection
Page 1
Choose Page Layout
Choose a layout for the current page:
OK
Cancel
Tips...
Title
Bulleted List
2-Column Bullets
1 Chart
2 Charts
4 Charts
Bullets & Chart
Bullets & Symbol
Organization Chart
Table
Basic Layout
[None]
Choose a Look for Your Presentation
Choose a look for your presentation by selecting a SmartMaster set:
tube.mas
vertbar.mas
waffle.mas
wave.mas
world1.mas
world2.mas
Directory...
SmartMaster with blank background
"Click here..." Text Block
Ready
Tips...
Humble Op
Click here to type subtitle
Click here to add symbol
Page Layout...
Add Symbol to Page
1. Choose a symbol category:
shapes.sym
animals.sym
arrows.sym
asia.sym
asiamap.sym
2. Choose a symbol (1 of 24: scroll for more)
New Page...

PART I

Quick Start

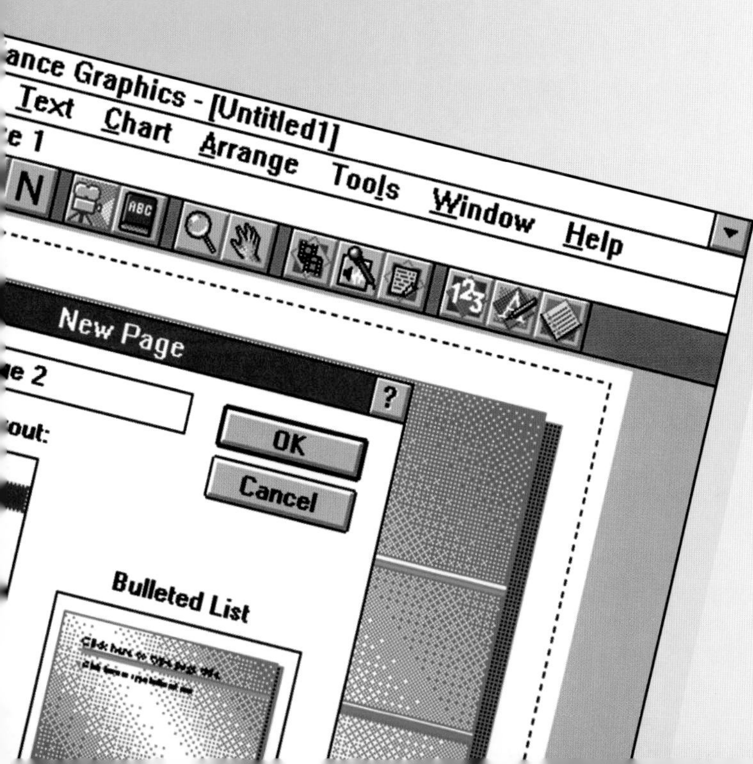

Freelance Graphics enables you to create presentations quickly and easily by supplying page layouts, backgrounds, and fill-in-the-blank steps for creating titles, bulleted lists, tables, and a variety of charts. With Freelance, you can produce professional-looking presentations that display on-screen or print in color or black and white.

When you start Freelance, the program displays dialog boxes that offer choices for creating and modifying presentations. All you have to do is answer the questions. Suppose you want to start a new presentation. Indicate the choice in the first dialog box, and Freelance displays a list of various backgrounds, or SmartMaster Sets, you can use for your presentation.

SmartMaster sets are color backgrounds, including a city skyline, mountains, the globe, continents, and miscellaneous line and geometric designs. Additionally, you can choose to use a blank background so you can design your presentation's look. You can scroll through the list of backgrounds and preview each one before making your choice. When you find a background that suits your presentation topic, select it and choose OK to continue. If you change your mind about the background later, you can easily select another.

The next step is to select a page layout. In the Choose Page Layout dialog box, you choose the *layout*, or page design, that best fits the information you plan to use. You can select any of eleven layouts, including charts, tables, bulleted lists, and so on. Suppose, for example, you want the first page of the presentation to display the company's name and logo. Use the Title page layout. Each page layout includes text that is already formatted with different type sizes, bold or italic attributes, bullets, and more. Additionally, each page layout is applied to the SmartMaster background you selected.

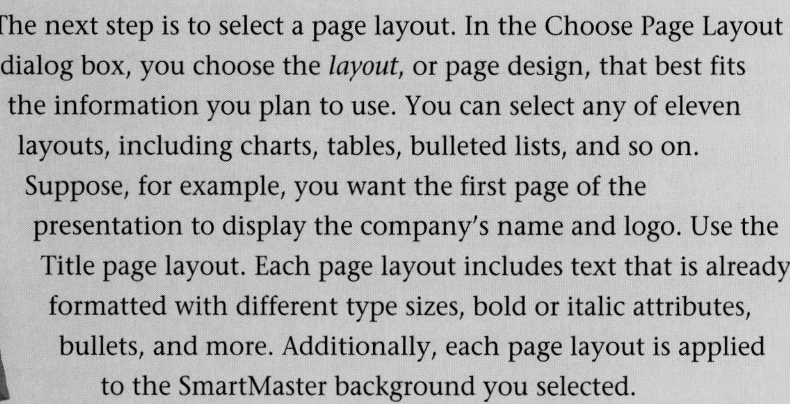

Next, you enter the text for your presentation. To help you, Freelance supplies instructions on each page. The title page, for instance, displays text, formatted in a large font for the title, that states "Click here to type presentation title." When you place the mouse pointer on the text and click the mouse button, a text box appears and you enter the text for the title. Choose OK, and the text is formatted in a font and size that suit the page design.

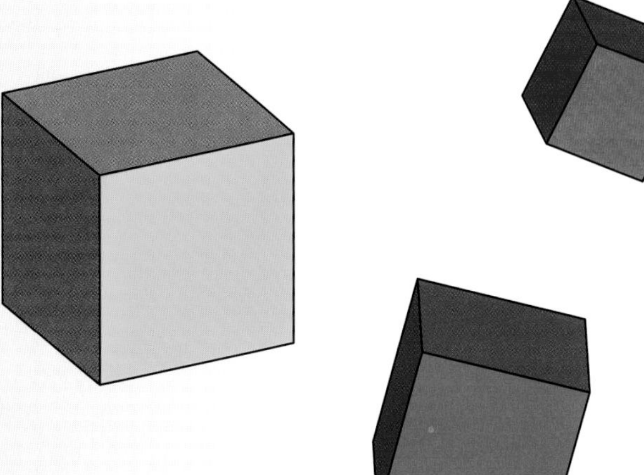

With these few steps, you can create an eye-catching, knock-out presentation in very little time. Of course, you can do much, much more with the program—including formatting your own pages, changing type size, adding images and symbols, and so on. These options are discussed throughout this book.

This part of the book shows you how to quickly create a presentation using Freelance's ready-made backgrounds, page designs, and fill-in-the-blank defaults.

TASK 1

Starting Freelance Graphics

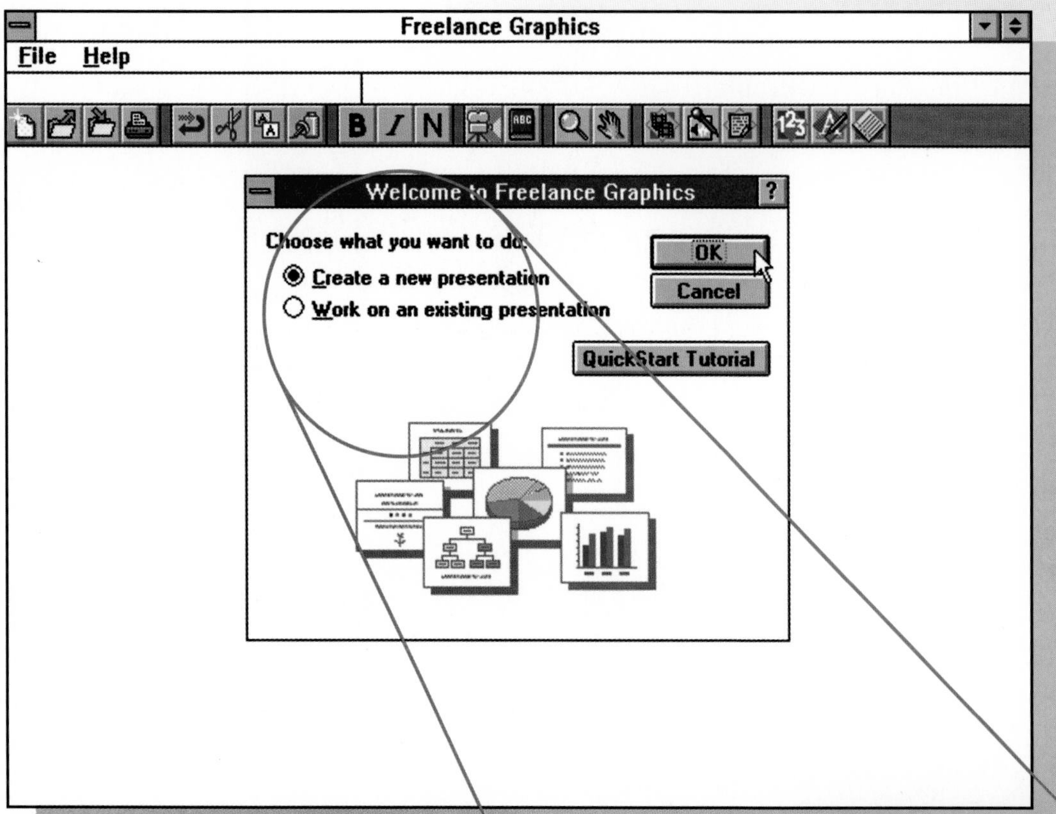

"Why would I do this?"

To use Freelance Graphics' powerful, step-by-step features, you must first start the program. When the program starts, you can choose to either start a new presentation or work on (open) an existing presentation. Your other choices include viewing a brief tutorial or getting specific help for various procedures.

The following task shows you how to start a new presentation.

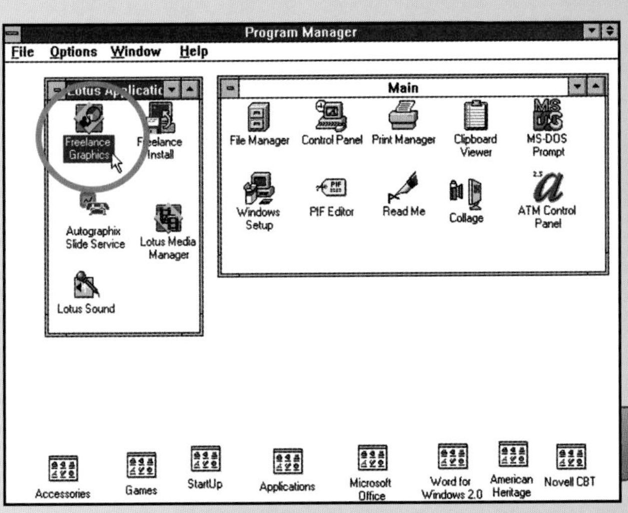

1 Point to the **Freelance Graphics** icon in the Program Manager of Windows and double-click. This step opens the Freelance program. As the program opens, the registration information screen appears briefly.

2 The Welcome to Freelance Graphics dialog box appears. Choose **Create a New Presentation**. After you have created and saved a presentation in Freelance, you can choose **Work On an Existing Presentation** to open the saved presentation file. Choose **OK**.

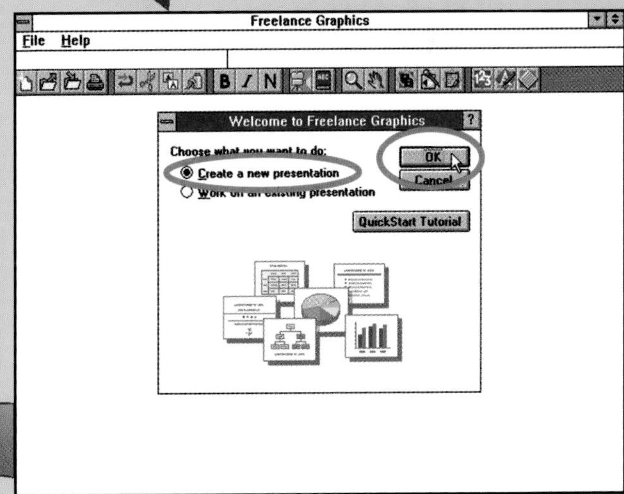

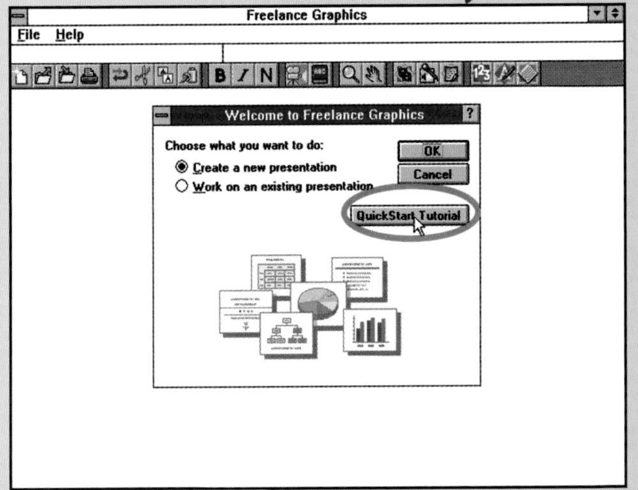

3 Or, you can choose to take the QuickStart Tutorial, which provides several activities and a quick tour of the program. Select the **QuickStart Tutorial** command button in the Welcome to Freelance Graphics dialog box. Follow the directions on-screen. When you quit the QuickStart program, Freelance returns you to the Welcome screen; you can then choose to create a new presentation.

TASK 2

Choosing a Background

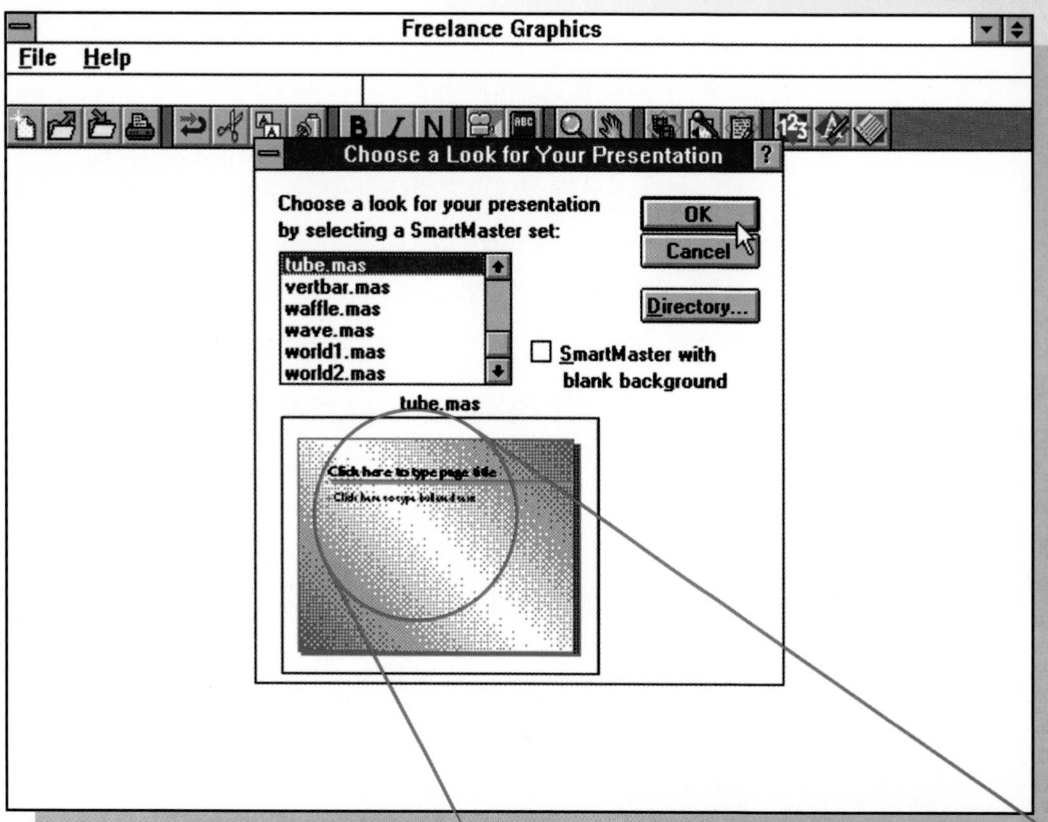

"Why would I do this?"

Freelance Graphics provides over sixty SmartMaster backgrounds you can use for your presentations. The background sets the mood of the presentation and suggests something about your company. One background may say "Our company is straight-forward and conventional"; another may say "Our company is flexible and open to change." Choose the background that best suits your company and the information contained in your presentation.

Task 2: Choosing a Background

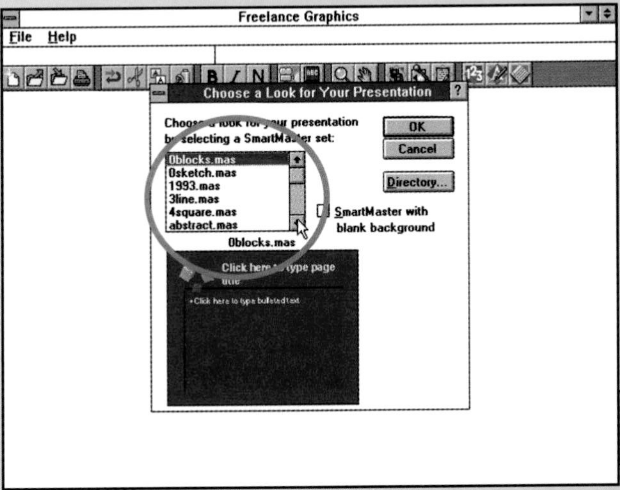

1 When you choose to create a new presentation, Freelance prompts you to choose a background. In the Choose a Look for Your Presentation dialog box, select any SmartMaster set from the list, and view the example in the preview area. The background provides color, images, or lines, and fill-in-the-blank, preformatted text for your convenience. Click the down arrow on the scroll bar to view the list of backgrounds.

2 The blank.mas set does not provide the formatted text with a colorful background. Use this set only if you plan to use colorful charts and images or if you design your own background.

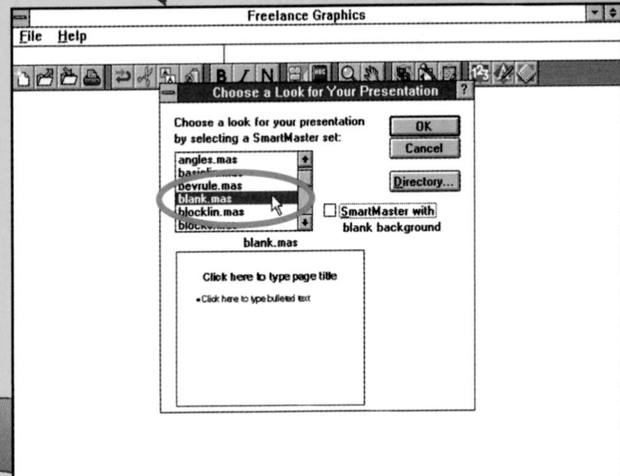

NOTE

The SmartMaster with Blank Background option provides a white background with the formatted text, graphic lines, and symbols contained in the SmartMaster set you choose.

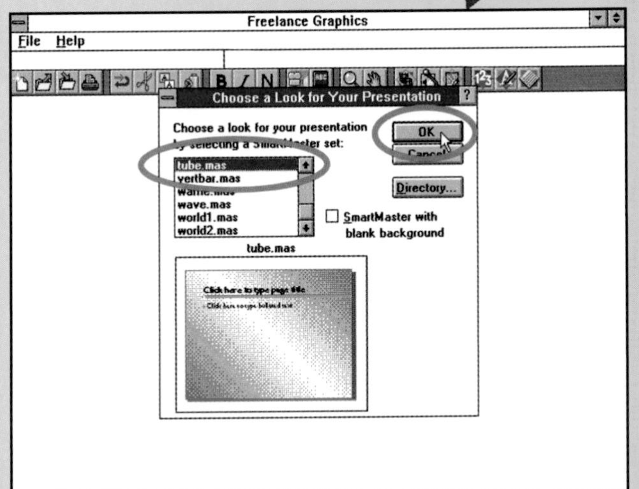

3 Select the **tube.mas** SmartMaster background for use in this presentation and choose **OK**.

WHY WORRY?

If you decide to change the background while creating your presentation, open the Style menu, choose SmartMaster Set, and then select a new background from the list.

TASK 3

Choosing a Page Layout

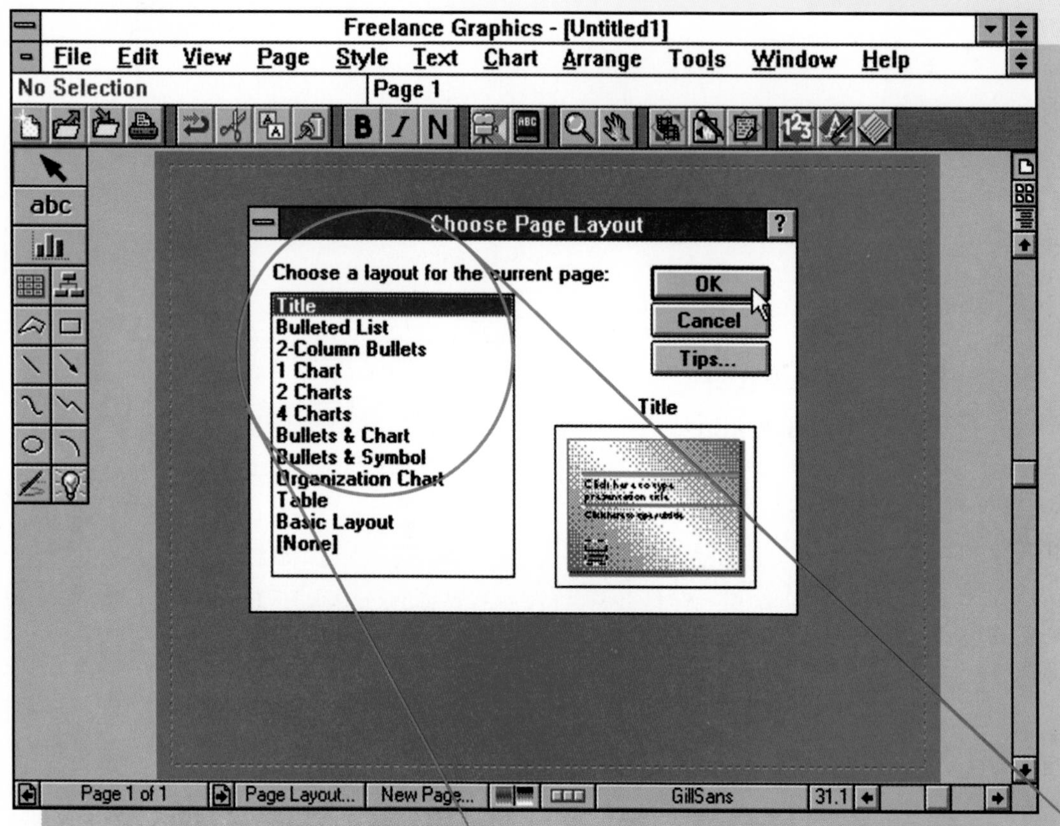

"Why would I do this?"

Choose the page layout you want to use for the first page of your presentation. Most presentations begin with a title page in which you display the company name and logo, the title of the presentation, or other pertinent information.

You can use different page layouts for pages two, three, and so on, or you can repeat page layouts if you want.

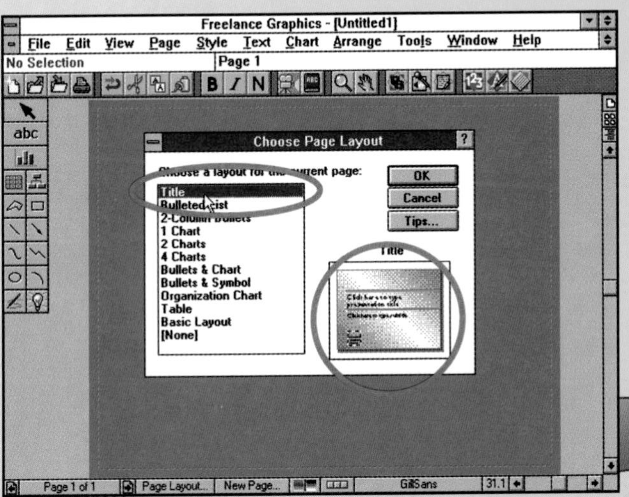

1 Now that you have chosen a background for the presentation, Freelance prompts you to choose a page layout. Select the **Title** page layout from the list. Freelance displays the page design in the preview box with the SmartMaster background you chose.

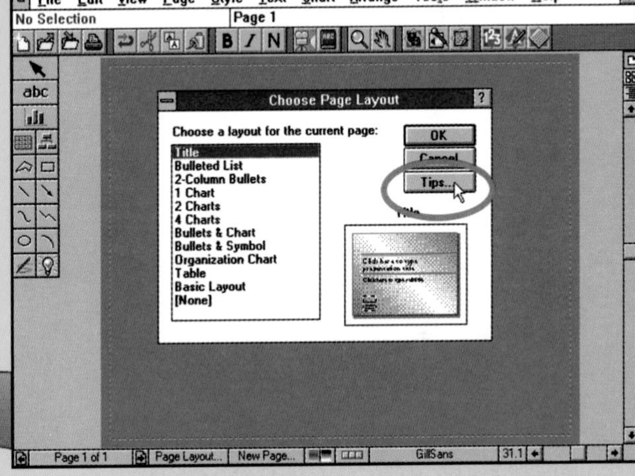

2 Choose the **Tips** command button. Helpful information about the dialog box appears on-screen. After reading the Tip, choose **OK** to close the dialog box and return to the Choose a Page Layout dialog box.

NOTE

Many dialog boxes in Freelance contain a Tips command button you can choose at any time for help.

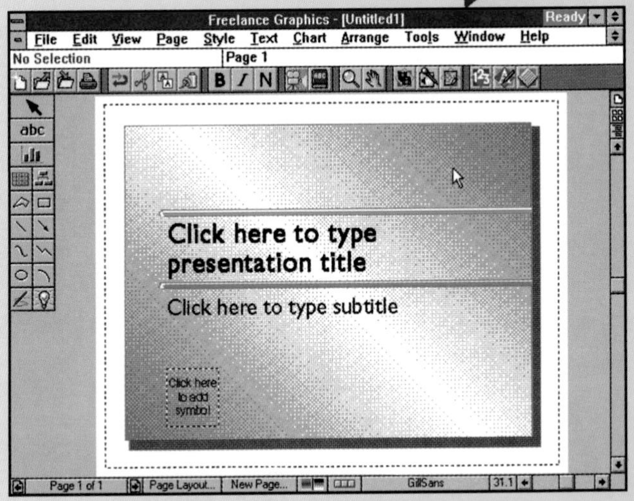

3 Choose **OK** to accept the page layout. Freelance displays the Freelance screen with the first page, the title page, of your presentation.

NOTE

You can use the mouse pointer to select various screen elements, such as menus, tools, and areas on the page.

TASK 4

Entering Text

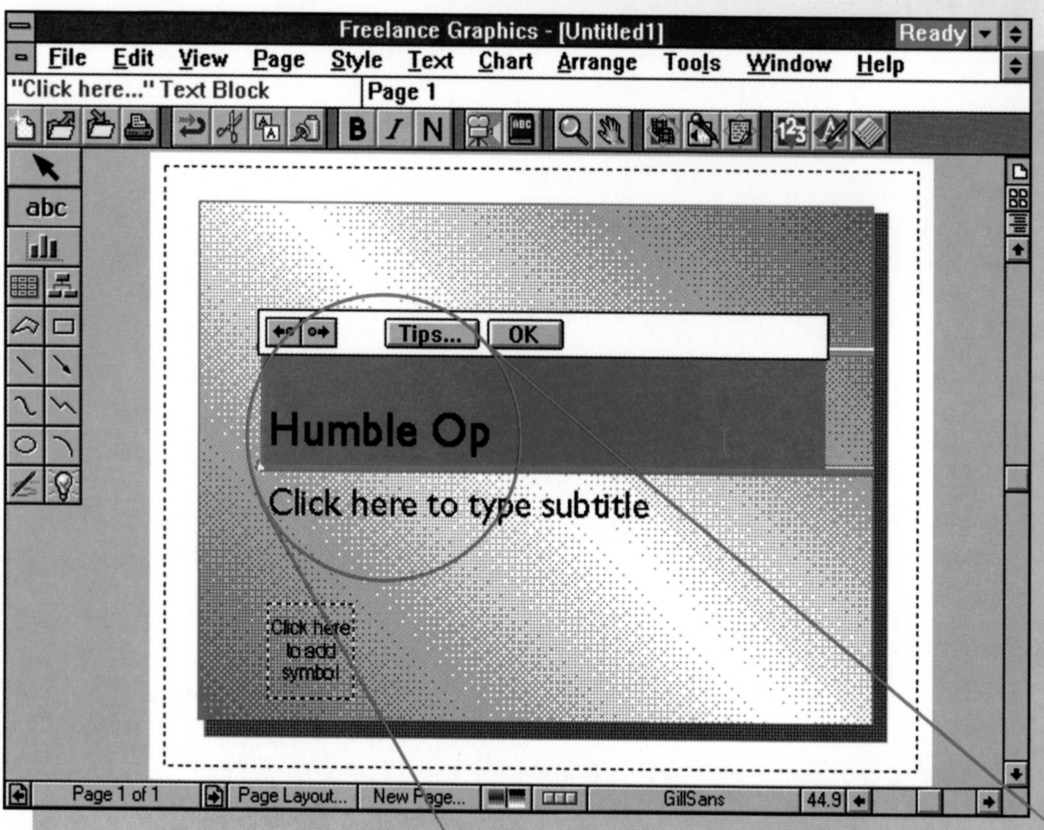

"Why would I do this?"

Freelance Graphics supplies text boxes in which instructions—"Click here to type presentation title," for example—help you enter text. The format—font, type size, alignment, and so on—of the instruction text is applied to any text you enter in that text box. A SmartMaster set contains similar text formatting throughout the page layout designs to create consistency in your presentation.

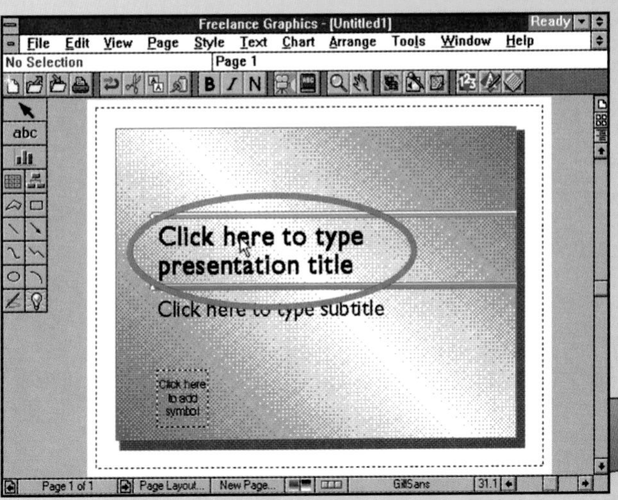

1 Click the first set of instruction text, **Click here to type presentation title**. The text changes to a text block in which you can enter your own text, and the mouse pointer changes to an I-beam, indicating you can click anywhere in the box to reposition the text cursor.

2 Enter the text **Humble Opinions Corporation**. Choose **OK**. Freelance inserts the text on the page.

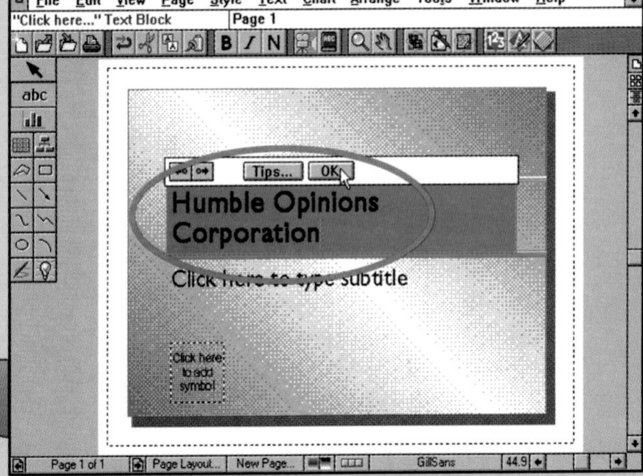

WHY WORRY?

The text box enlarges to accommodate the text you enter, so if you have more than one or two lines of text, simply continue to type. Freelance uses automatic word wrap to break lines. If you need to start a new line of text, press Enter.

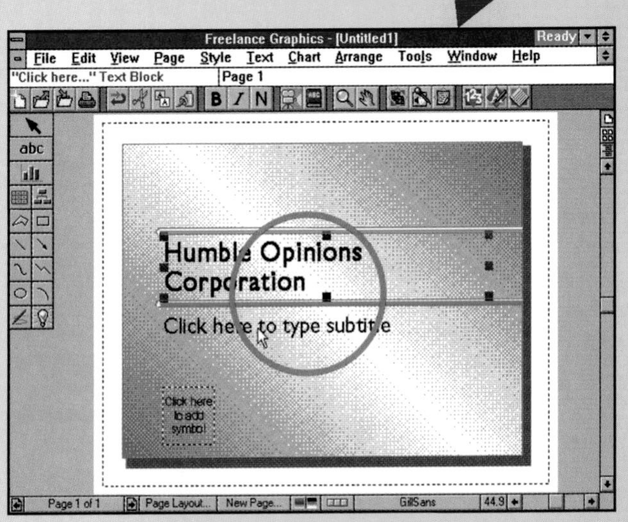

3 Click the text **Click here to type subtitle**, and enter **Software Training and Consulting**. Choose **OK**. Small square boxes, or *handles*, appear around the text block. Click anywhere outside of the text block to hide the handles.

WHY WORRY?

If you do not enter text in a text box, the instruction text does not print or show on-screen during a presentation, so you do not need to delete the text boxes.

TASK 5

Adding a Symbol

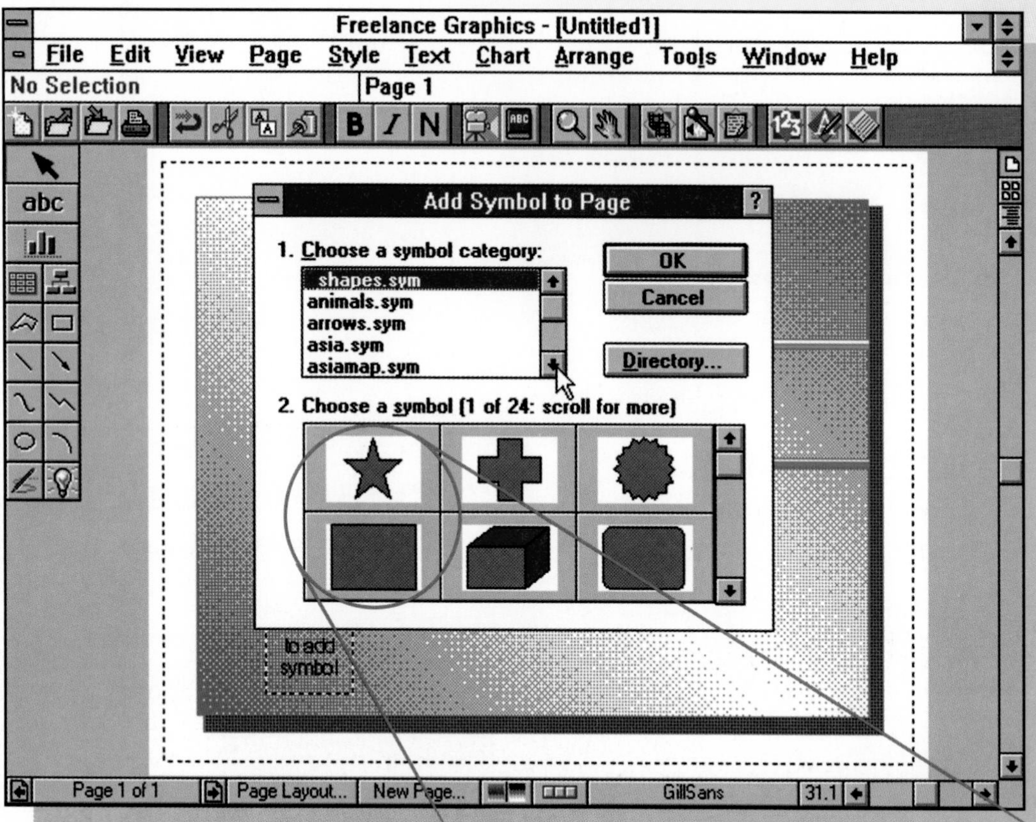

"Why would I do this?"

You can add symbols—stars, arrows, pointing hands, hearts, check marks, and so on—as well as images—boats, animals, people, maps, and so on—to any page in your presentation. Symbols and images emphasize important points, illustrate items, and enhance the design of the page.

Several page layouts, such as the Title page layout, present an option for inserting a symbol.

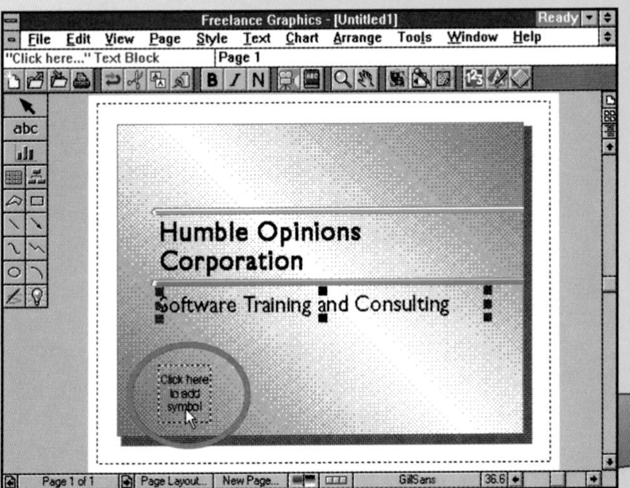

1 Click the text **Click here to add symbol**. The Add Symbol to Page dialog box appears. Choose a symbol category, such as stars, shapes, animals, and so on, in the first list box. Samples of the category appear in the bottom list box.

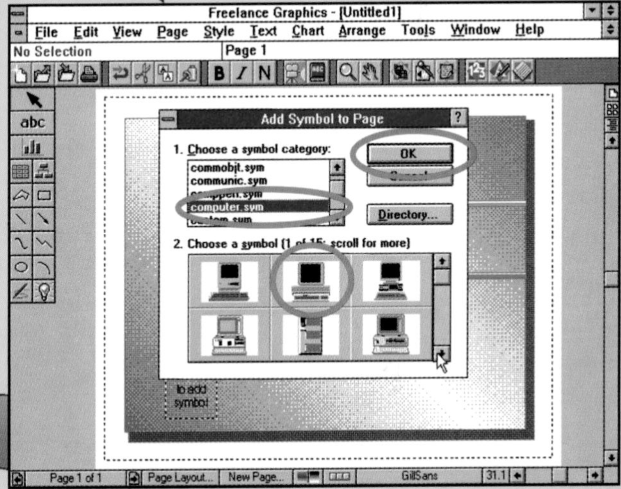

2 Choose **computer.sym** in the symbol category list by clicking the down arrow of the category scroll bar. Scroll to the last set of computers in the bottom list box, and choose the middle computer on the top row. Choose **OK** to accept the selected image.

3 Freelance closes the dialog box and displays your computer image in the title page. Drag a handle to resize the symbol.

WHY WORRY?

If you can't find a symbol or image you want to use in the Add Symbol to Page dialog box, choose the Directory button. In the Directory dialog box, choose another drive and directory to use other program files.

TASK 6

Adding a New Page

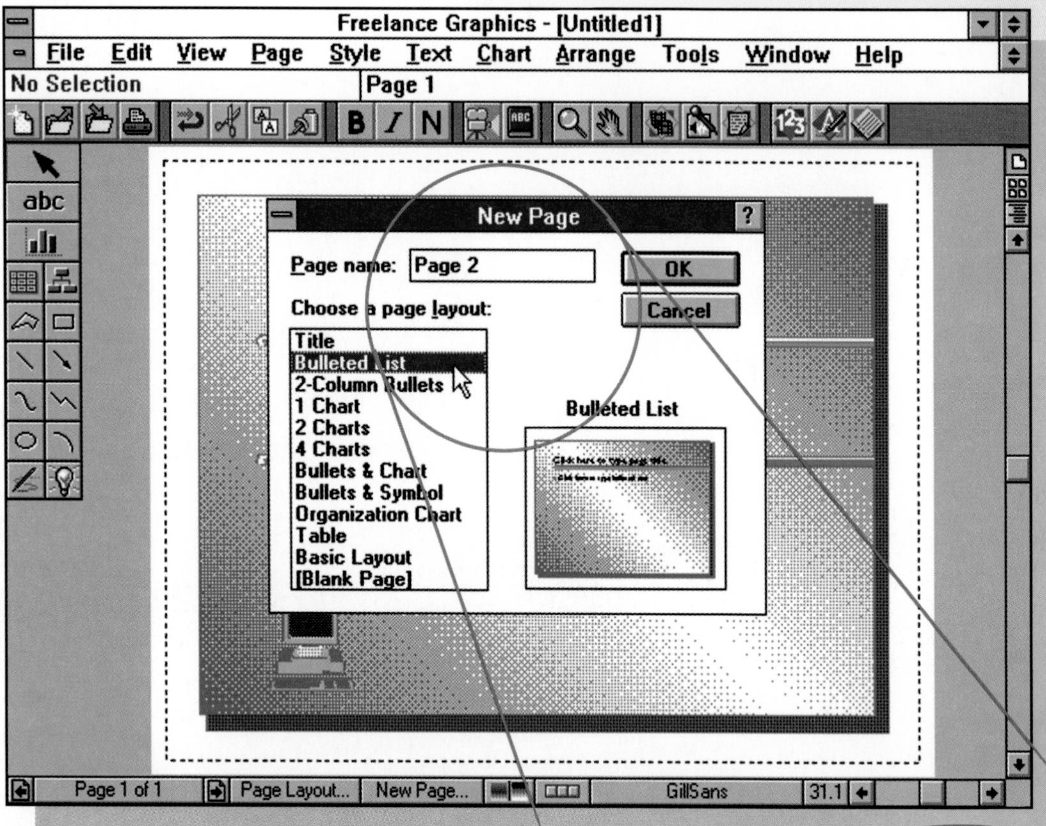

"Why would I do this?"

The first page of a presentation is usually a title page that introduces the subject of the presentation or the company. The next pages usually contain data and information in the form of lists, tables, charts, and so on. You can add pages in Freelance to continue the presentation.

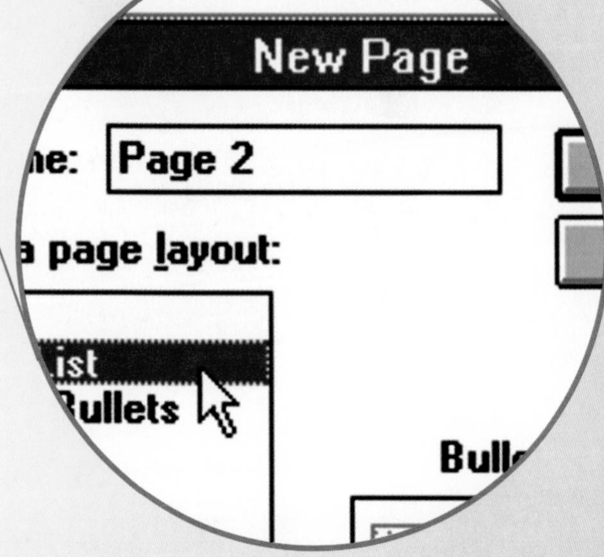

Task 6: Adding a New Page

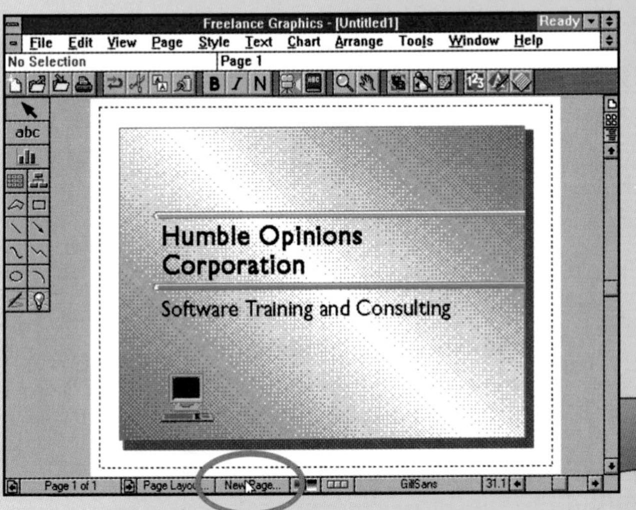

1 Place the mouse pointer on the **New Page** button that appears in the status bar at the bottom of the Freelance screen. Click the button to display the New Page dialog box.

2 In the New Page dialog box, choose **Bulleted List** as the page layout for page 2. An example of the page design appears in the preview box. Choose **OK** to add the second page.

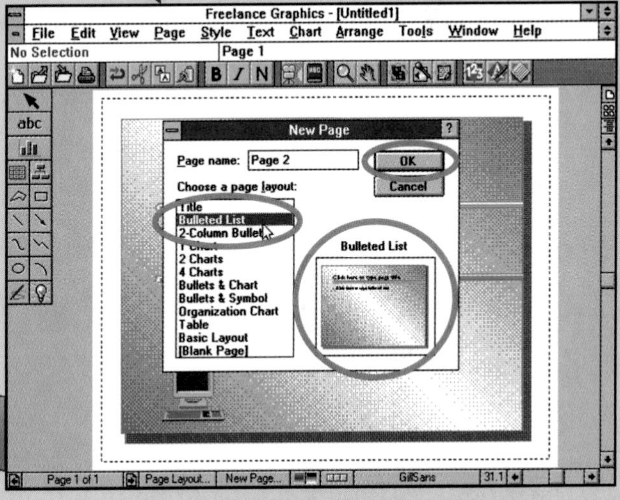

3 Freelance inserts the second page after page one. Page two contains similar instruction text as page one contained.

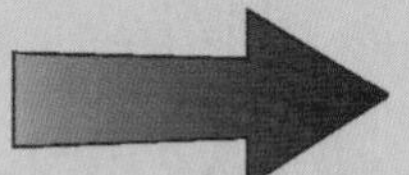

Task 6: Adding a New Page

4 Click the instruction text **Click here to type page title** to display the text box. Enter the text **We offer training in most popular software programs....** Choose **OK**.

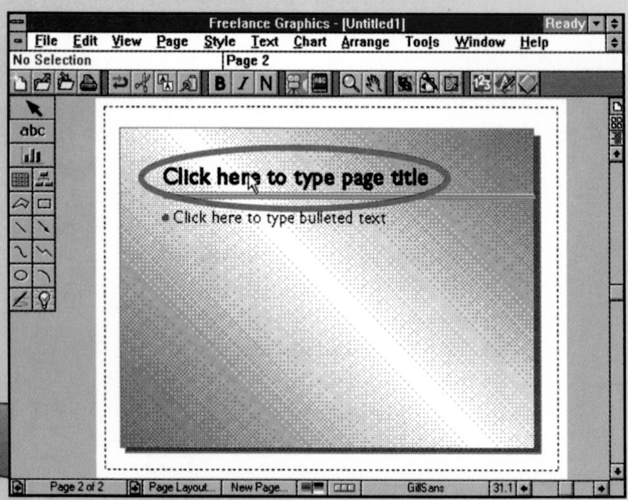

NOTE

The status bar displays which page is showing. If you want to move to the previous page, click the left arrow in the left corner of the status bar. To move to the next page, click the right arrow.

5 Click the text **Click here to type bulleted text** to display the text box. Enter the text **Freelance Graphics 2** to create the first bullet.

6 Press **Enter** to start a new line preceded by a bullet. Enter the following text, pressing **Enter** after each program name: **Ami Pro 3.0**, **Lotus 1-2-3 Rel. 4**, **SmartSuite 2.1**, **Organizer 1.1**.

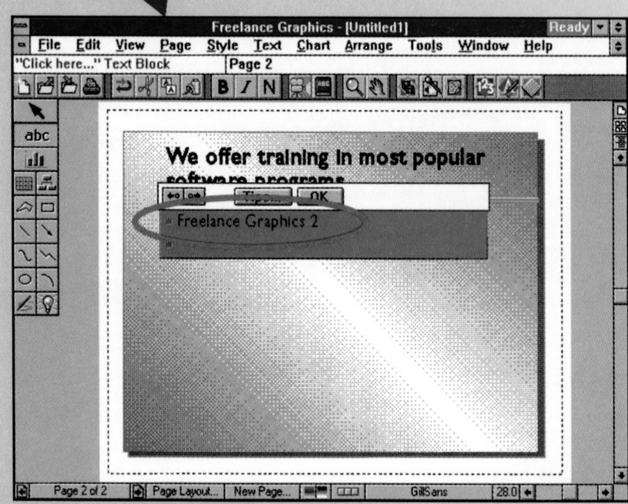

NOTE

If you want to add a line of text that is not preceded by a bullet, press Ctrl+Enter to start the line.

TASK 7

Saving a Presentation

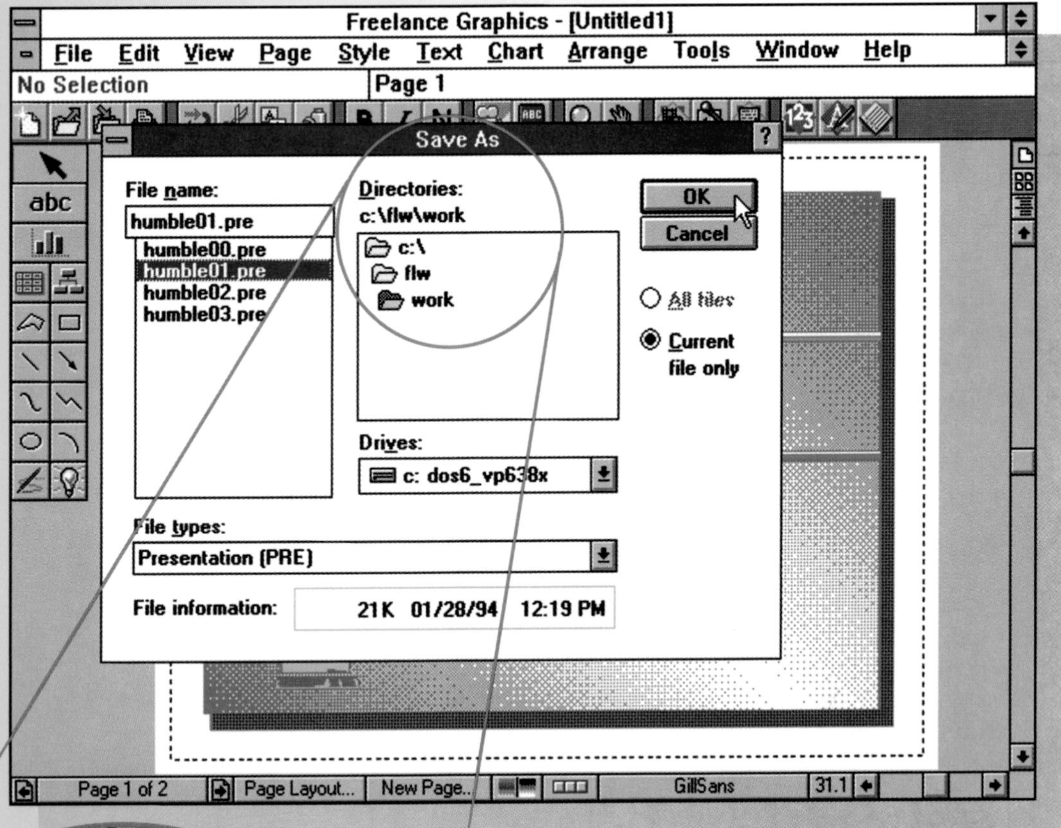

"Why would I do this?"

Save your presentations early and often to prevent loss of your work. If, for example, your computer experienced a power failure now, you would lose the two pages of this presentation. To be safe and to preserve your hard work, save often.

Task 7: Saving a Presentation

1 Open the **File** menu and choose **Save As** to save a file by assigning a name and a location. The Save As dialog box appears.

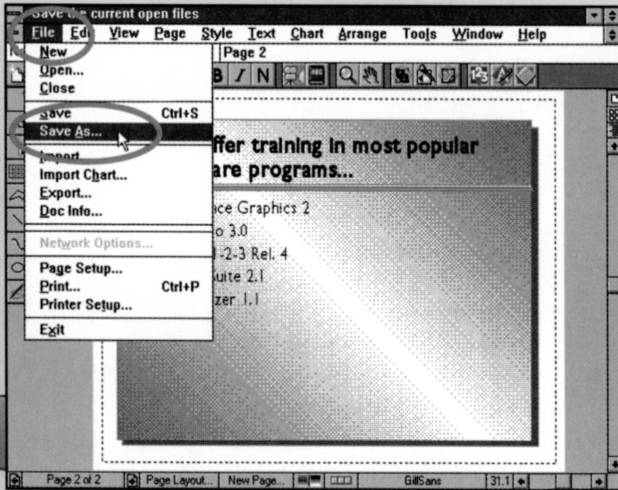

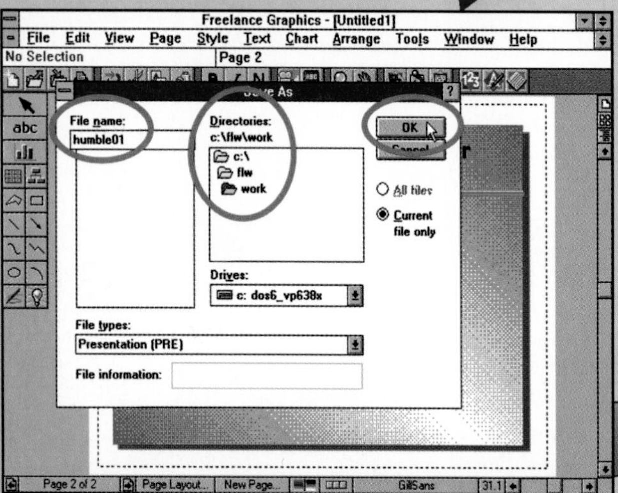

2 Enter **humble01** in the **File Name** text box to name the file. Freelance will automatically add the PRE extension to save the file in Presentation format so that you can open it in Freelance at any time. Additionally, Freelance automatically uses the c:\flw\work directory as the location for saving your presentation files. Choose **OK** to save the file.

3 Freelance returns to the presentation screen and displays the name of the document in the title bar.

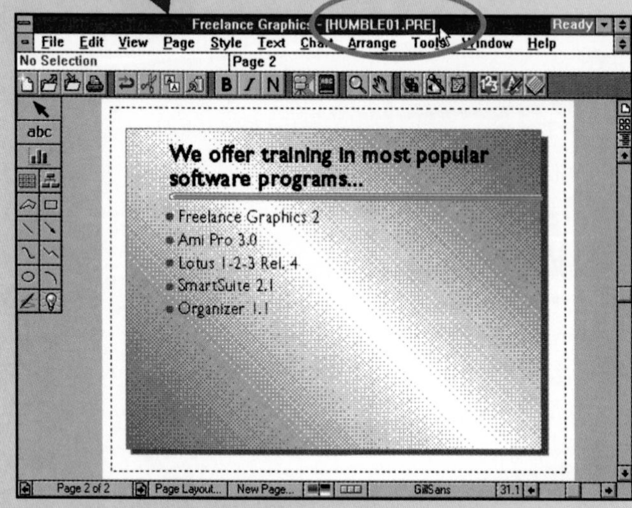

WHY WORRY?

After you have saved a file by naming it, you can quickly save edits and additions by choosing File Save; or, press the keyboard shortcut Ctrl+S to quickly save the file.

TASK 8

Printing a Presentation

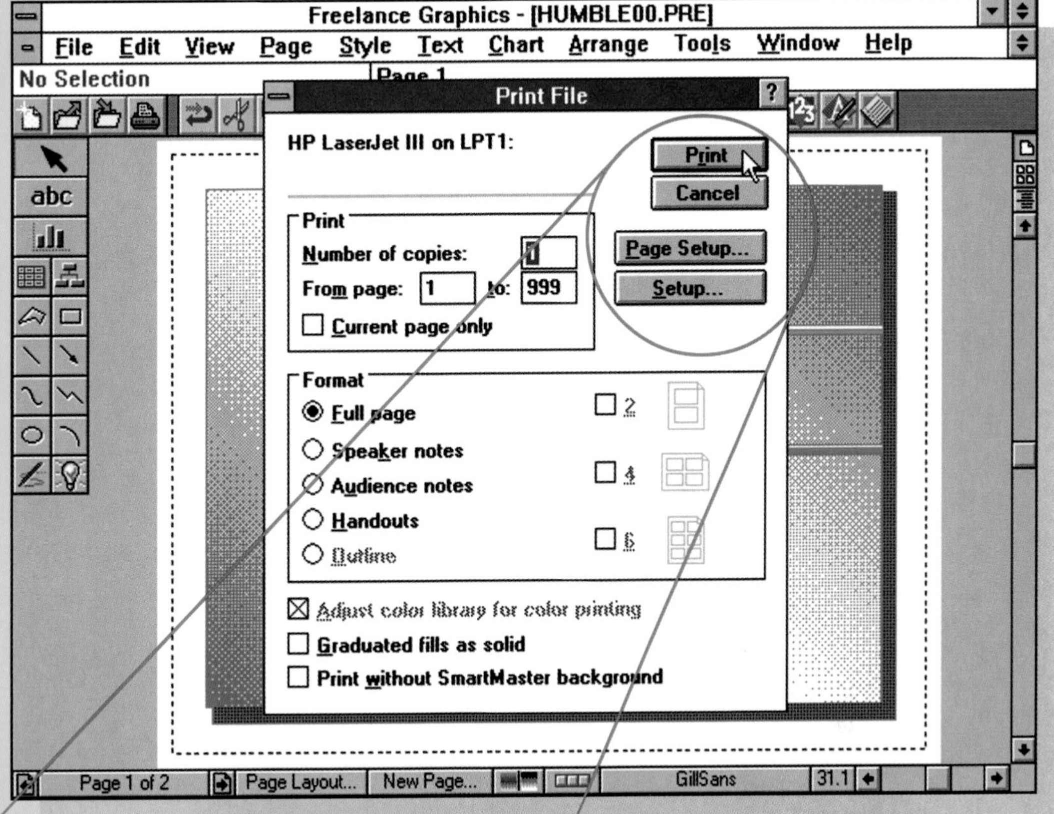

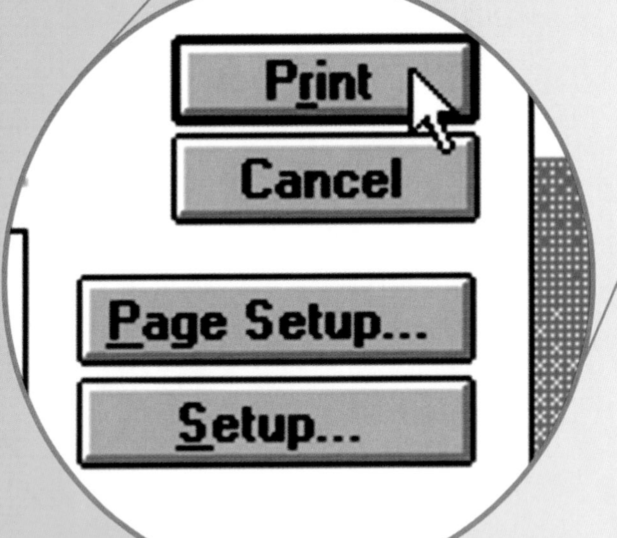

"Why would I do this?"

You may want to print your presentation for a variety of reasons. First, you can use the printed pages for proofreading and checking data. Second, you can print your presentation for use in a notebook presentation. Finally, you may want to print your presentation to transparencies.

You can print your presentation to a black-and-white printer or a color one. Naturally, presentations printed in color will be more impressive.

Task 8: Printing a Presentation

1 Open the **File** menu and choose **Print**, or press **Ctrl+P**. The Print File dialog box appears. Make sure your printer is plugged in, turned on, and has paper in it.

Freelance uses the printer specified in your Windows program.

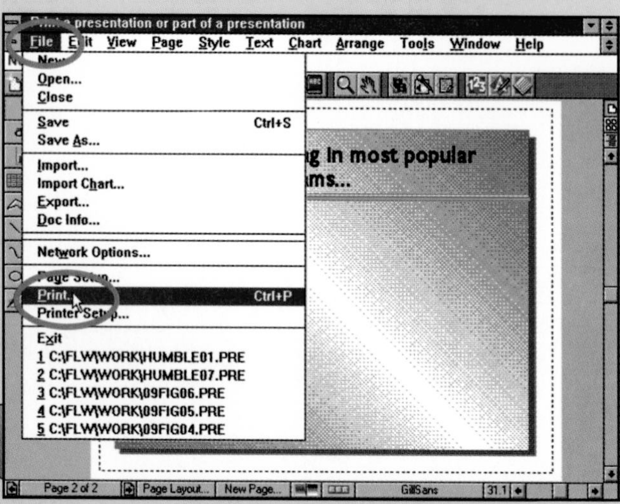

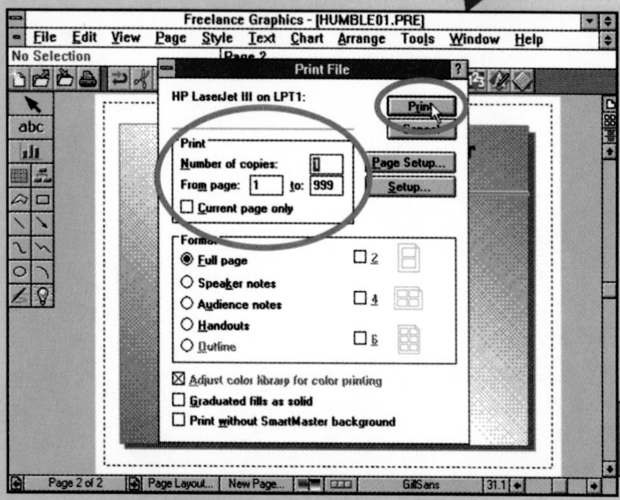

2 Enter the **Number of Copies** you want to print; one copy is the default. Specify the pages you want to print. By default, Freelance prints all the pages. You can choose to print the current page only, or you can print particular pages. To print specific pages, enter the first page number in the **From Page** text box and the second page number in the **To Page** text box.

3 Choose **Print**. The Printing Status dialog box appears. You can choose **Cancel** to stop the Print command.

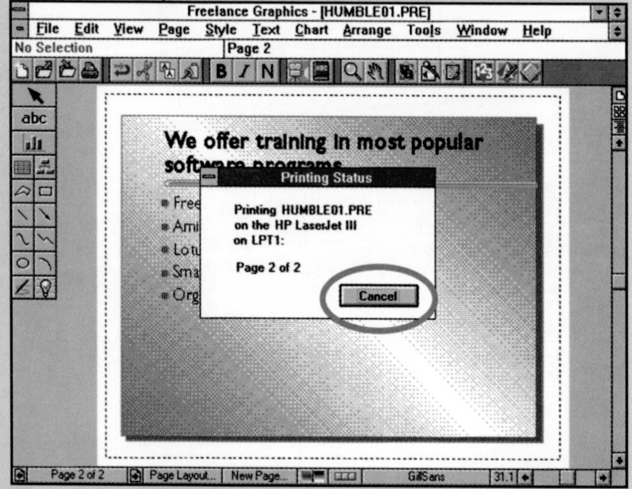

TASK 9

Closing a File

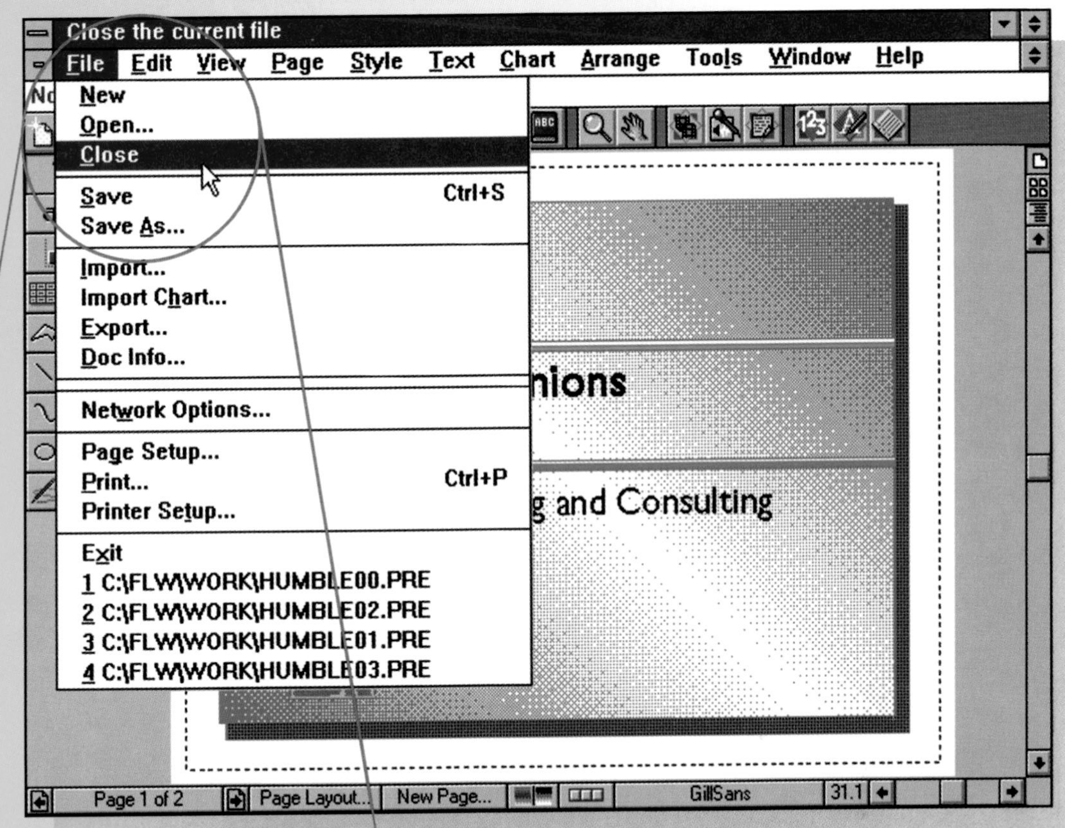

"Why would I do this?"

After you finish a presentation, you can close it to get it out of the way, and then work on another presentation if you want. Closing a completed presentation serves two purposes: it keeps you from accidentally altering the open file, and it conserves computer memory for other presentations and open Windows programs.

Task 9: Closing a File

1 To close a file, open the **File** menu and choose **Close**. Freelance closes the file if you have recently saved your presentation file.

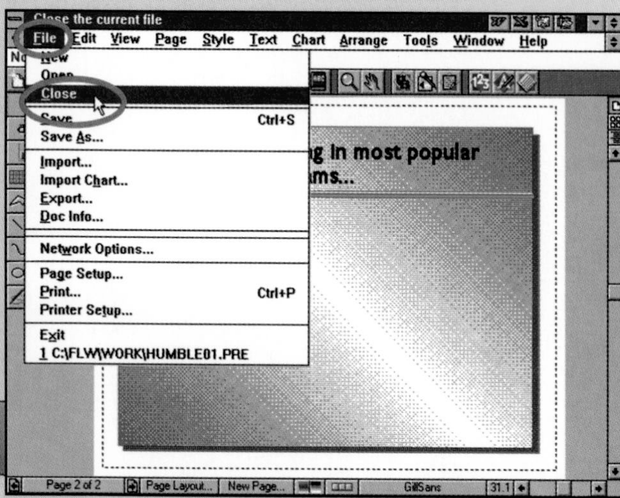

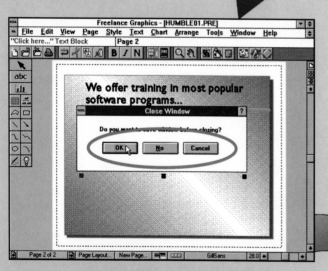

2 If you have not saved the file, Freelance displays the Close Window dialog box. Choose **OK** to save the presentation; choose **No** to abandon the recent changes; or choose **Cancel** to return to the presentation.

NOTE

If you choose to save a presentation that has not been named and assigned a location on disk, Freelance displays the Save As dialog box.

3 Freelance displays the screen with only the toolbar and two menus: File and Help. You now have three choices. You can start a new file, open an existing file, or exit the program.

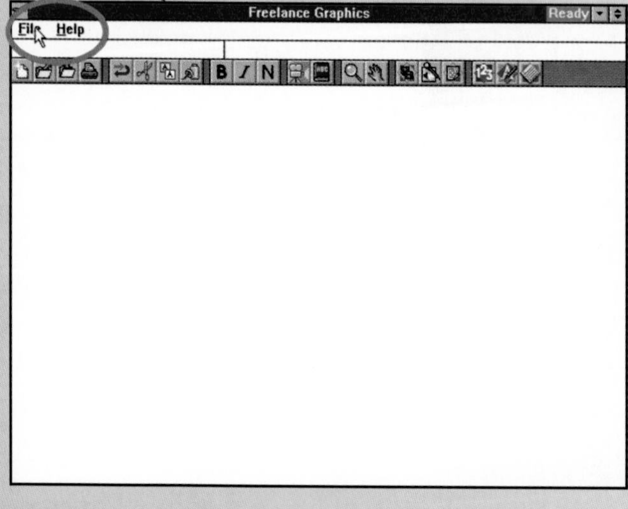

TASK 10

Starting a New File

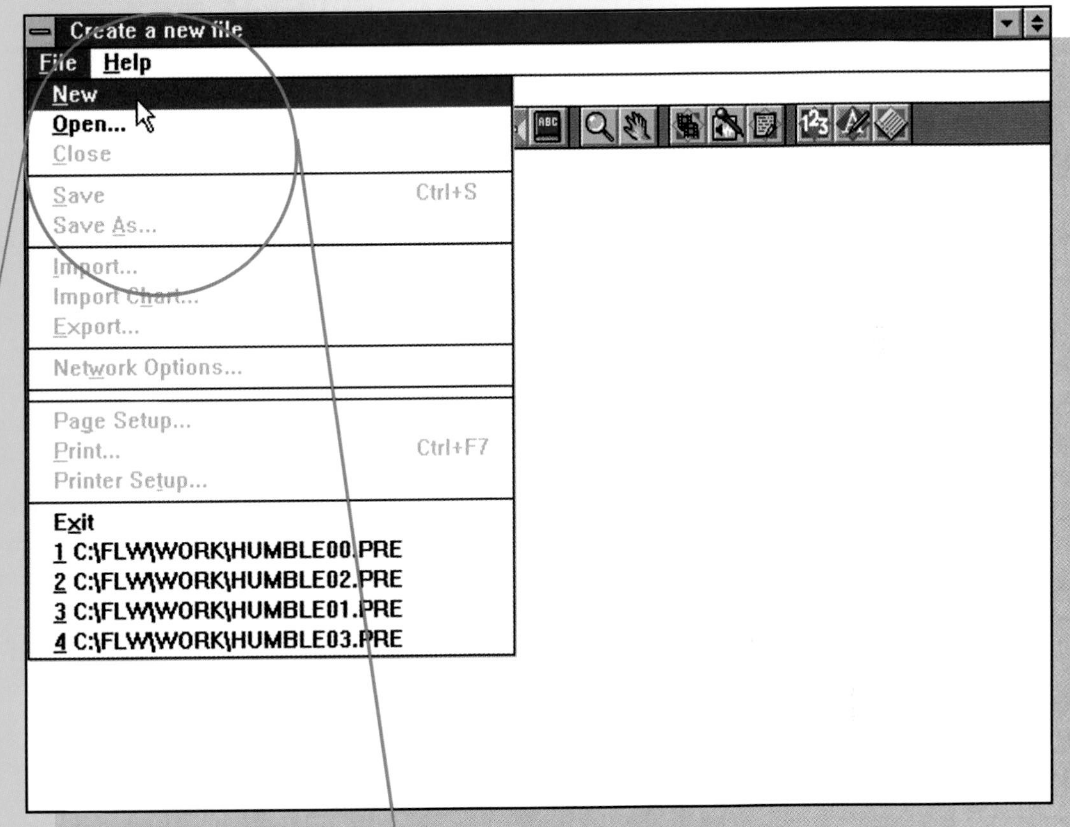

"Why would I do this?"

Before you can begin working on a new presentation, you must start a new file. You can start a new file by starting the Freelance program; the program displays the Welcome to Freelance Graphics dialog box. You then choose to create a new presentation. But what if you want to create a new presentation after closing the one you just finished? Freelance provides a command for this purpose.

Task 10: Starting a New File

1 Open the **File** menu and choose **New** to start a new presentation file.

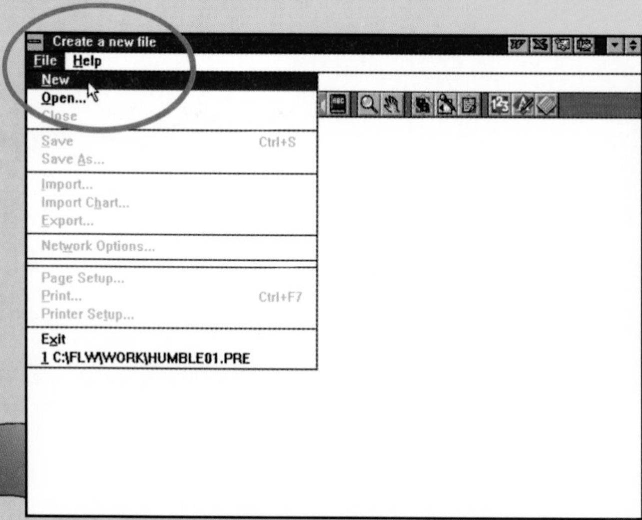

NOTE

You can choose the New command any time you are in Freelance: while you are working on a presentation, before saving the current presentation, and when you have several other presentation files open.

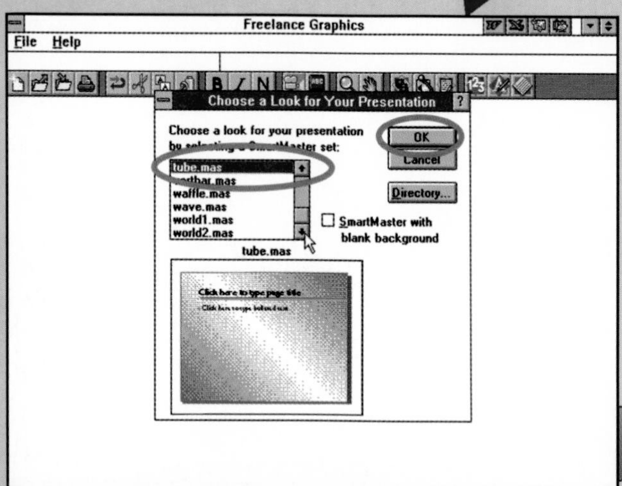

2 The Choose a Look for Your Presentation dialog box appears, with the last SmartMaster background set you used selected. Choose the set you want to use for the new presentation by scrolling the list, and choose **OK**.

3 Freelance displays the Choose Page Layout dialog box. Choose the page design for the new presentation, and then choose **OK**. Freelance displays the background on-screen, ready for your new presentation.

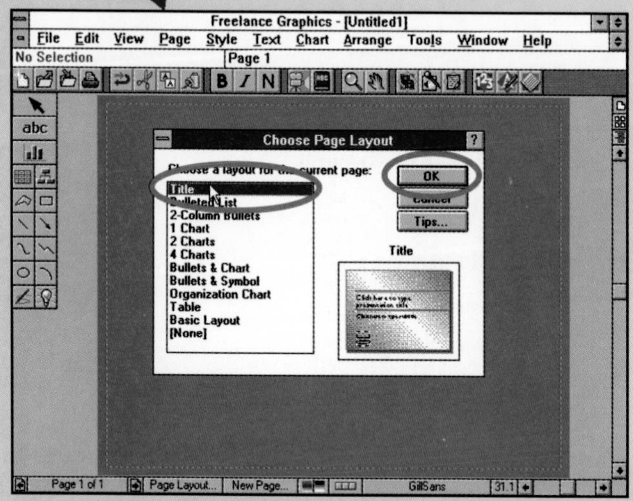

NOTE

If you start a new presentation by following steps 1 through 3 and do not make changes to the page, you can close the file and Freelance will not prompt you to save.

TASK 11

Opening an Existing Presentation

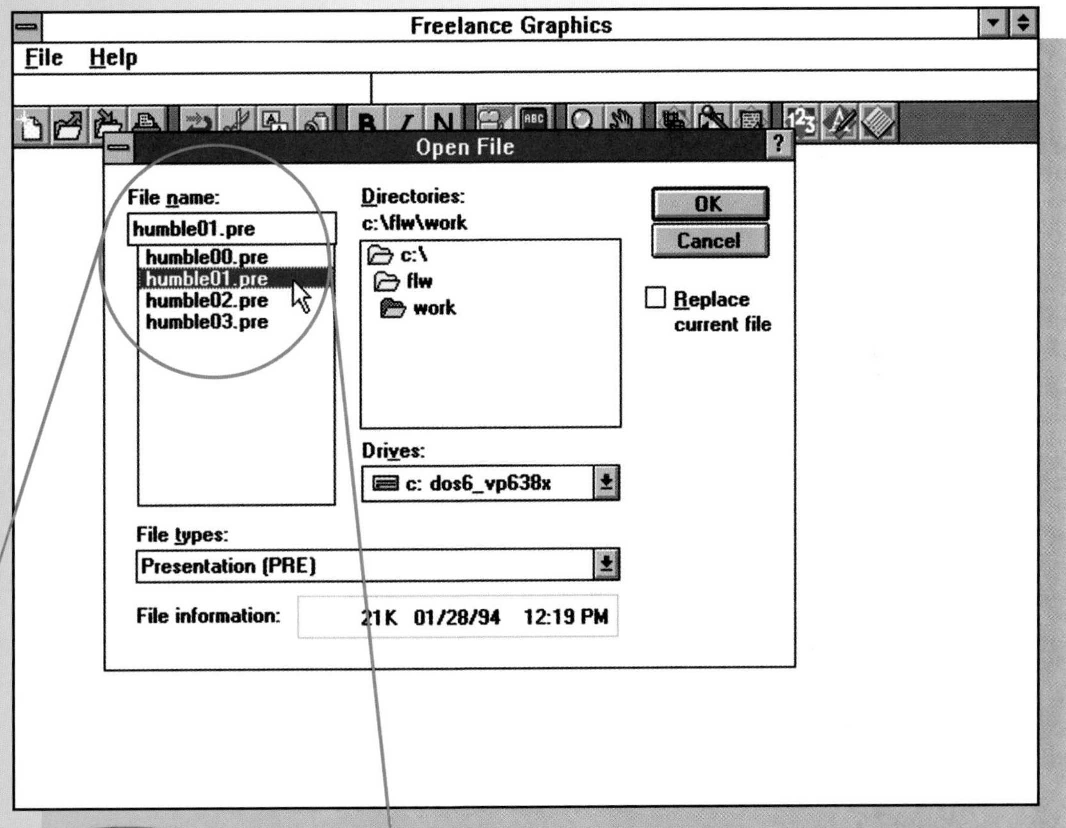

"Why would I do this?"

You will often want to open presentations to add to, delete from, or modify the information in the presentation, or to print or display the presentation on-screen. Freelance stores all your presentations in the same place so you can easily locate them (unless you changed the directory when you saved the file).

Task 11: Opening an Existing Presentation

1 Open the **File** menu and choose **Open** to display the Open dialog box.

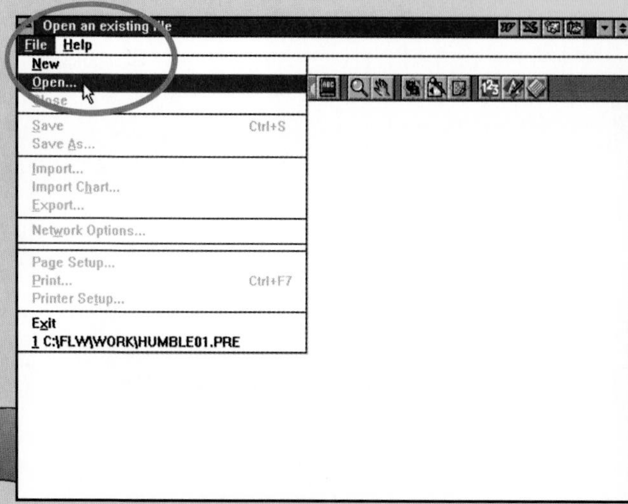

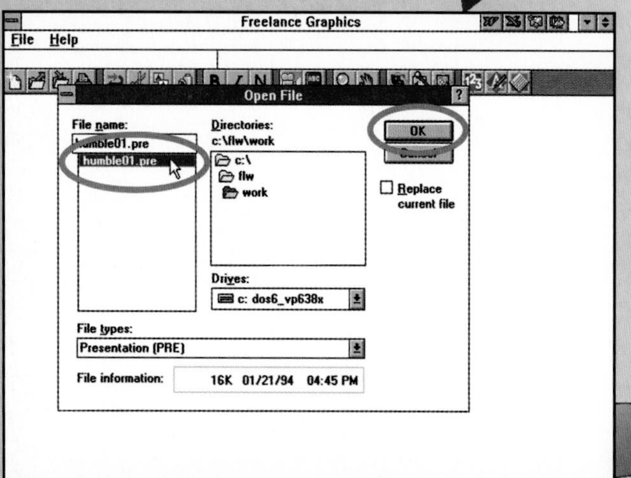

2 Select the name of the file, **humble01.pre**, in the **File Name** list; or, you can type the file name in the **File Name** text box. Choose **OK** to open the file.

WHY WORRY?

If you saved the file to a directory other than c:\flw\work, you must change directories or drives to display the file name in the list.

3 The dialog box closes and the presentation appears on-screen. The page that was displaying when you closed the presentation is the page that displays when you open the presentation.

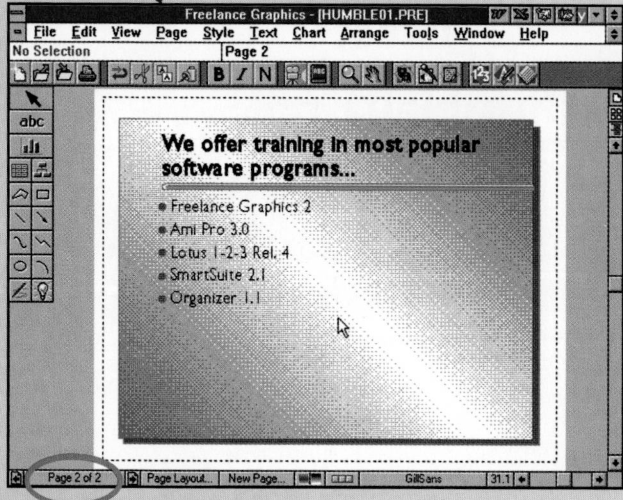

TASK 12

Quitting Freelance Graphics

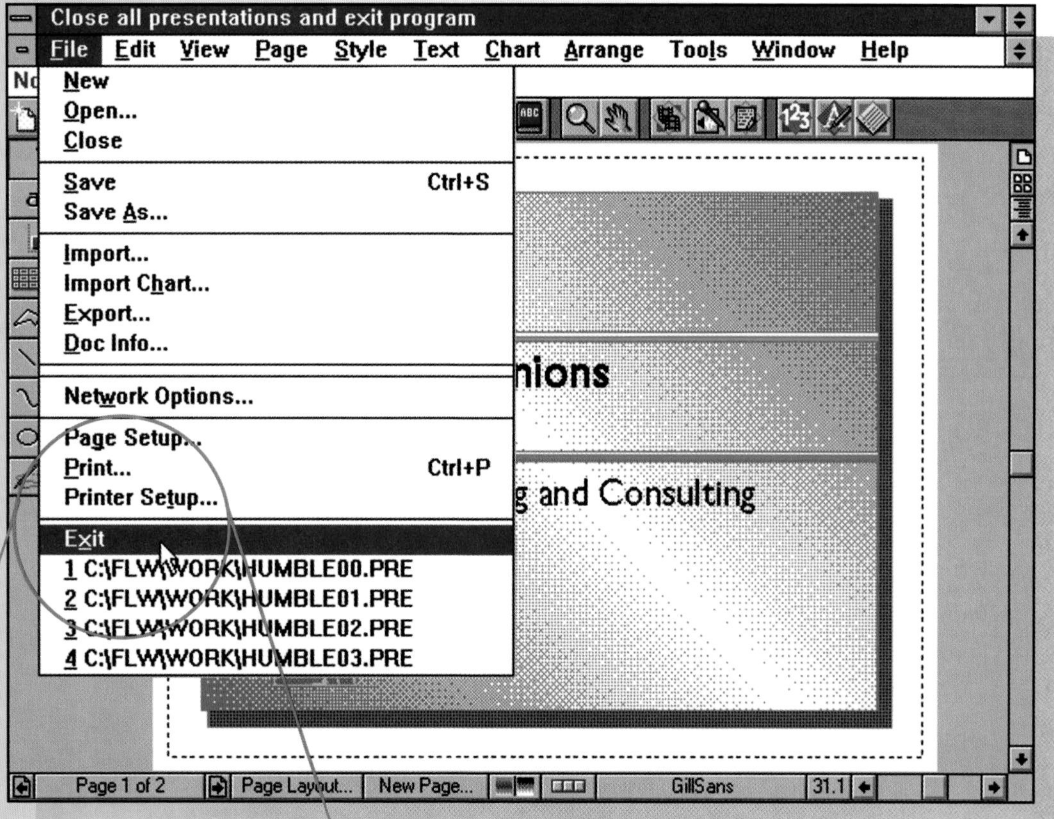

"Why would I do this?"

When you are finished working in the Freelance program, you exit the program. If you turn off your computer before exiting Freelance and Windows, you will lose any unsaved data. You can quit, or exit, Freelance without first closing all of your open presentations.

Task 12: Quitting Freelance Graphics

1 To exit Freelance, open the **File** menu and choose **Exit**.

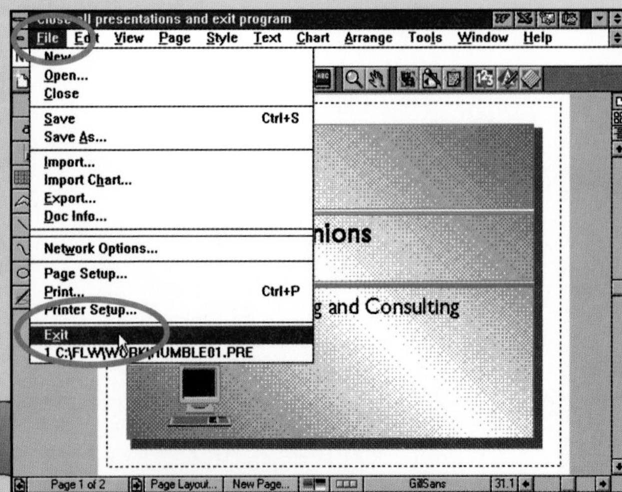

2 If you have not saved the open presentation, Freelance displays the Exit Freelance dialog box, prompting you to save the file. Choose **OK** if you want to save; choose **No** if you want to abandon the changes; or choose **Cancel** to return to the document.

3 The Freelance program closes and returns to the Program Manager. If you are finished working, open the **File** menu and choose **Exit Windows** to close the Windows program. Windows displays the Exit Windows confirmation dialog box. Choose **OK** to exit Windows.

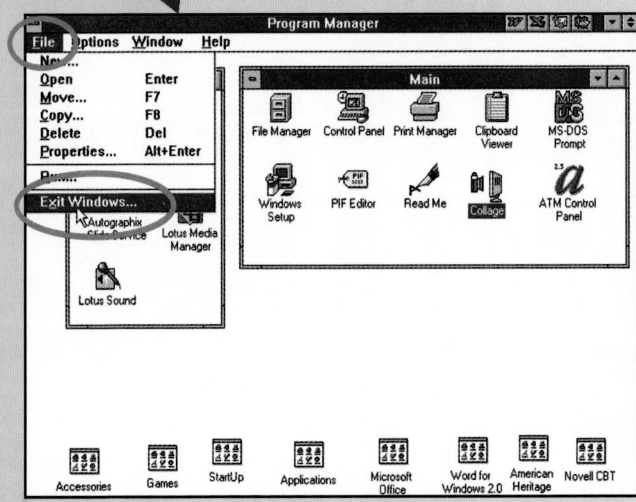

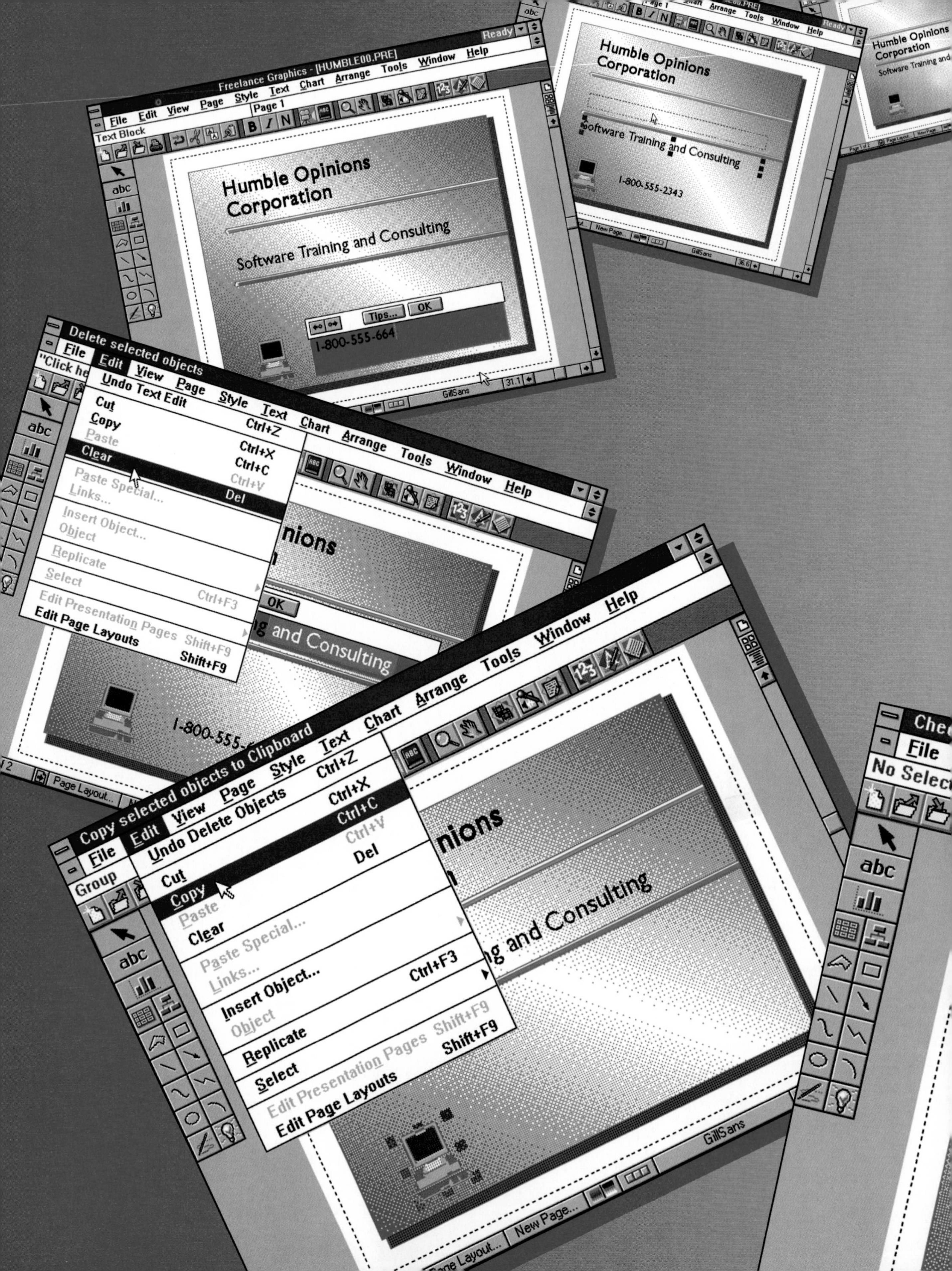

Freelance Graphics - [HUMBLE00.PRE]
Ready
File Edit View Page Style Text Chart Arrange Tools Window Help
Page 1
Text Block
Humble Opinions Corporation
Software Training and Consulting
Tips... OK
1-800-555-664
1-800-555-2343
GillSans
Delete selected objects
Undo Text Edit Ctrl+Z
Cut Ctrl+X
Copy Ctrl+C
Paste Ctrl+V
Clear Del
Paste Special...
Links...
Insert Object...
Object
Replicate
Select
Edit Presentation Pages Shift+F9
Edit Page Layouts Shift+F9
Copy selected objects to Clipboard
Undo Delete Objects Ctrl+Z
Cut Ctrl+X
Copy Ctrl+C
Paste Ctrl+V
Clear Del
Paste Special...
Links...
Insert Object... Ctrl+F3
Object
Replicate
Select
Edit Presentation Pages Shift+F9
Edit Page Layouts Shift+F9
Group
No Selec
Page Layout...
New Page...

PART II

Entering, Editing, and Formatting Text

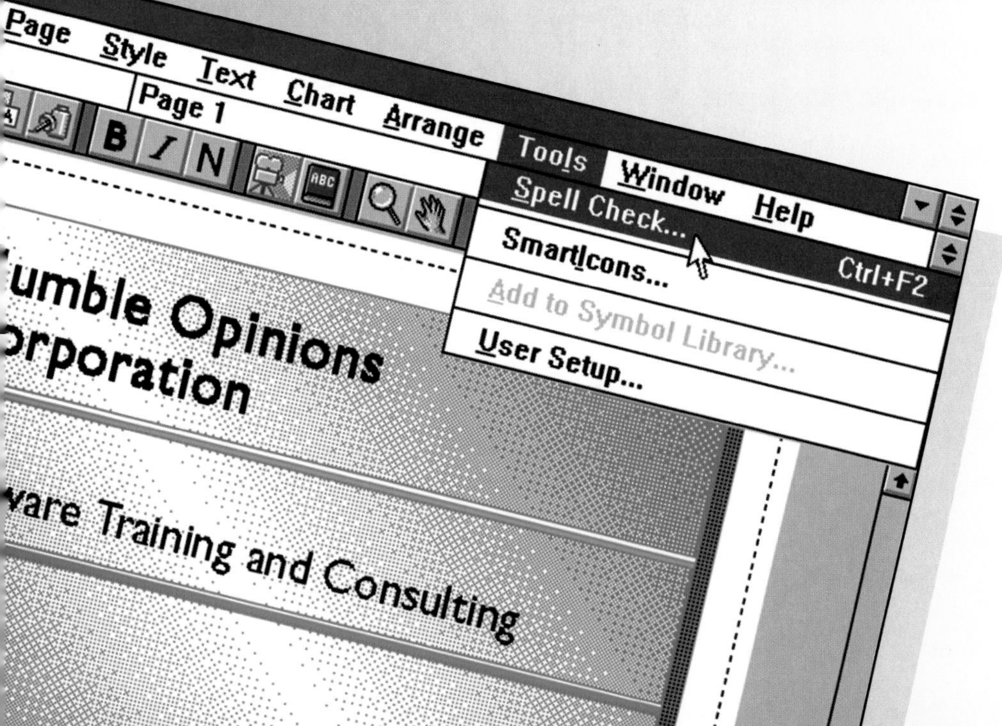

Freelance Graphics provides a variety of page layouts for you to use with your presentations. Each page layout contains various type sizes and text enhancements, such as bold, italic, bullets, and so on. Freelance's layout designs are attractive and professional—and they help you complete your work quickly.

There will be situations, however, when you want to add more text to a page, center a title that was left-aligned, use a different font, or copy information from one page to another. Freelance enables you to enter, edit, and format text in addition to the text already in the page layout.

abc

Suppose you want to type additional text on the title page of a presentation. You can create a text block—just like those Freelance supplies for you—enter the text in the text block, and move the block around on the page. You can even move Freelance's supplied text blocks, as well.

Freelance also includes several handy editing commands you can use when designing a presentation. Using the Edit menu, or various shortcuts, you can cut or copy items from the page and then paste those items elsewhere in the presentation, or even paste them in another presentation.

Cut, copy, and paste are editing tools that make use of the Windows Clipboard. When you select an item—text, a symbol, or a chart, for example—and cut or copy that item, the item is stored in the Windows Clipboard until you paste it or cut or copy a different item to replace the original item.

You can, therefore, select a chart, bulleted list, symbol, or other item on the page and move or duplicate the item on another page of the presentation.

Freelance provides other editing tools you can use to help speed up your work, including the Undo and Replicate commands. The Undo command enables you to cancel or erase the last change you made to the document. The Replicate command copies the selected item to the current page without first moving it to the Clipboard. Using the Replicate command, therefore, saves whatever item is on the Clipboard for later use.

Another useful editing tool in Freelance is the Spell Check. You can use the Spell Check to review all text in a presentation or just selected text. If the Spell Check finds a word that is not in Freelance's dictionary, it displays the word in a dialog box, suggests alternative spellings, and lets you decide if there is an error.

After you enter, arrange, and edit the text, you may want to change the format of the text. You format text by changing font, type size, and alignment, and by applying attributes such as bold, italic, underlining, and so on. Additionally, you can choose to add any of a variety of bullets, and even change the bullet color and size.

Freelance supplies the tools and commands you need to customize a presentation so that it fits your needs exactly. This part of the book shows you how to enter, edit, and format text in a presentation. For the following tasks, you can use the file HUMBLE01.PRE, which you created in Part I.

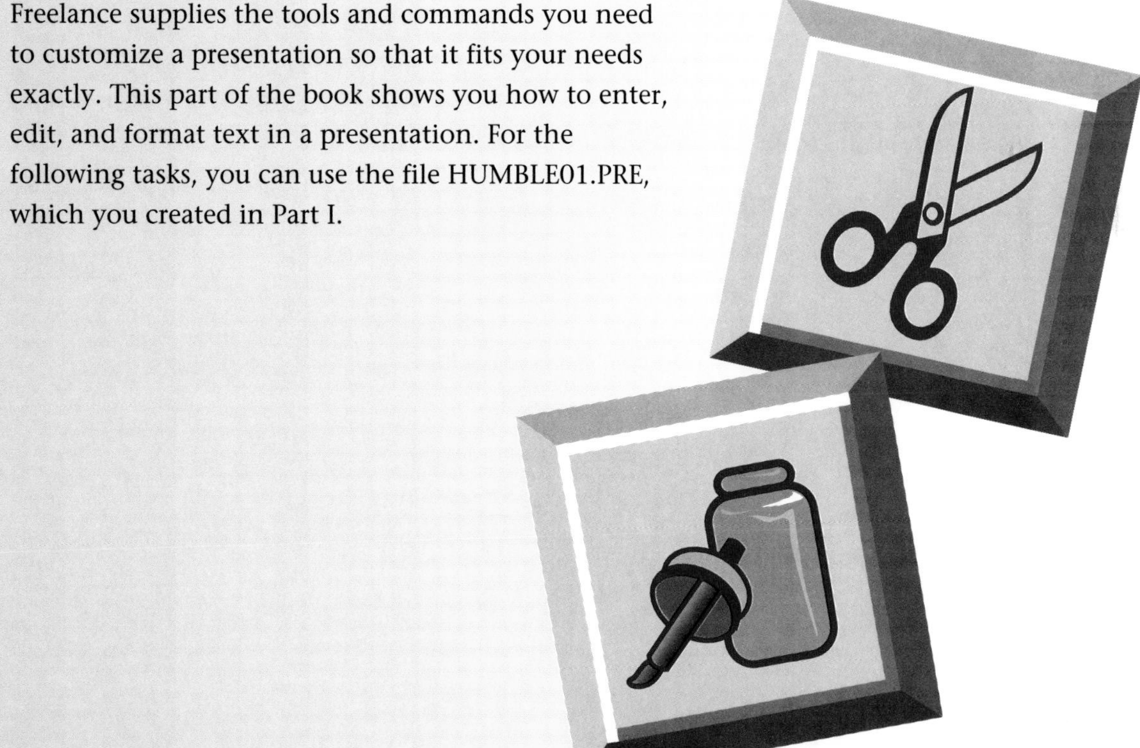

TASK 13

Creating a Text Block

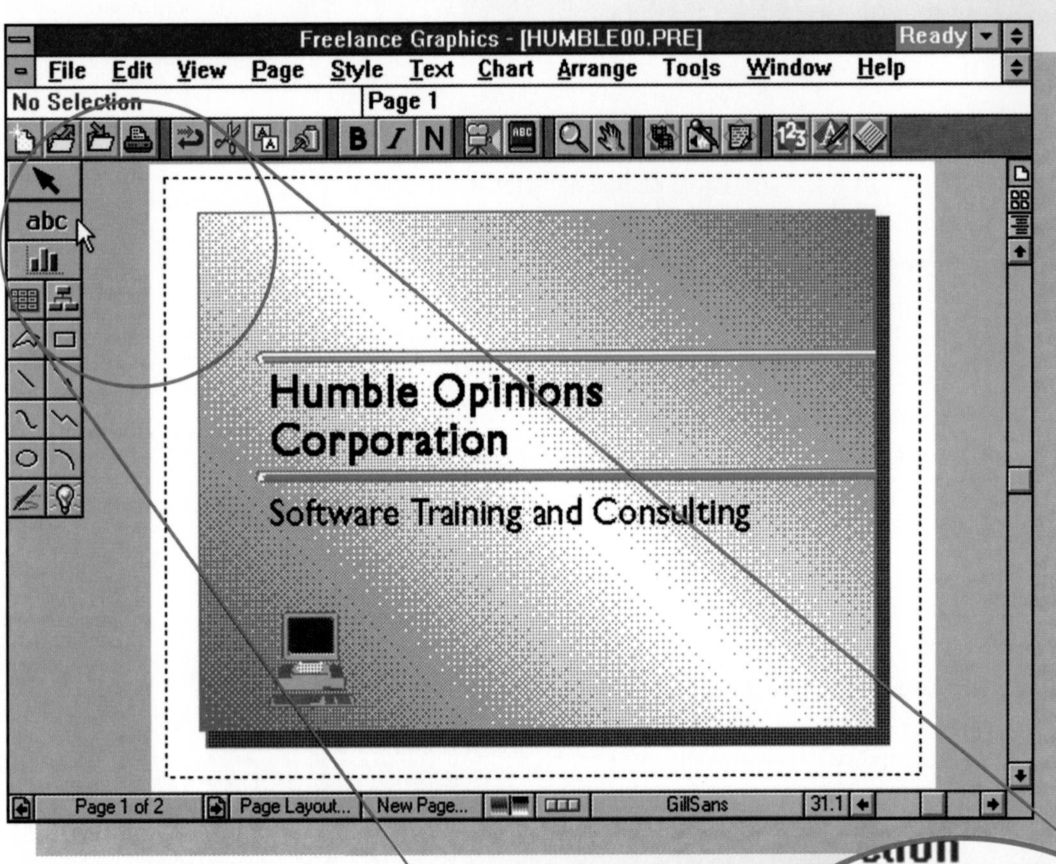

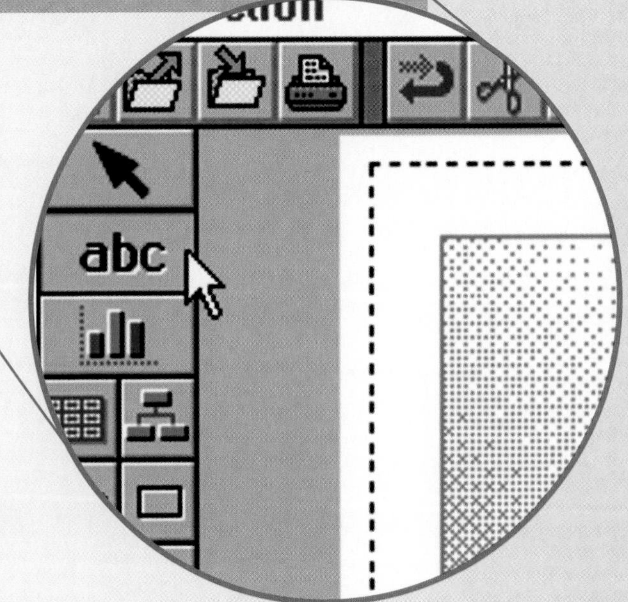

"Why would I do this?"

You can create a text block on any page of a presentation to add text. Freelance Graphics may not always supply enough text blocks for the text you need. The text block you create looks and acts like any of Freelance's default text blocks. Enter the text and choose OK when you are finished; Freelance closes the text block and displays the text on the background.

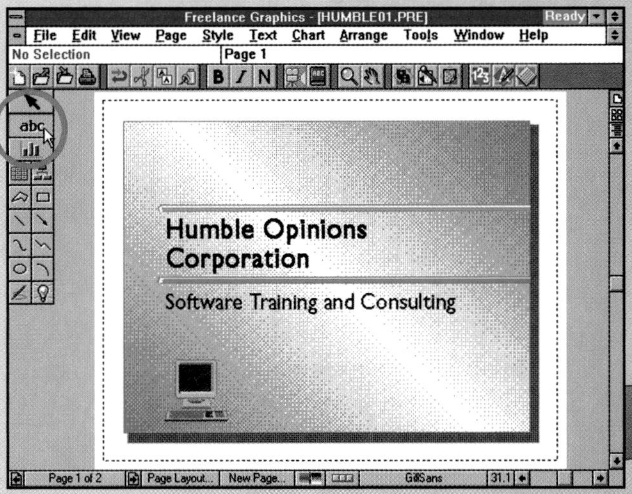

1 To add a text block to a page, you must first choose the **Text** button. The Text button is the button with abc on it. The button is located on the toolbar on the left side of the screen. Place the mouse pointer on the Text button and click the left mouse button once.

WHY WORRY?

If you don't like the position of a text box, don't worry. You can move the text block by dragging it to the new position.

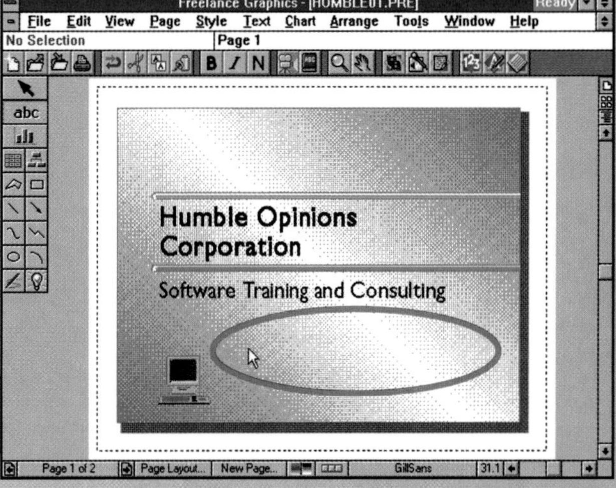

2 Move the mouse pointer to the location where you want the text to begin—do not position the pointer on top of an existing text block. Press and hold the mouse button while you drag a rectangle across the area. When the rectangle is large enough to hold the text you want, release the mouse button.

WHY WORRY?

If the rectangle is too small for the text, the text block enlarges as you enter more and more text.

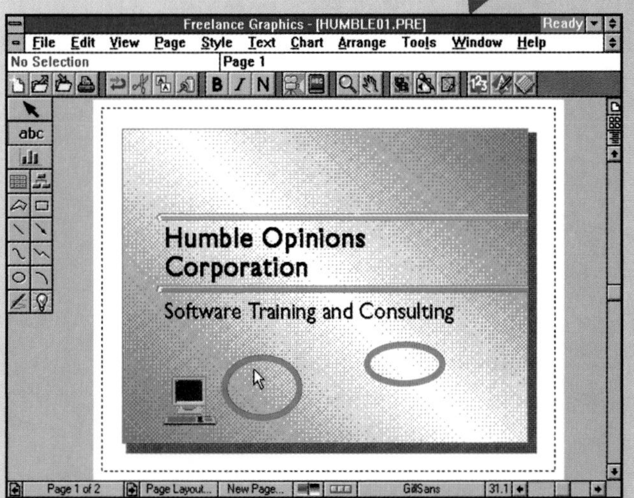

3 A text block appears with a blinking cursor. Enter the text **1-800-555-2343**. Choose **OK** to insert the text and close the text block.

TASK 14

Moving a Text Block

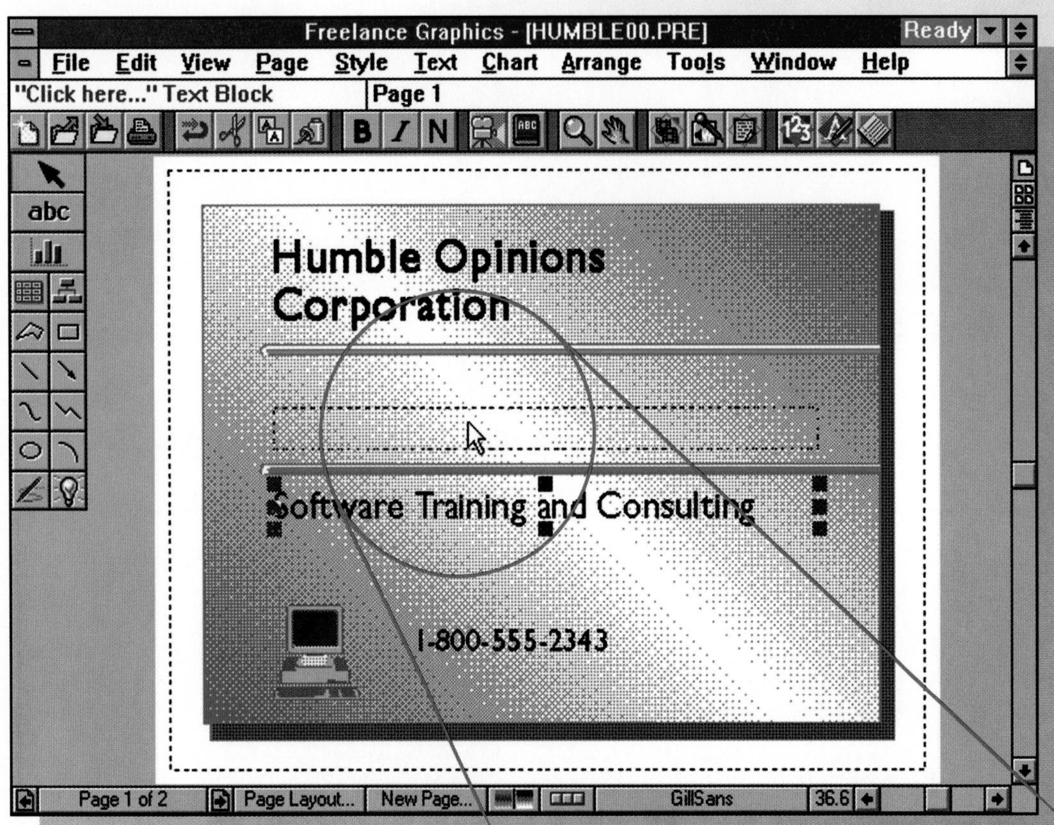

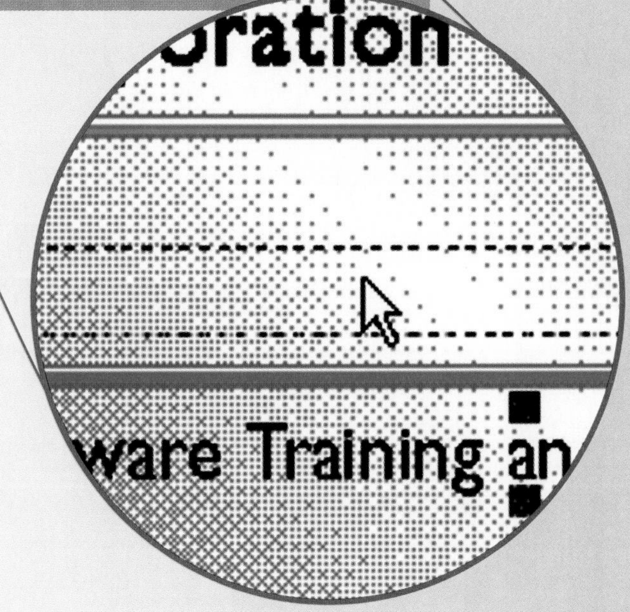

"Why would I do this?"

You can move any text block on the page, whether it is text you added or text from a "Click here..." text block. You may want to rearrange the text, make room for another text block or a symbol, or change the design of the page by moving the text. You can also move other items on the page, including symbols, charts, and so on.

Task 14: Moving a Text Block

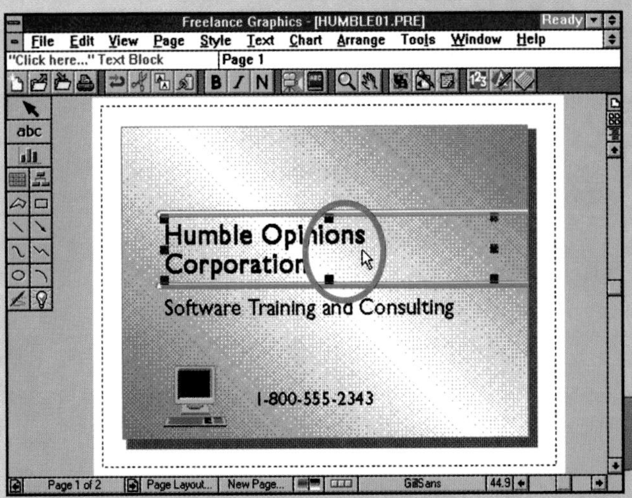

1 Click anywhere within the Humble Opinions Corporation text block to select it. When you click, small boxes, or *handles*, appear on the corners and sides of the text block. These handles indicate the block is selected.

2 With the mouse pointer positioned anywhere inside of the text block, click and drag the text box to a new location. As you drag, a dotted rectangle moves with the mouse pointer so you can see the new placement. When you reach the new location, release the mouse button.

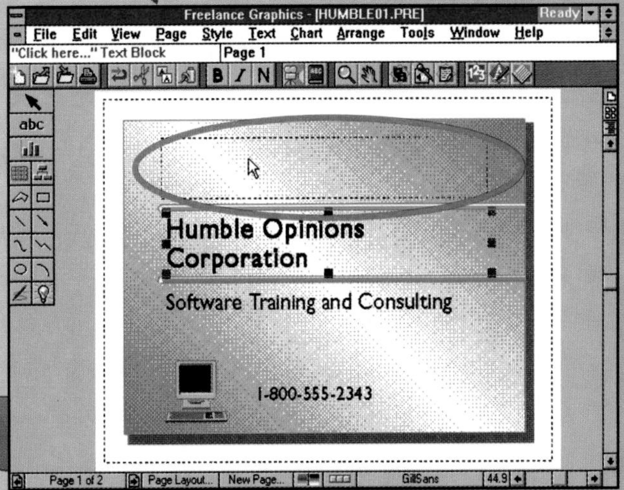

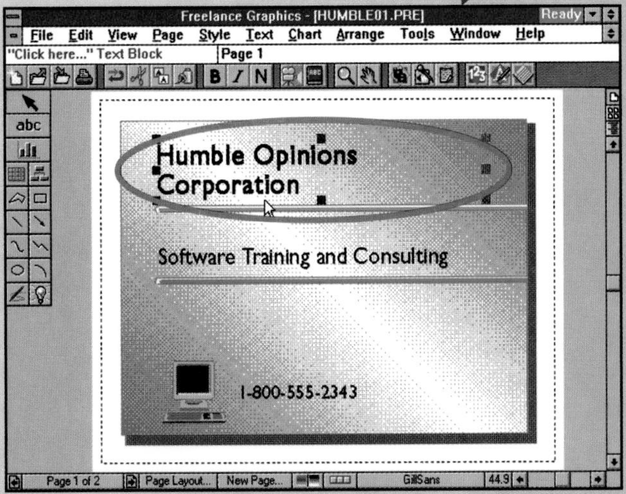

3 When you release the mouse button, the text block appears in the location of the dotted rectangle. To deselect the text, click anywhere on the page.

NOTE

To save time formatting text, drag the text box you created into a text block containing the "Click here..." instructions. The created text takes on the formatting of the "Click here" text block.

TASK 15

Editing a Text Block

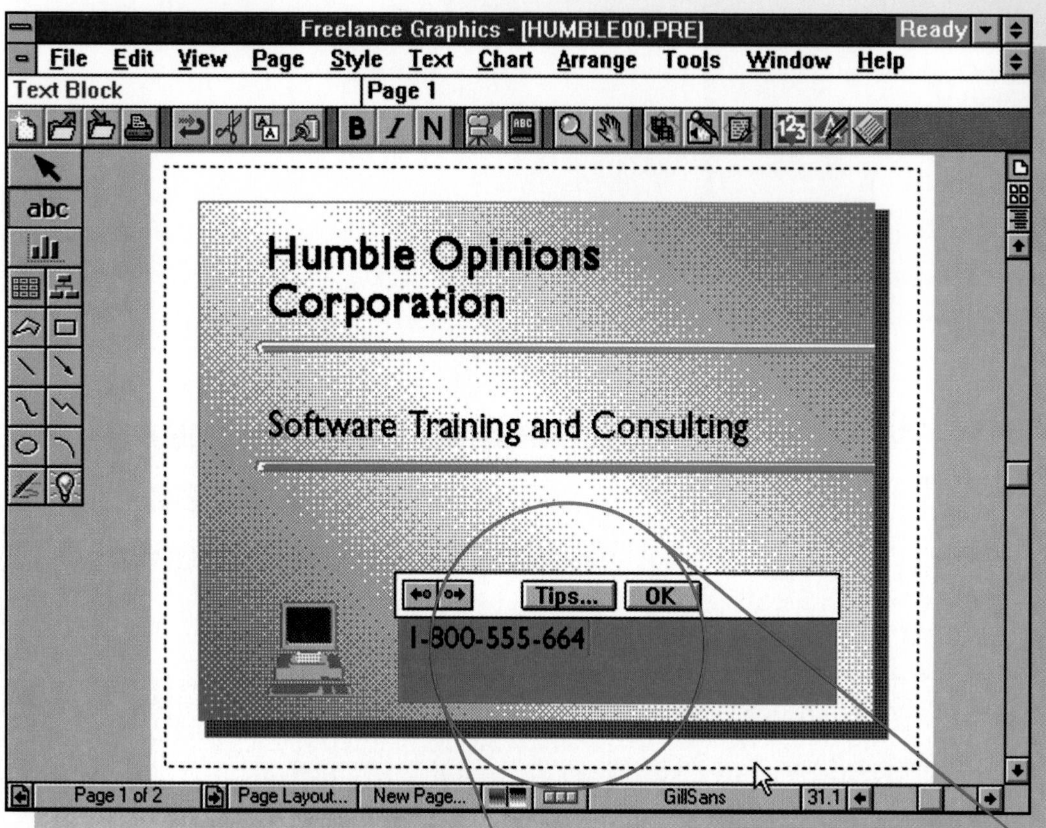

"Why would I do this?"

If you find you have made an error when entering text or if you want to add text to a text block, you can edit the text in any block. You can use the Backspace or Delete key to remove unwanted characters, and then you can position the cursor and enter new text, if you want.

Task 15: Editing a Text Block

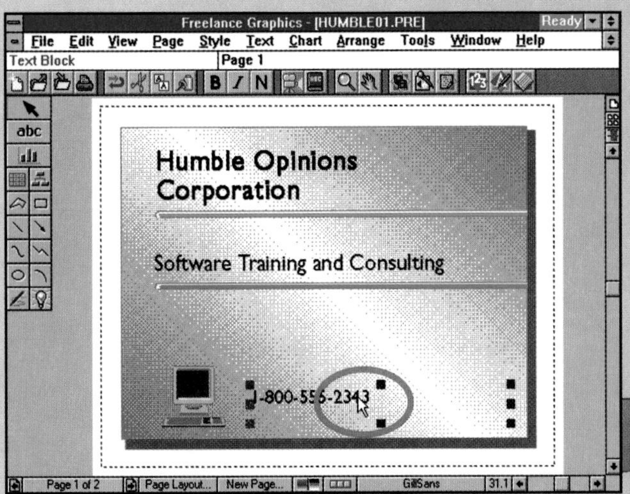

1 Click the text to be edited, **800-555-2343**, to reveal the selection handles. The handles appear on the corners and sides of the text block.

NOTE

If you click a text block with the right mouse button, you reveal a quick menu that enables you to edit the text block. Choose Edit from the quick menu.

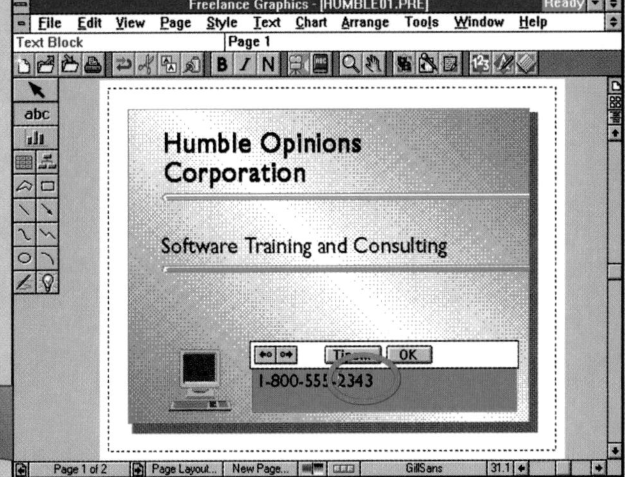

2 Click the text again to reveal the editing text block. The I-beam and blinking cursor appear in the text block. Position the I-beam in front of the **2** to begin editing.

WHY WORRY?

If you click the selected text block too quickly, as in a double-click, or if you click near the edge of the text block, you may display the Paragraph Styles dialog box. Choose the Cancel button.

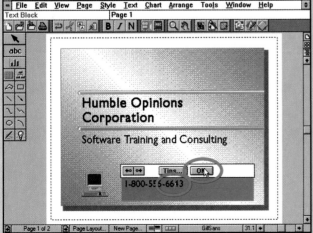

3 Press the **Delete** key twice to delete the 2 and the 3. Type **66** to replace the deleted characters. Choose **OK** when you are finished editing the text.

NOTE

Make sure you save your presentation periodically so if there's a power failure you won't lose the changes. To save changes, you can press Ctrl+S.

TASK 16

Deleting Text

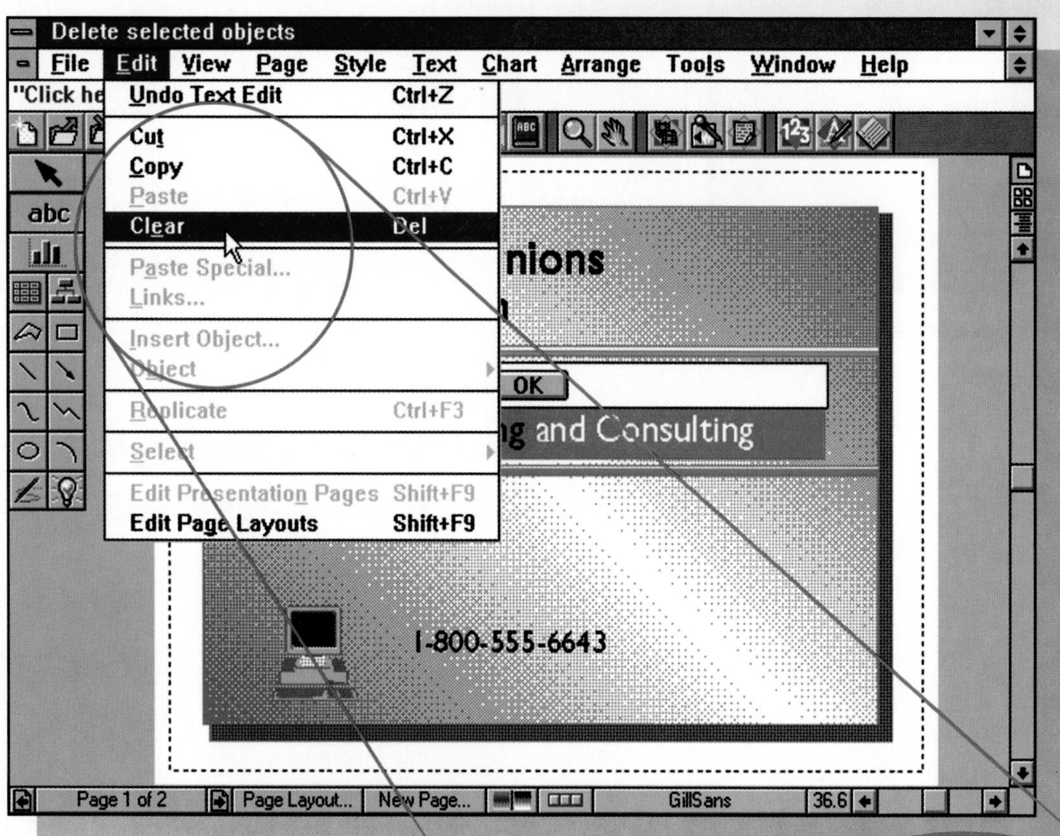

"Why would I do this?"

You may want to delete the text on a page if you want to enter all new text or if some of the text must be replaced or corrected. You can delete text from a text block so the formatting remains, or you can delete an entire text block. If you delete the text block, you may need to change the font, type size, alignment, and so on of any text you create.

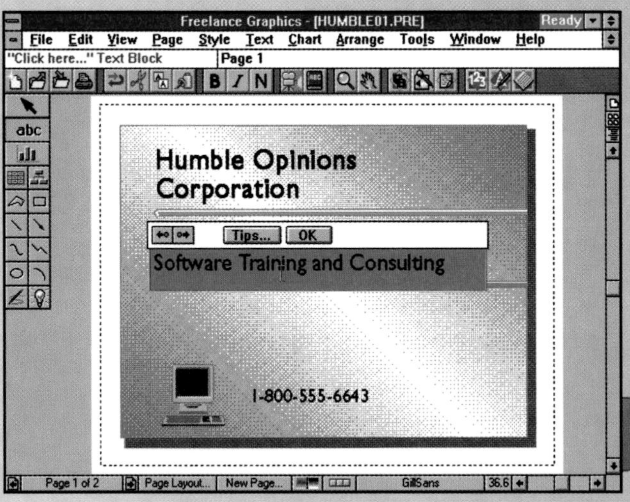

1 To select the text to delete but leave the formatting, click the text **Software Training and Consulting** to select the block. Click again to reveal the text block. The text block appears with the I-beam and the blinking cursor.

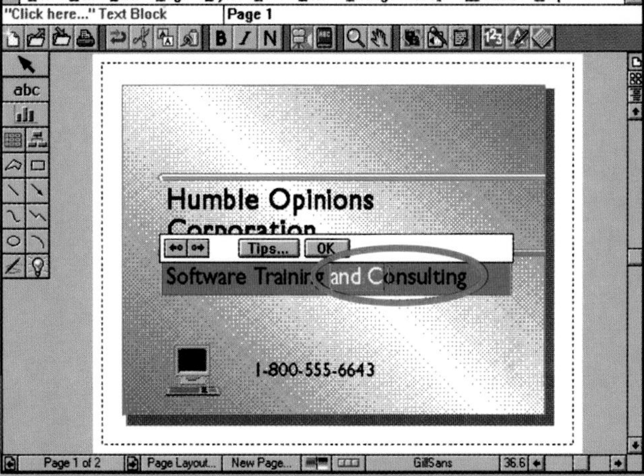

2 Select the text **and Consulting** by positioning the I-beam at the beginning of the text. Click and drag the mouse to the end of the text. The selected text appears in reversed video.

WHY WORRY?

If you have trouble dragging, click the mouse button at the beginning of the text. Hold the Shift key and move the I-beam to the end of the text and click.

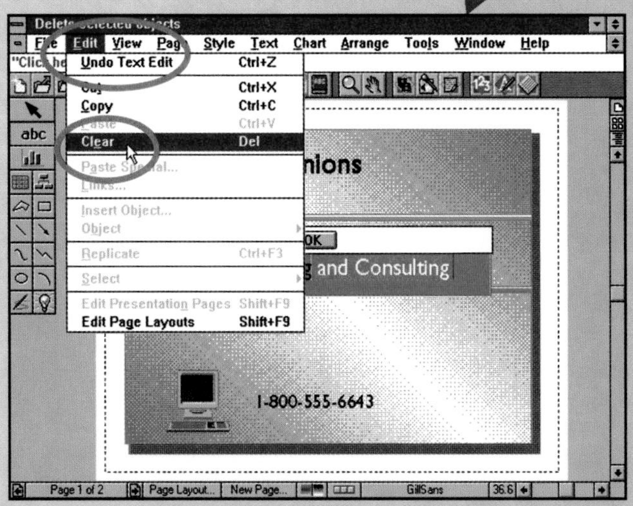

3 Open the **Edit** menu and choose **Clear**; or, press the **Delete** key. If you accidentally delete the wrong text, open the **Edit** menu and choose **Undo Text Edit**.

When using Edit Undo, you can only reverse the last command or action.

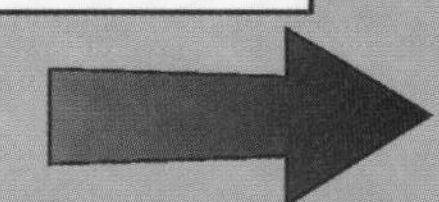

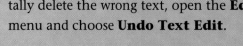

Task 16: Deleting Text

4 The text is erased, but the formatting and the text block remain. You can enter new text or choose **OK** to close the text block.

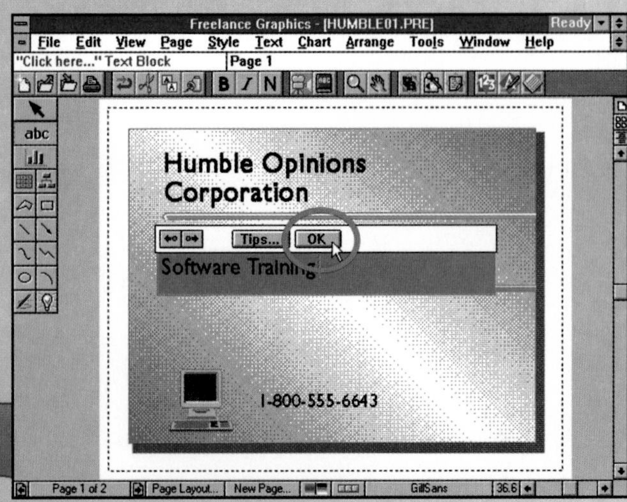

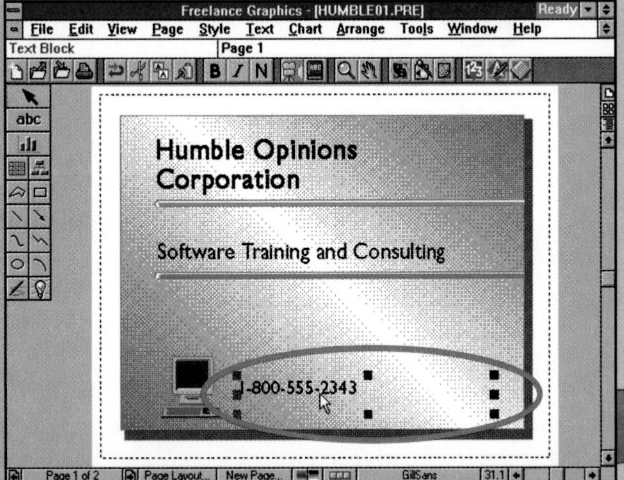

5 To delete an entire text block, click the text block containing the 800 number. Selection handles appear around the text block.

6 Press the **Delete** key to erase the entire text block. The text disappears from the page.

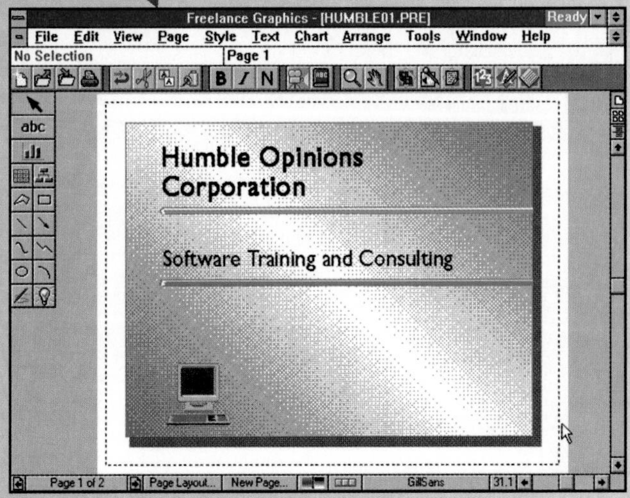

TASK 17

Cutting, Copying, and Pasting

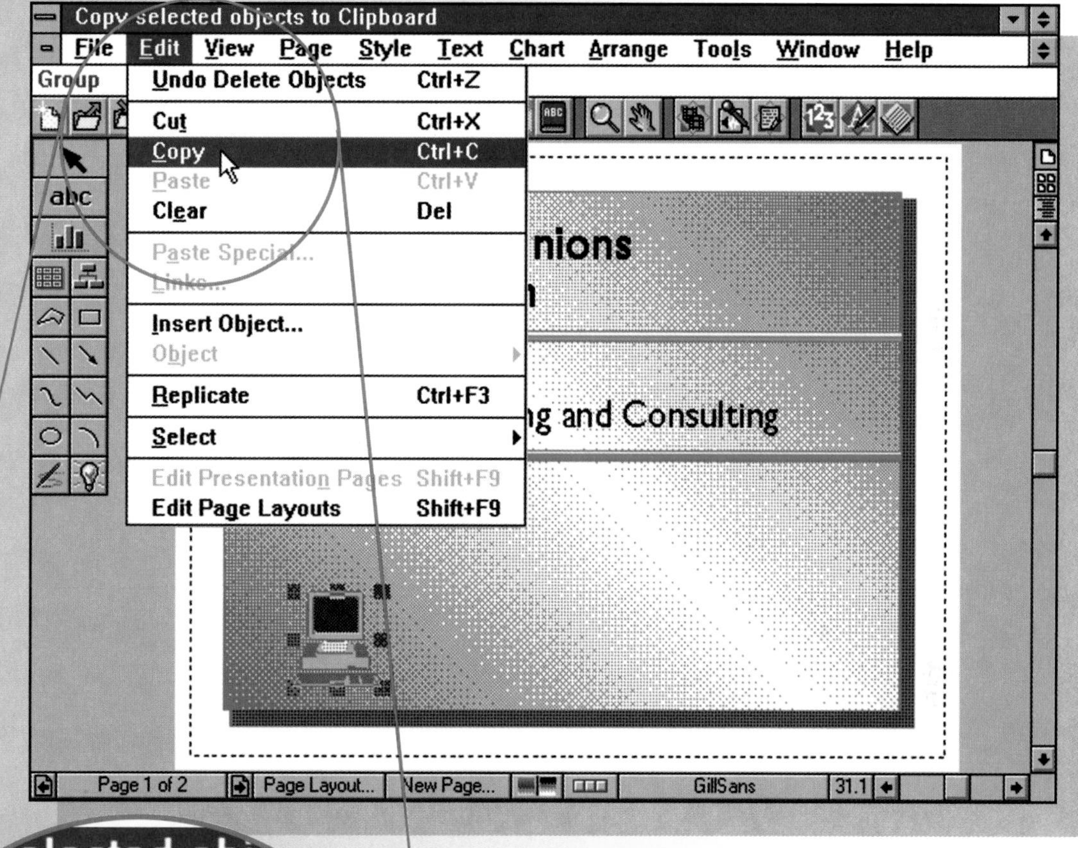

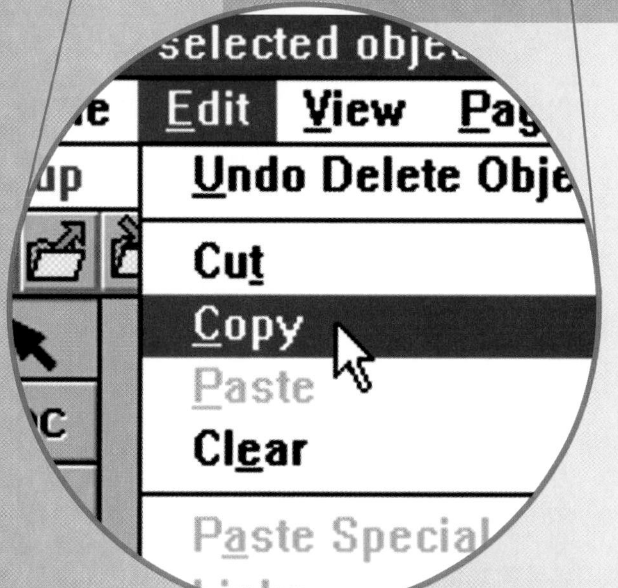

"Why would I do this?"

Suppose you wanted a symbol or logo to appear on another page of your document; it's easier to copy and paste the symbol than to use the Add Symbol to Page dialog box and select the category and symbol again. You can copy and paste text or other items on the same page, from one page to another, or from one document to another. You also can move text or other items from one page or document to another. Freelance supplies editing tools to make your job easier.

Task 17: Cutting, Copying, and Pasting

1 To copy the computer symbol to page two of the presentation, select the symbol by clicking the image. Handles appear, indicating the object is selected.

NOTE

You cannot only copy symbols and images, you can copy text blocks or specific portions of text, charts, bullets, and so on.

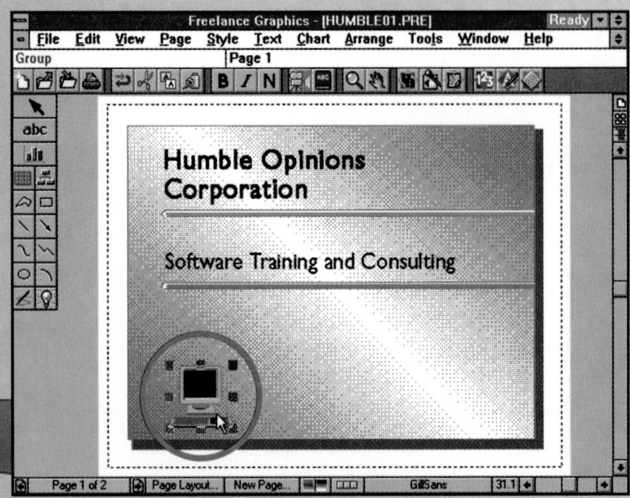

2 Open the **Edit** menu and choose **Copy**; or, press **Ctrl+C**. Either of these actions places a duplicate of the symbol on the Windows Clipboard.

NOTE

When you cut or copy an item to the Clipboard, the item remains there until you cut or copy another item. You can, however, paste that same item on the Clipboard over and over until you cut or copy something else to the Clipboard.

3 Place the mouse pointer on the **page arrow** in the status bar and click to move to page two; or, you can press the **PgDn** key.

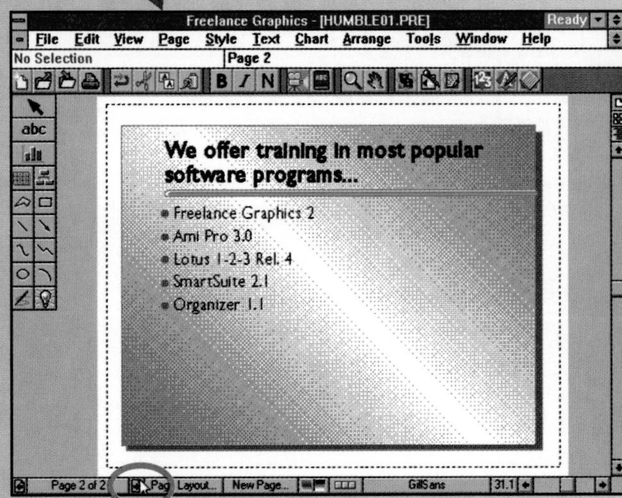

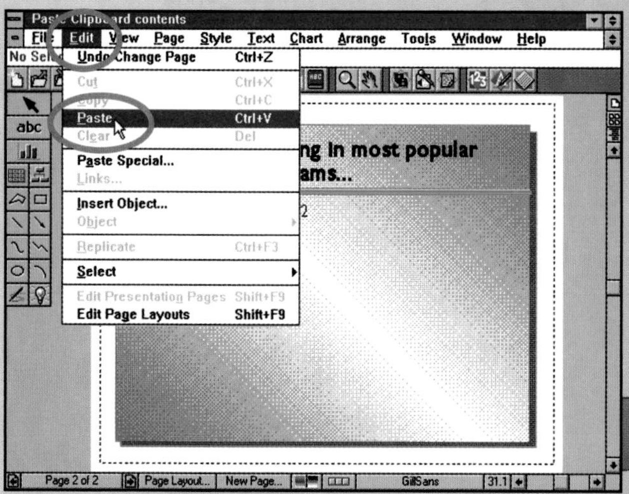

4 Open the **Edit** menu and choose **Paste**; or, you can press **Ctrl+V**.

NOTE

If you click a text block with the right mouse button, you display a quick menu that enables you to choose Cut, Copy, or Paste.

5 Freelance pastes the symbol in the exact position it held on the original page. When the object is pasted, it appears with handles. You can move the symbol by dragging it.

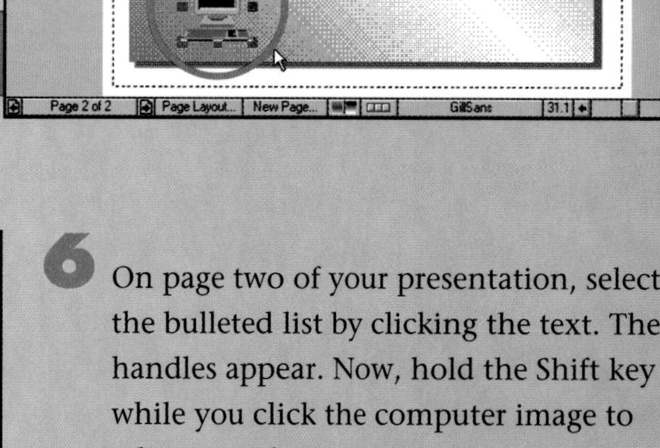

WHY WORRY?

If you want to keep the item on the Clipboard so that you can paste it again but you want to copy another item, use the Edit Replicate command.

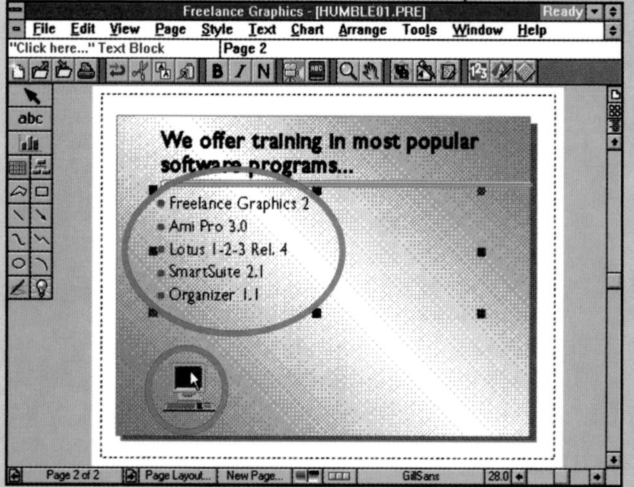

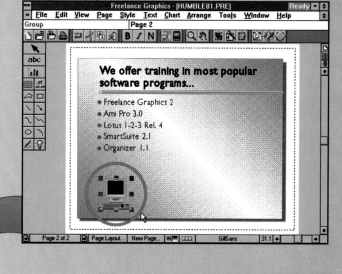

6 On page two of your presentation, select the bulleted list by clicking the text. The handles appear. Now, hold the Shift key while you click the computer image to select two objects.

WHY WORRY?

To deselect an item you did not mean to select, hold the Shift key while clicking the object. The rest of the objects remain selected.

Task 17: Cutting, Copying, and Pasting

7 Open the **Edit** menu and choose **Cut**; or, press **Ctrl**+**X**. The objects disappear from the page and are cut to the Clipboard.

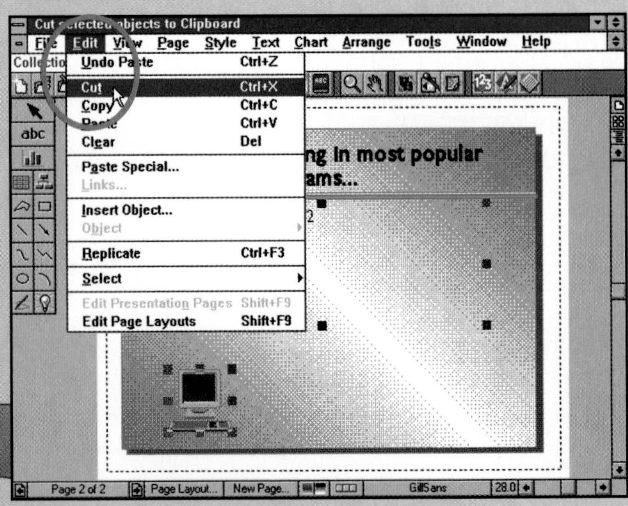

8 Click the **New Page** button in the status bar.

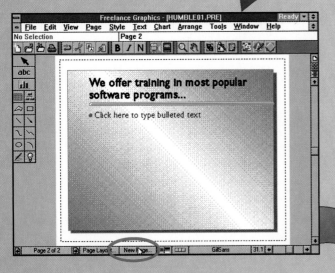

9 The New Page dialog box appears. Choose the **Basic Layout** page layout, and choose **OK** to close the dialog box and display the new page.

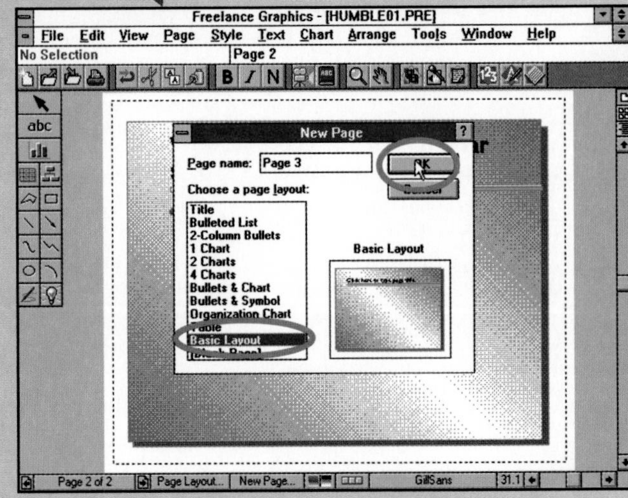

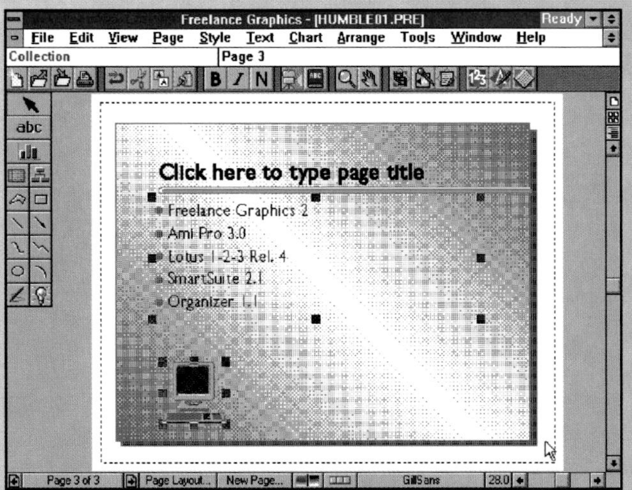

10 Press **Ctrl+V**, the shortcut for the Edit Paste command. The two cut items appear on the new page. You can now enter a title. Type **Learn Lotus...**.

TASK 18

Checking Spelling

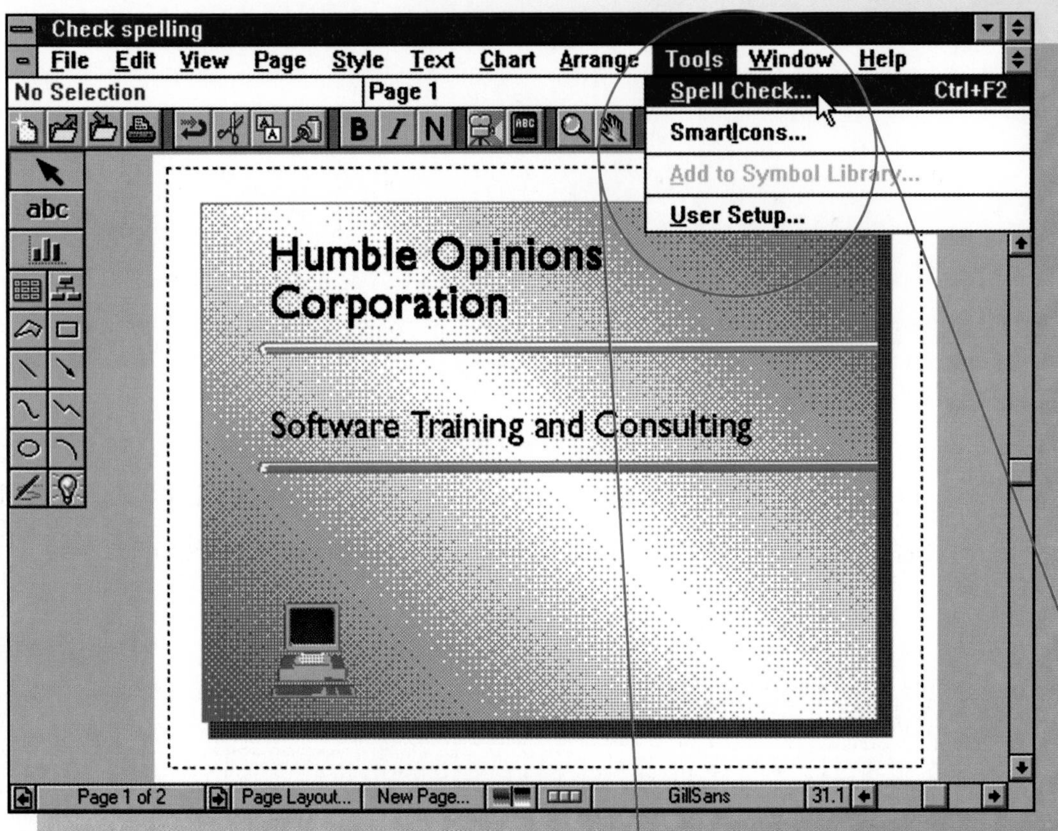

"Why would I do this?"

You can read and re-read the text in your presentation, but chances are, if you typed it, you will probably miss a misspelled word. Freelance's Spell Check feature can check for most misspelled words and alert you to the problem. It's fast, it's easy, and it's necessary for presenting a professional presentation.

Task 18: Checking Spelling

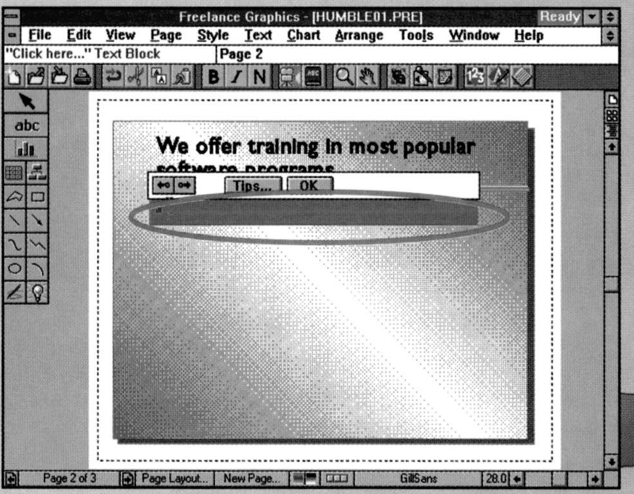

1. Press the **PgUp** key to move to page two. Click the **Click here to type bulleted text** text block that Freelance created when you cut the previous text in the last task. Enter the following text and typos as the bulleted list, pressing **Enter** after each item: **Word Porcessing**, **Spreadsheets**, **Databases**, **abd Desktop Publishing**. Choose **OK** to close the text block, and click anywhere on the page to deselect the text block.

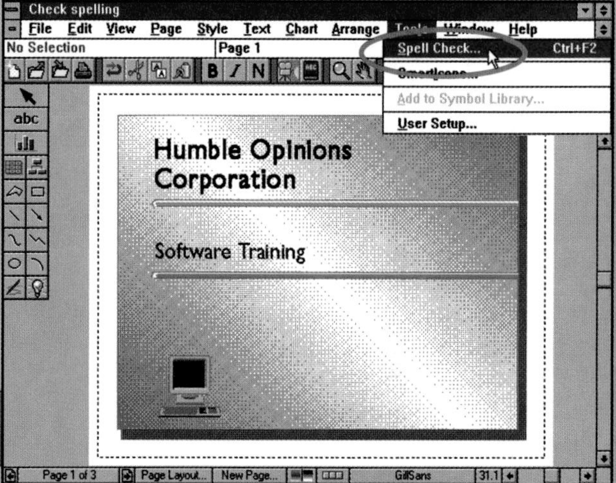

2. Press the **PgUp** key to move to page one of the presentation. Open the **Tools** menu and choose **Spell Check**; or you can press **Ctrl+F2**.

3. The Spell Check dialog box appears. In the Check Spelling Of option group, choose **Entire Presentation** and choose **OK**.

WHY WORRY?

You can, alternatively, check the spelling of only the selected text or the current page.

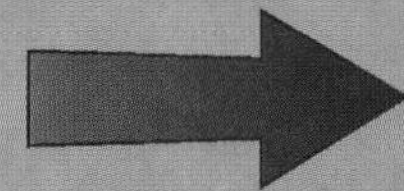

Task 18: Checking Spelling

4 The Spell Check dialog box appears when the program finds a misspelled word. The dialog box identifies the page and the title on the page. In addition, the Spell Check displays the questionable word in a box in its context. Next, the Spell Check suggests a word to replace the misspelled word as well as a list of alternatives from which you can choose. Select **Processing** from the list.

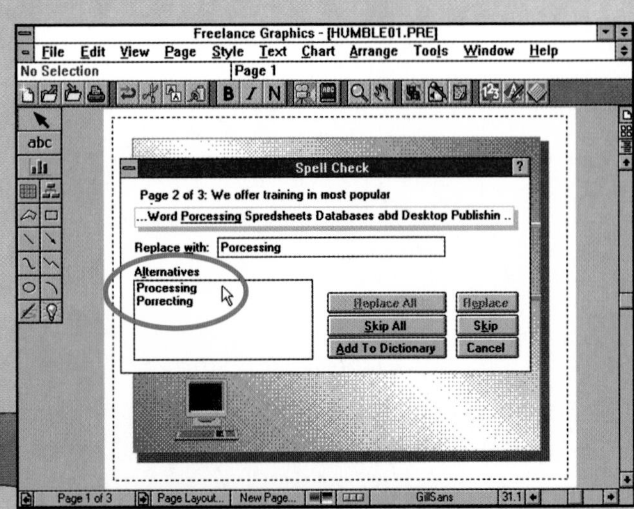

5 When you select Processing, the Spell Check activates the Replace and Replace All command buttons. Choose **Replace** and Freelance replaces the misspelled word with the selected alternative.

NOTE

You can choose Replace All to instruct the program to replace all instances, in this presentation, of "Porcessing" with "Processing."

6 The Spell Check continues and displays the misspelled word abd. In this case, the correct word is not in the list of alternatives, so you must enter the correct spelling. The cursor is already in the Replace With text box. Press the **Backspace** key to erase abd, and type in **and**. Choose **Replace**.

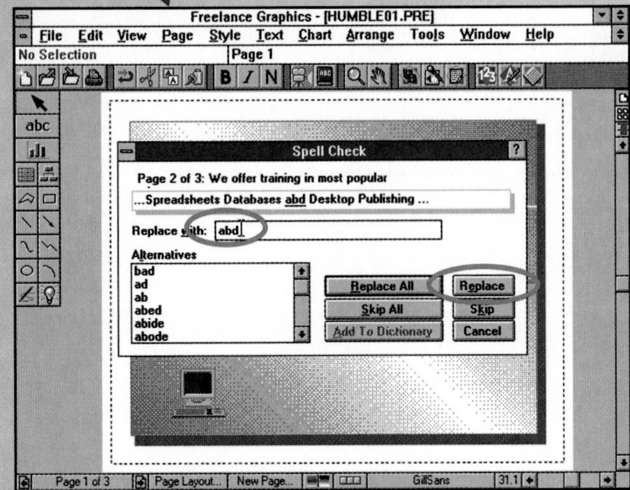

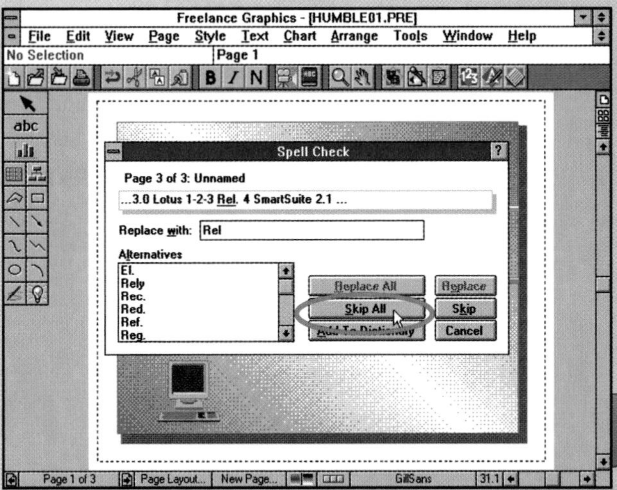

7 Spell Check discovers a word not in its dictionary, but nonetheless a correctly spelled word. Choose **Skip All** to ignore this word and continue the spell check.

8 Spell Check also questions the spelling of SmartSuite. If this is a word you use in many presentations, you can choose to add the word to the dictionary. Freelance then appends the dictionary so the Spell Check no longer questions this spelling. Choose **Add To Dictionary**.

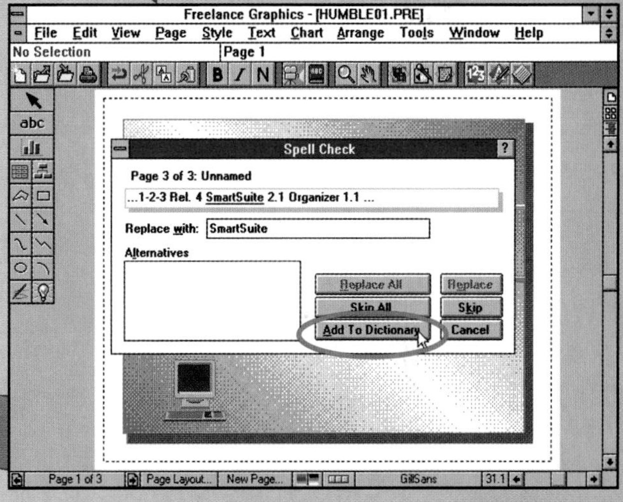

9 The Spell Check is finished and displays a message box. Choose **OK** to complete the task and return to the presentation.

TASK 19

Making Text Bold, Italic, or Normal

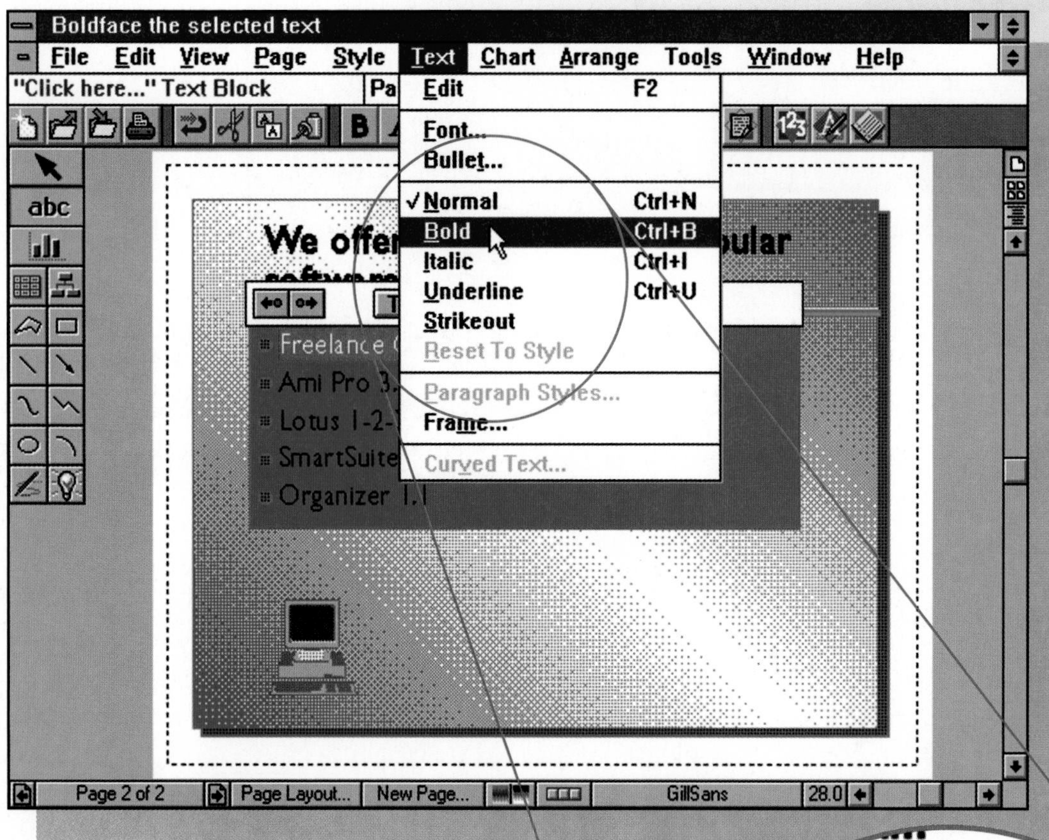

"Why would I do this?"

Often you will want to enhance specific text to make it stand out in the presentation. Headlines, for example, or key words, are frequently bolded to emphasize their importance. Freelance Graphics enables you to apply several text attributes to selected text: bold, italic, underline, strikeout, and normal. Choose Normal when you want to revert the text back to its original attribute setting.

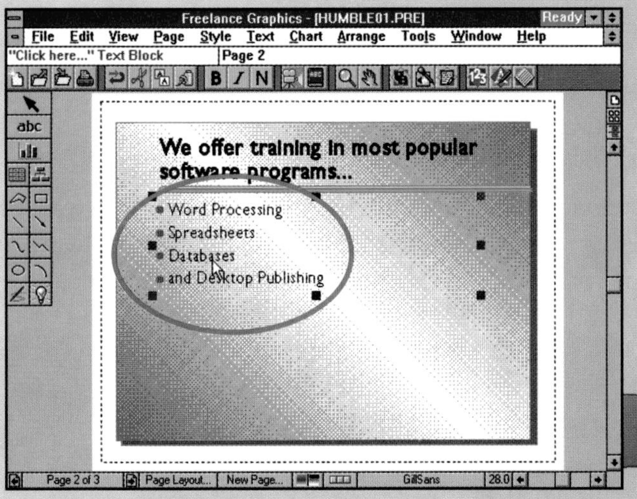

1 On page two of your presentation, click the bulleted list twice to display the text block.

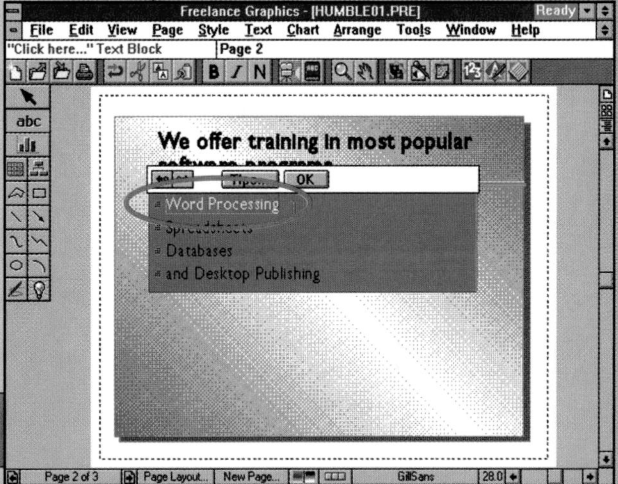

2 Select **Word Processing** by dragging the I-beam across the text. The text appears in reversed video.

3 Click the **B** button in the SmartIcons, the icons appearing across the top of your screen, below the title and menu bars. B stands for Bold.

NOTE

You also can apply the italic attribute by clicking the I button. The N button returns any text with applied attributes to normal.

Task 19: Making Text Bold, Italic, or Normal

4 Click outside of the selected text to deselect it and view the bold attribute.

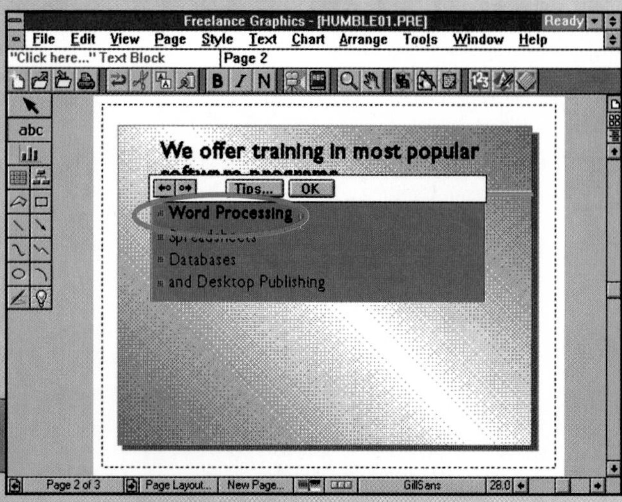

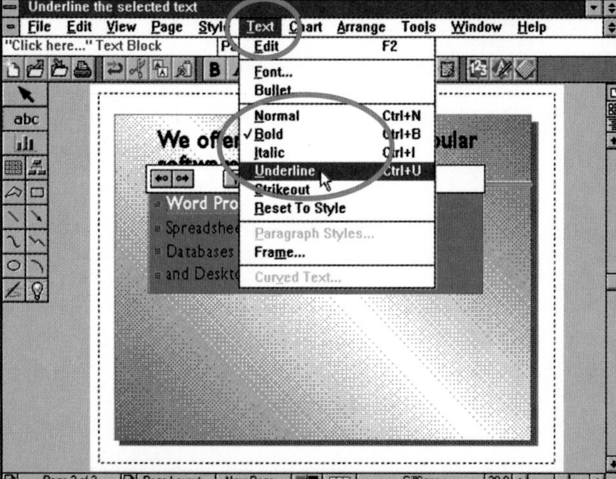

5 Select the words **Word Processing** again. Next, open the **Text** menu and choose **Underline**. Notice the other attributes you can apply to the text. Applied attributes are indicated by a check mark to the left of their names, such as the Bold attribute.

NOTE

You can also use the shortcut keys listed to the right of the commands in the Text menu to apply attributes to selected text.

6 Click outside the text so you can view the attributes. Select the modified text and press **Ctrl+N** to change it back to normal again.

WHY WORRY?

You can apply an attribute to one character, one word, or all of the text. If you change your mind at any time, select the text and choose the N button or press Ctrl+N to return the text to its normal state.

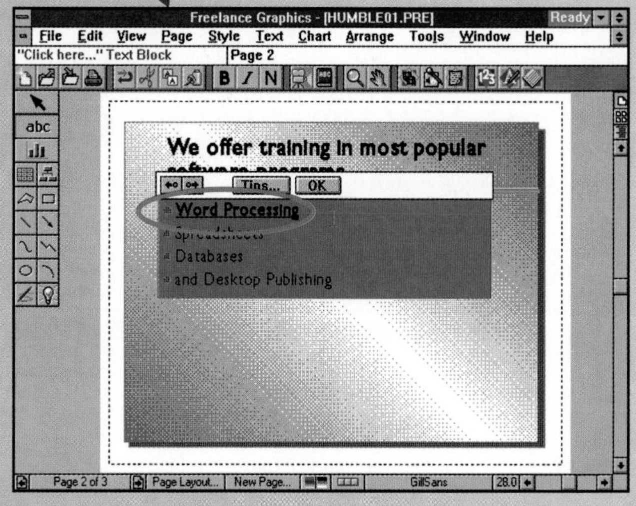

TASK 20

Changing the Font and Font Size

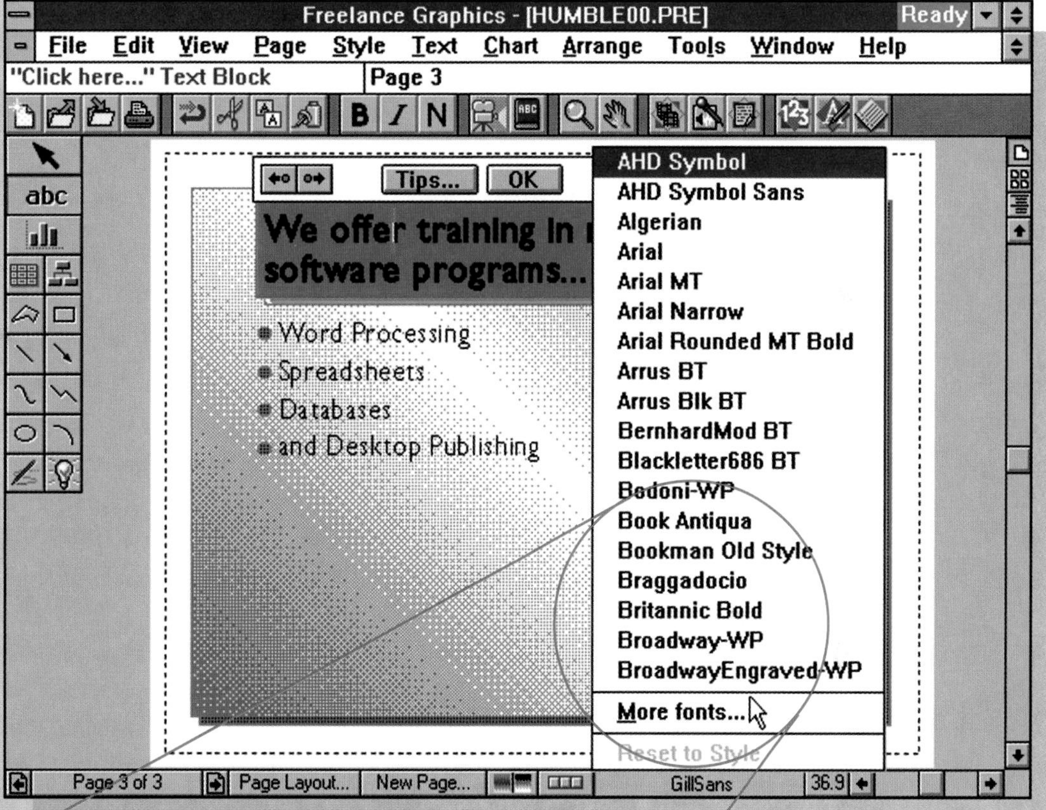

"Why would I do this?"

A *font* is a typeface, such as Times New Roman, Arial, GillSans, and so on. You use different fonts to spice up a presentation, attract attention, emphasize important titles, or to create a mood. You can change the font at any time to create some excitement in your presentation. You can also change the size of the text. If you need to fit more text on the page, for example, you can make the type smaller. Or, you may want to make a title or other important text larger.

Task 20: Changing the Font and Font Size

1 On page two of your presentation, click the title text block to display the handles, indicating the text is selected.

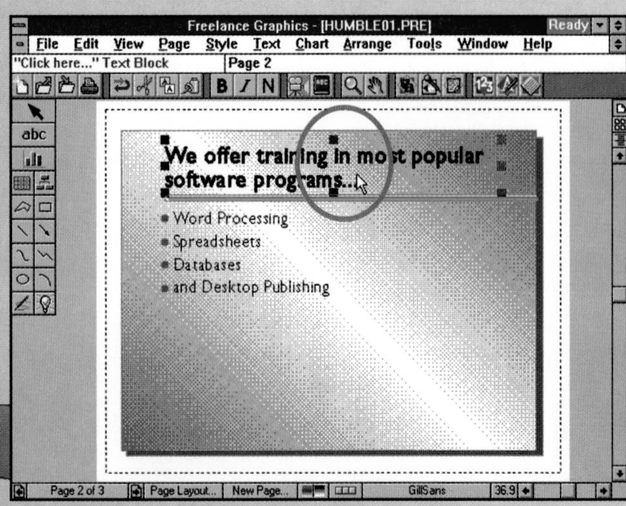

NOTE

You can select text either by clicking the block and displaying the handles, or by clicking the block twice and dragging the I-beam over the text so it appears in reverse video.

2 Click the font name **GillSans** in the status bar. An alphabetical list of available fonts appears. You can choose from the listed fonts or choose to view more fonts.

WHY WORRY?

If you click GillSans in the status bar and nothing happens, make sure you have selected the text. This step only works when text is selected.

3 Choose **More Fonts** in the list. The More Fonts dialog box appears. Scroll through the available fonts.

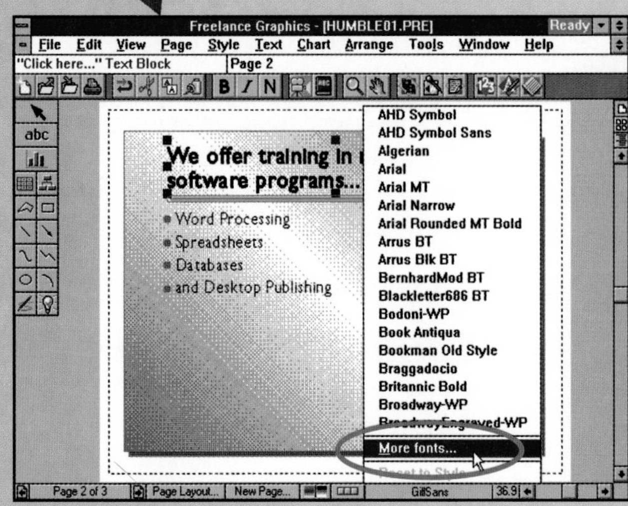

NOTE

Freelance uses ATM (Adobe Type Manager) fonts, if you installed ATM with your Freelance program or other program. Additionally, Freelance uses TrueType fonts used with many Windows programs.

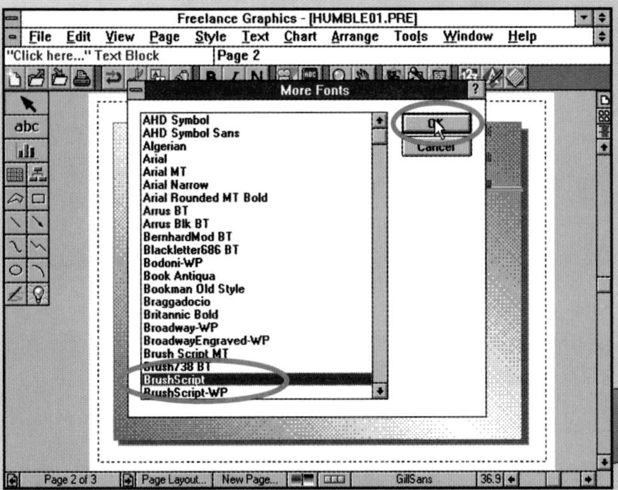

4 Select a font, such as **BrushScript**, and choose **OK**. The new font appears in the text block.

NOTE

Limit the number of different fonts you use in a presentation to no more than two. For example, use BrushScript for titles and GillSans for the bullet text, subtitles, and so on. Too much variety in fonts can be distracting.

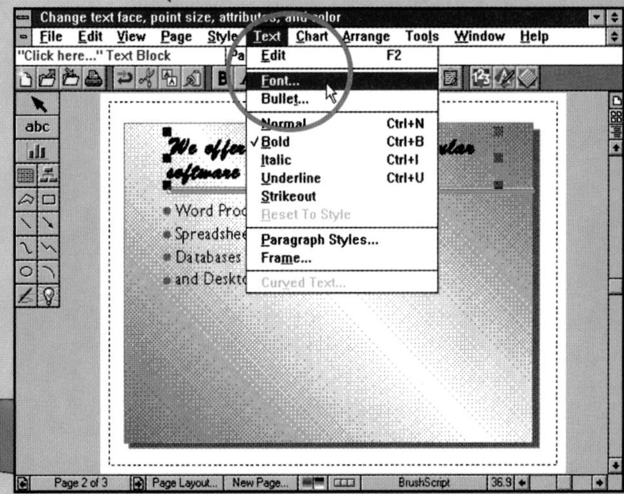

5 You can alternatively change fonts by opening the **Text** menu and choosing **Font** to display the Font dialog box.

NOTE

If you change the font on one page of the presentation—such as the title on page two—you should change all titles in the presentation so the pages look consistent.

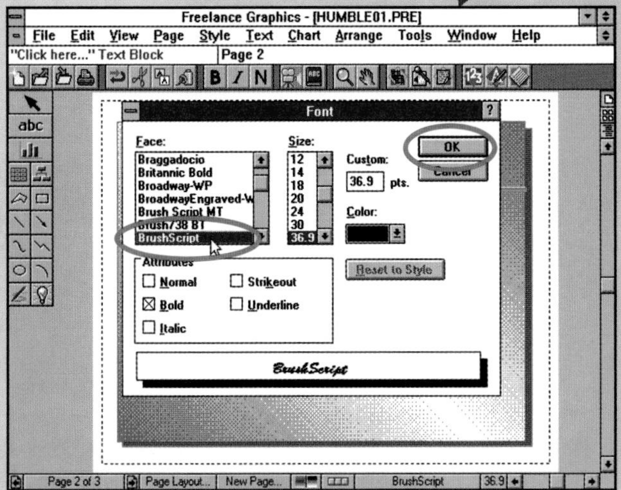

6 Select a font from the **Face** list in the Font dialog box; an example of the font appears at the bottom of the dialog box. Choose a font and choose **OK** to close the dialog box and apply the font.

NOTE

If you click a text block with the right mouse button, you reveal a quick menu that enables you to change fonts through the Font dialog box.

Task 20: Changing the Font and Font Size

7 On page one of the presentation, select **Software Training** by clicking the text box.

NOTE

You may need to enlarge text that appears smaller in one font than in another font, even though the font size is the same. Another reason to enlarge text is because you have room on the page.

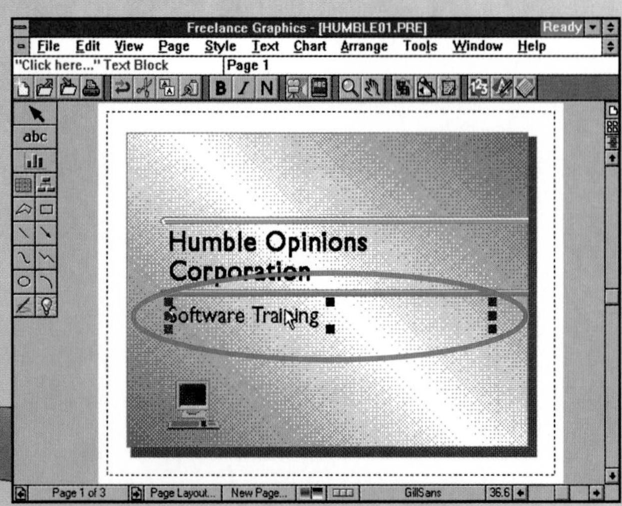

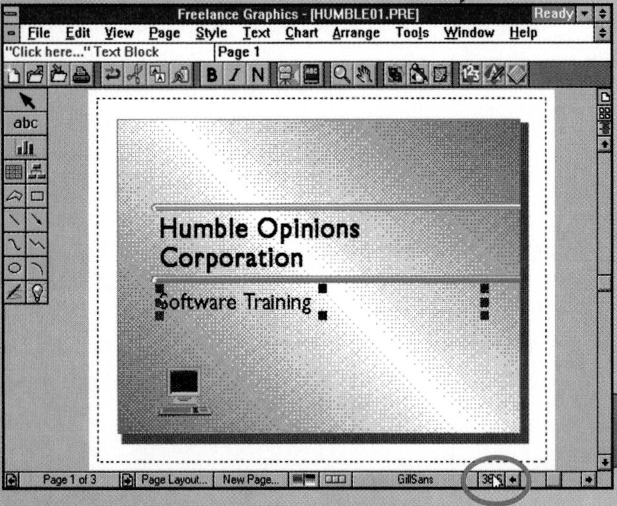

8 In the status bar, click the **Type Size** button, located next to the Font button. You can select any size listed in the size menu.

9 If the size you want is not listed, choose the option **Size** near the bottom of the list. The Text Size Other dialog box appears. In the **Size in Points** text box, enter **44** and choose **OK**.

NOTE

When you change the size of one title in your presentation, you should change the size of all titles to create consistency in your presentation.

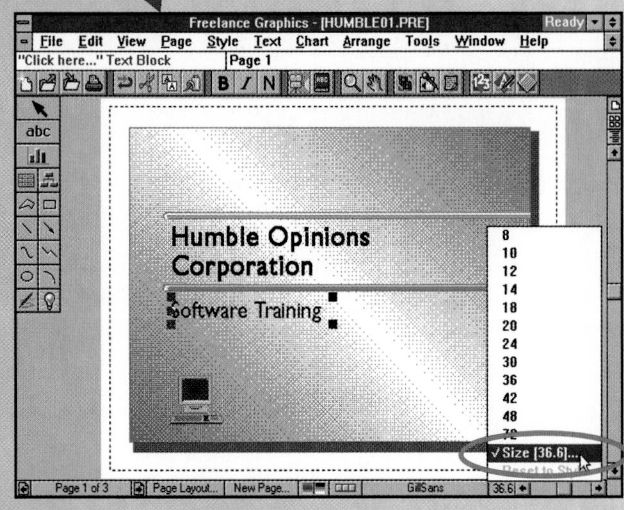

TASK 21

Adding and Modifying Bullets

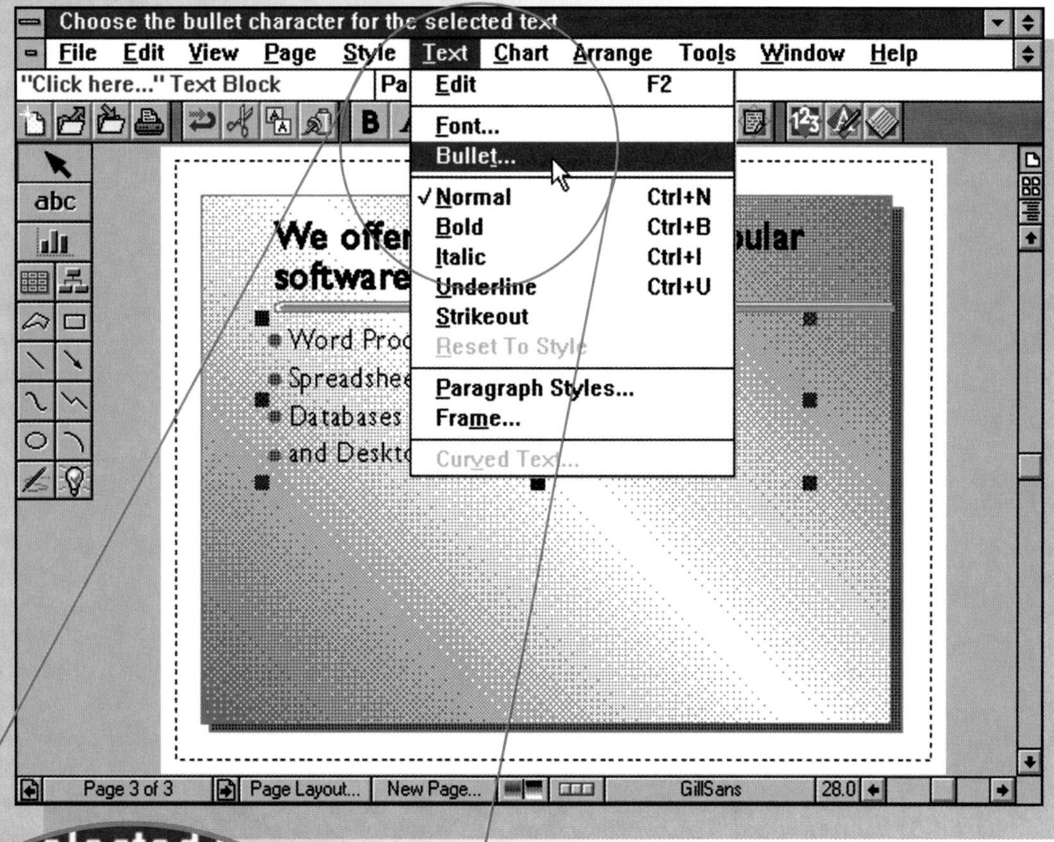

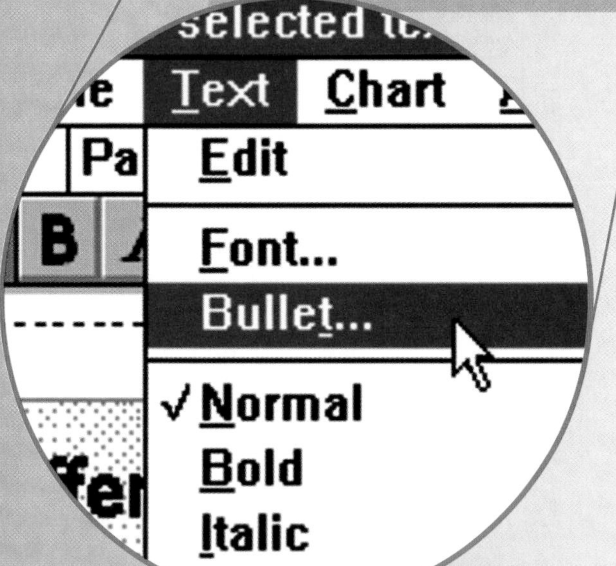

"Why would I do this?"

Freelance provides several different bullet styles—check marks, stars, arrows, and so on—you can use in place of the default bullet in a page layout. You may want to change the bullet style to fit the text and symbols you are using, or you may change the bullet style to attract more attention to the list. Additionally, you can change the color of the bullets to almost any color in the rainbow, and you can change the size of the bullets.

Task 21: Adding and Modifying Bullets

1 On page two of the presentation, select the bulleted list by clicking the text block.

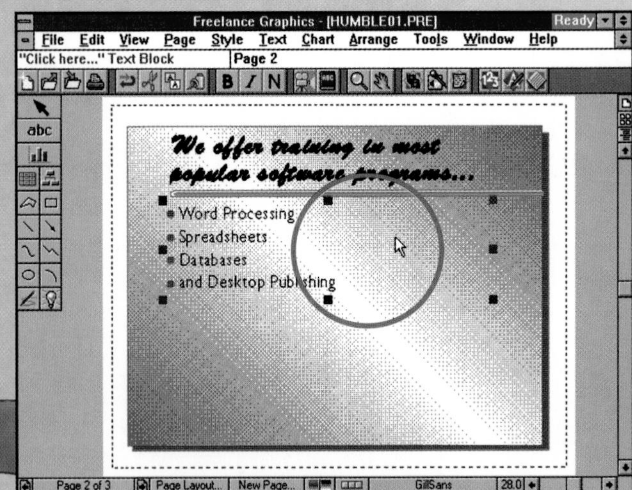

2 Open the **Text** menu and choose **Bullet** to display the Text Bullet dialog box.

3 The Text Bullet dialog box contains three options you can change: Style, Color, and Size.

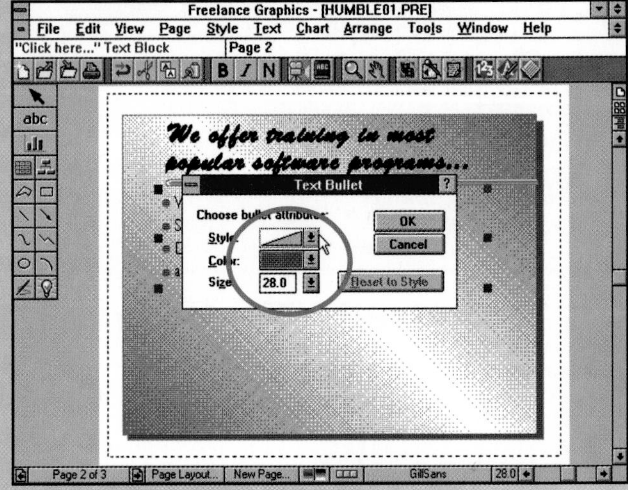

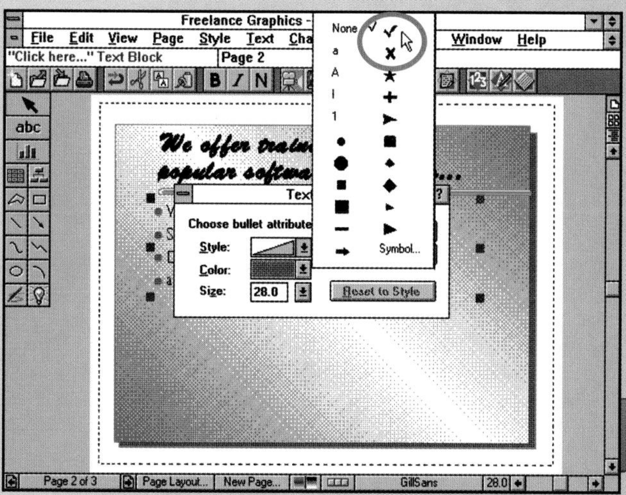

4 Choose **Style** to reveal the available styles for bullets. Choose the **check mark**.

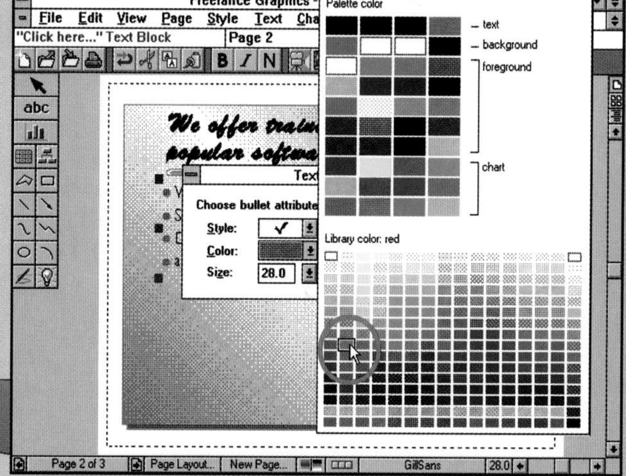

5 Choose **Color** to reveal the color palette. Choose **red**.

WHY WORRY?

If you decide the bullets are too small for the text, open the Text menu, choose Bullet, and change the size of the bullets. Bullet size is measured in points, just like type size.

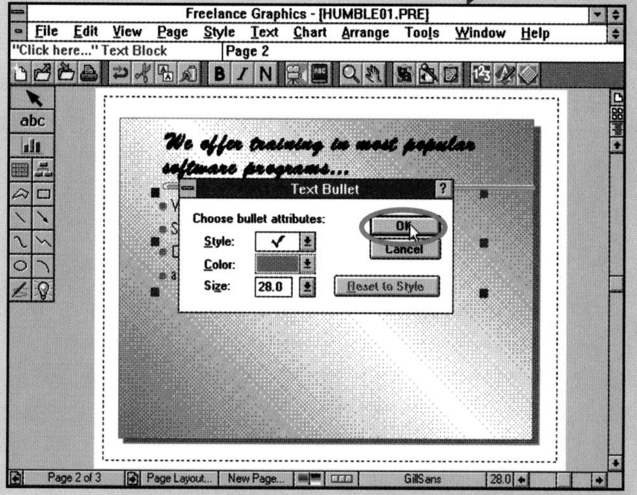

6 Choose **OK** to view the bullets in the text block.

NOTE

When you change the bullets on one page of your presentation, make all the bullets on all pages of the presentation the same, for consistency.

PART III

Formatting Styles

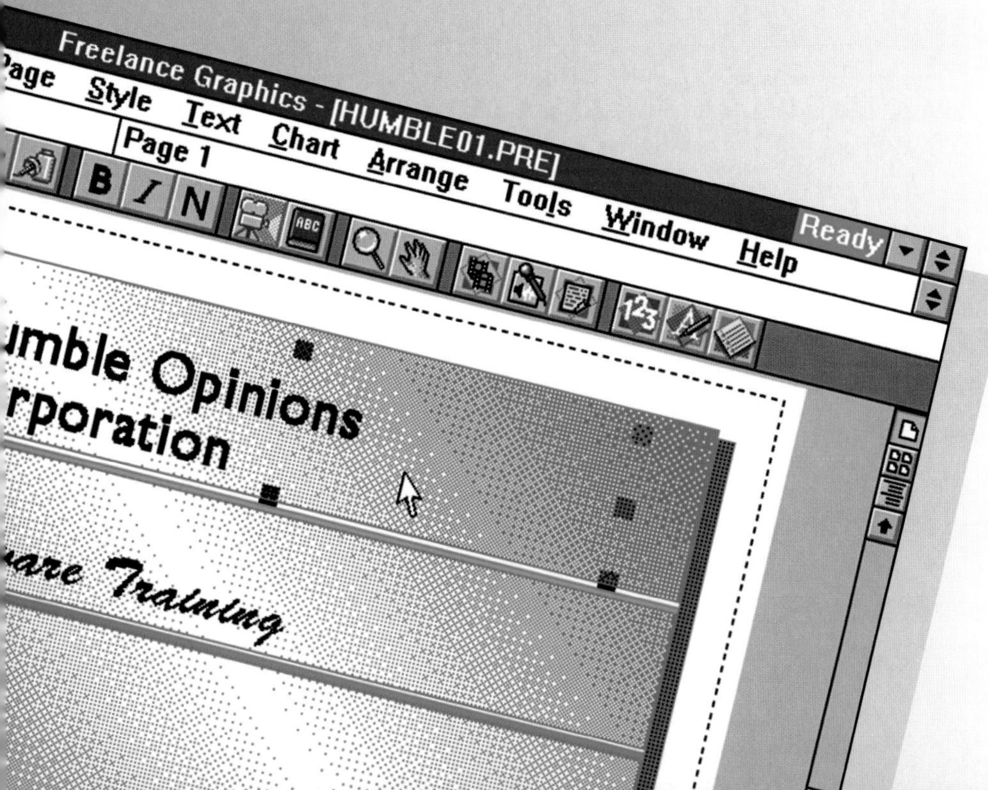

Each page layout design uses several default styles of type. A *style* is a predefined set of characteristics—such as font, type size, bullets, indent, and so on—assigned to the type. Freelance Graphics assigns styles to the type so that you can use a page layout for creating presentations without having to format the type yourself.

typestyle

In the tube.mas SmartMaster set, for example, the text for the bulleted list is 28-point GillSans normal, black, left-aligned, with a large, round, green bullet. The title style is 36.9-point GillSans, black, bold, and left-aligned. Freelance has already set these styles for you so that you can easily create a quick presentation; however, you can change the typeface, type size, type color, text alignment, and even the size, shape, and color of the bullet of any paragraph style.

bold

As you have seen, you can change the formatting of any text in Freelance to suit the presentation by using the Text menu. In addition, Freelance offers three styles, each with different formatting, from which you can choose in some of the text blocks. In the text blocks with bullets, for example, you can select a bulleted line of text and apply a style that indents the text and reduces the size of the bullet. Using the Promote and Demote buttons in a text block, you can quickly create an outline effect in your bulleted lists by applying one of the three supplied styles.

italic

In addition, you can apply various formatting to a style, using the Paragraph Styles dialog box, and that formatting applies to all text within that text block. A *paragraph* in Freelance is any one or more lines of text set off from other text by a carriage return. Suppose, for example, that you want to change the font, size, text color, or bullet color. You can change the attribute in one line of text, and the change applies to all text in the text block.

There may be times when you want to change the text alignment—perhaps center the text on the page, for example—or add space between the lines of text. What if you want to indent a bullet another half of an inch? You can apply any of these formatting changes using the Paragraph Styles dialog box.

Freelance lets you apply formatting changes and preview the changes before you decide on the final look of the text. If you decide you do not like the changes, you can cancel them or go back and modify the text until you are satisfied with it.

Finally, you can use the Paragraph Styles dialog box to modify styles in a specific page layout and then apply the changes to all styles in that same page layout throughout the presentation. Suppose, for example, that you changed the bullets on a Bulleted List layout page. If those changes were extensive—changing spacing, indents, bullet size and color, even text size and color—you change the Paragraph Styles within the bulleted list.

After changing the styles, you choose an option that applies the changes to every other Bulleted List layout page in your presentation. Therefore, you can change all bulleted lists in the presentation automatically, without moving to each individual page and making each change. Choosing this option not only saves you time creating your presentation, but it promotes consistency among page designs and formats.

TASK 22

Assigning Paragraph Styles

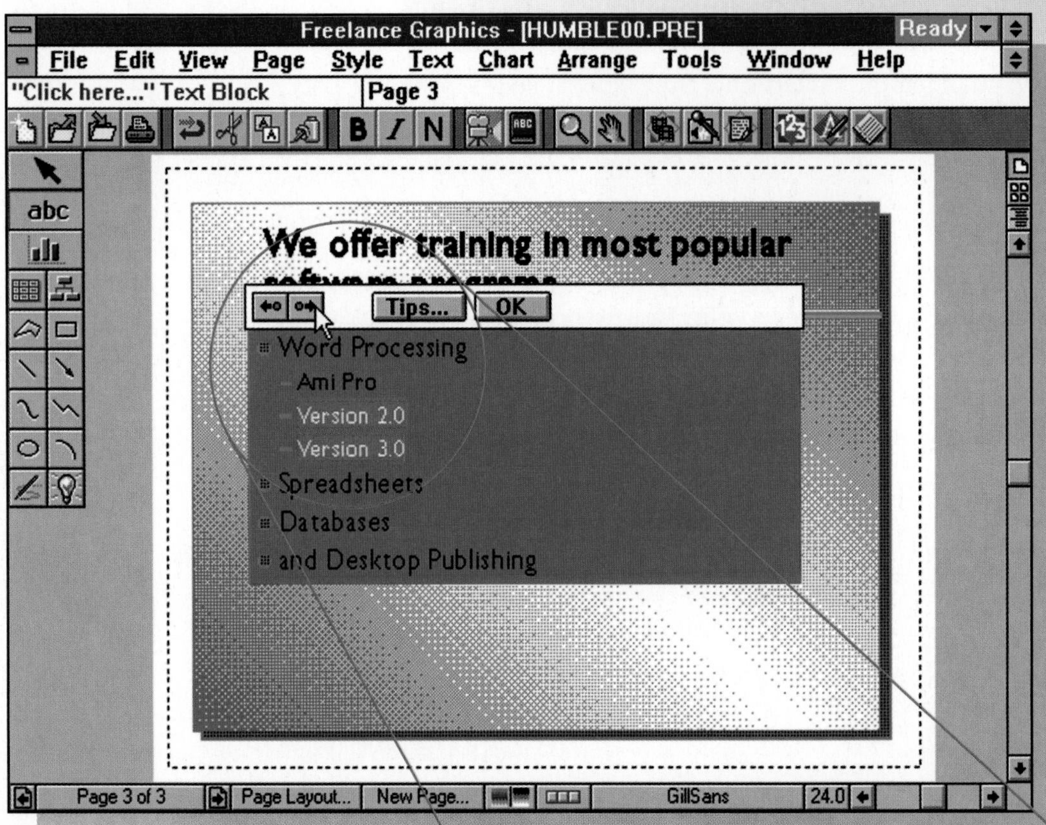

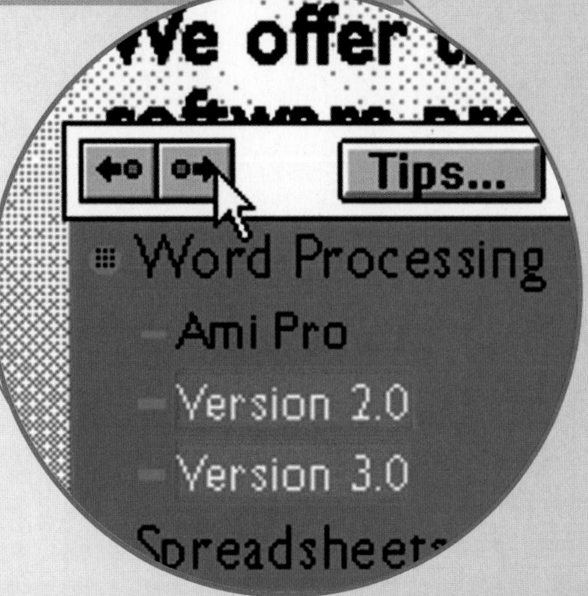

"Why would I do this?"

Freelance has preformatted some styles for you, so you can quickly create a presentation without the bother of selecting and modifying the text. Applying Freelance's preformatted paragraph styles enables you to apply a different font, type size, indent, or other formatting to the text in a text block. You can, for example, apply three different bulleted list styles to help you organize the text in a list.

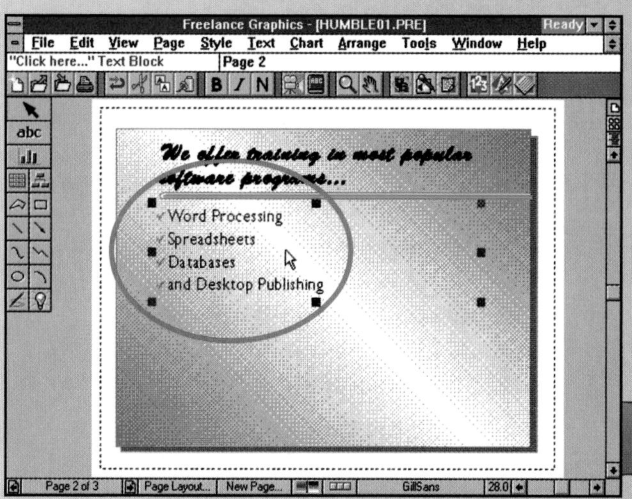

1 On page two of your presentation, click the bulleted list, and click again to display the editing text block.

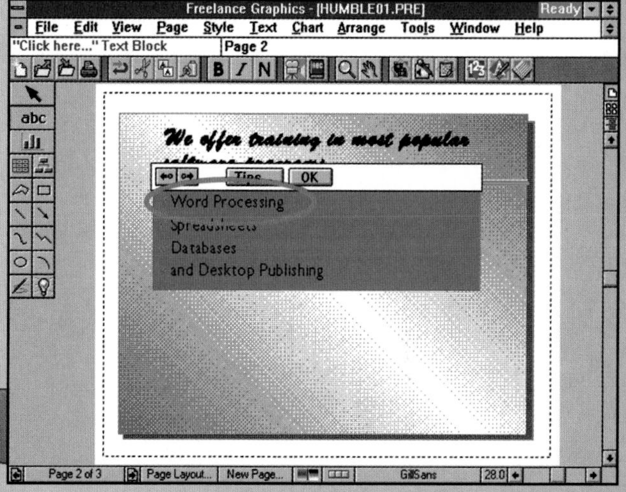

2 Position the insertion point after `Word Processing` and press **Enter**. Type **Ami Pro** and press **Enter**; **Version 2.0** (press **Enter**); **Version 3.0** (press **Enter**); **Word for Windows** (press **Enter**); **Version 2** (press **Enter**); **Version 6** (press **Enter**); and **WordPerfect 6.0**.

3 Select the seven new lines of text, beginning with **Ami Pro** and ending with **WordPerfect 6.0**, by dragging the I-beam across and down the text. The text appears in reverse video.

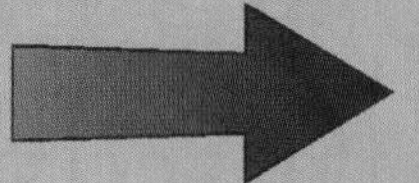

Task 22: Assigning Paragraph Styles

4 In the title bar of the text block, click the **Demote** button (the button to the left containing the right arrow). Freelance applies style 2 to the text, indenting the text one-half inch and reducing the type size.

NOTE

The Promote button (the button containing the left arrow) elevates the text to its former position in the outline. Promoting the text you just demoted removes the indent and enlarges the text.

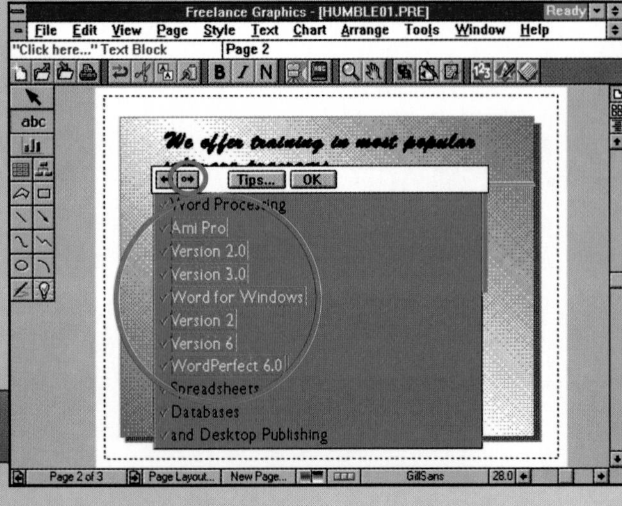

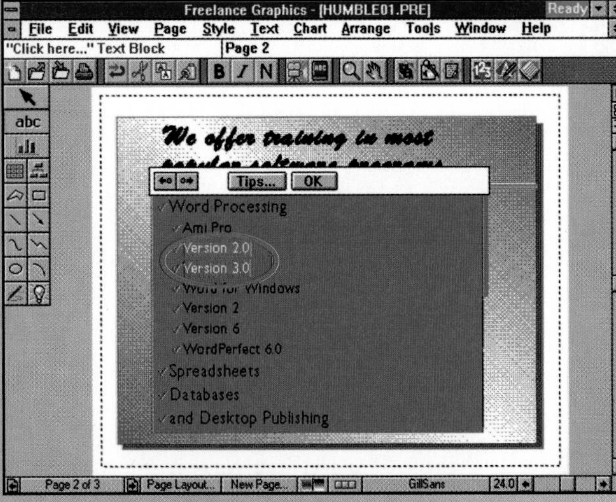

5 Select the two lines of text below `Ami Pro`, **Version 2.0** and **Version 3.0**.

6 Click the **Demote** button. Freelance demotes the two lines of text. Repeat steps 5 and 6 with the two lines of text below `Word for Windows`, **Version 2** and **Version 6**. Choose **OK**.

NOTE

To quickly demote or promote bullets in a text block, click the line of text to be modified, and press Tab to demote the bullet or press Shift+Tab to promote the bullet.

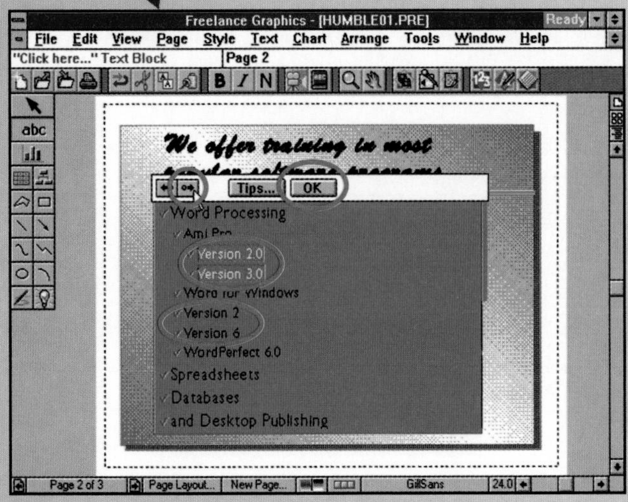

TASK 23

Changing Font Attributes

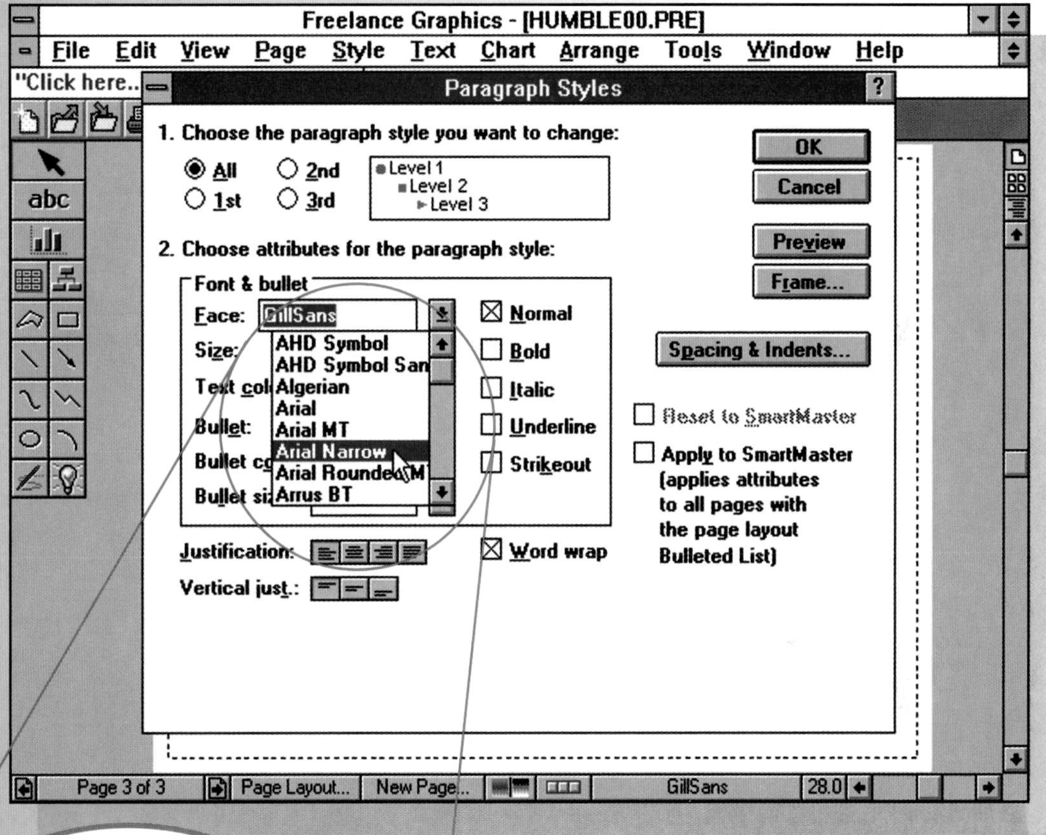

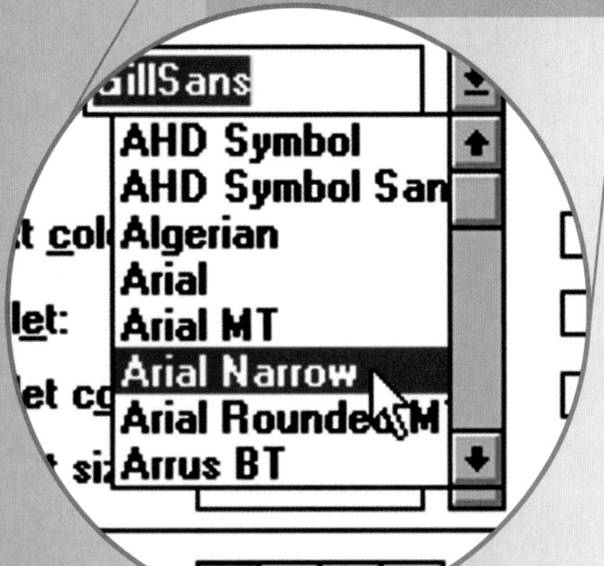

"Why would I do this?"

You can quickly change the font, type size, text color, and enhancements (bold, italic, and so on), of all text in a text block, using the Paragraph Styles dialog box. Suppose you want to change the text to Times Roman or make the size of all the text the same. You can make the changes in one dialog box that affect all the text in the block. Paragraph styles make text formatting in Freelance quick and easy.

Task 23: Changing Font Attributes

1 On page two of your presentation, double-click the bulleted list text block.

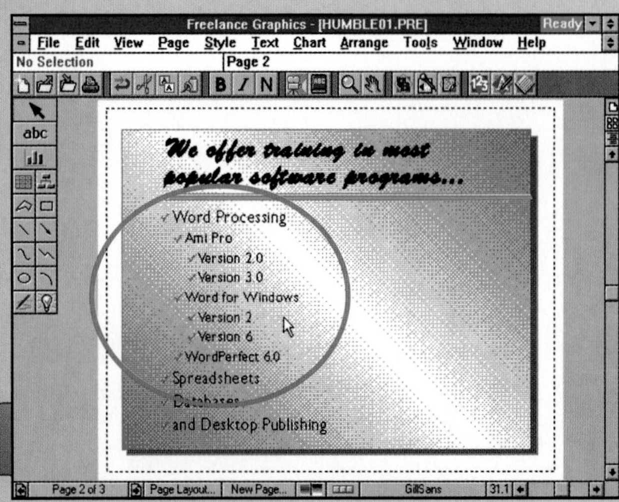

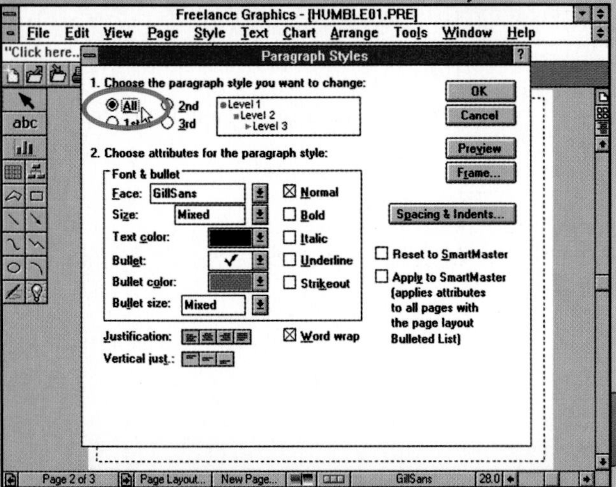

2 The Paragraph Styles dialog box appears. In the first option group, you can choose the paragraph style you want to change. The default, All, applies any changes you make in the dialog box to all paragraph styles in the selected text block. For now, leave the selection as **All**.

WHY WORRY?

If you want to make a change only to one level of the bullets in your list, select one of the following options: 1st, 2nd, or 3rd.

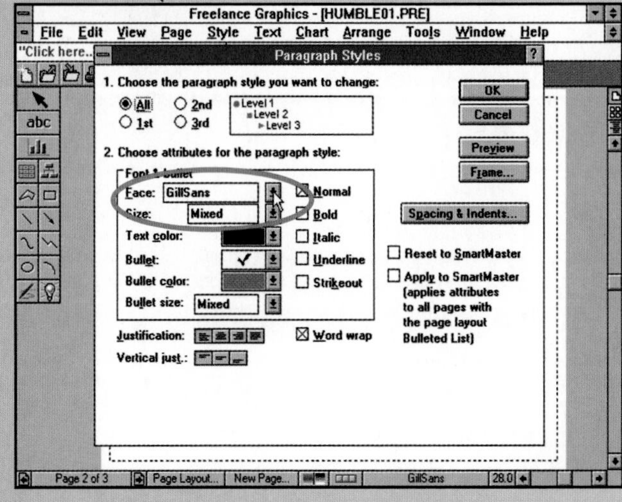

3 In the second option group, you can choose the attributes for the fonts in the selected text block. Scroll through the **Face** drop-down list of typefaces, or fonts. Choose **Arial MT**, **Arial Narrow**, or, if you do not have Arial, choose another font in the list.

The font you select applies to *All* of the text in the selected text block.

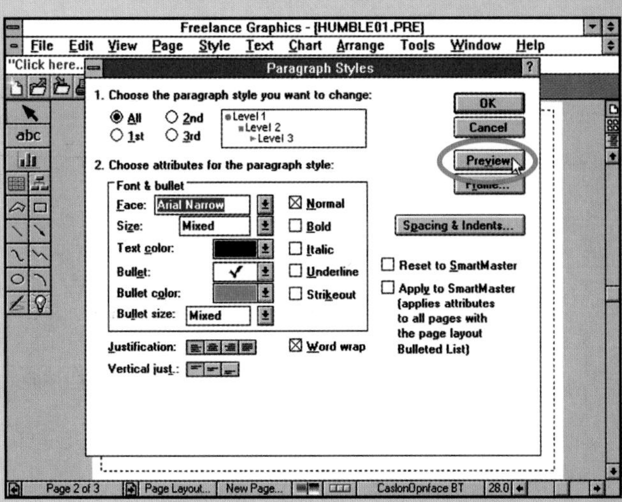

4 Choose the **Preview** command button, located in the upper right corner of the dialog box. Using Preview, you can see the results of your changes.

5 The Preview view shows the changes you have made to the text. Choose **Change** to return to the Paragraph Styles dialog box.

NOTE

You can choose OK to accept the changes and return to the document. The Tip button reveals a shortcut for viewing the preview. In the Paragraph Styles dialog box, click Preview, holding down the mouse button. Freelance displays the preview.

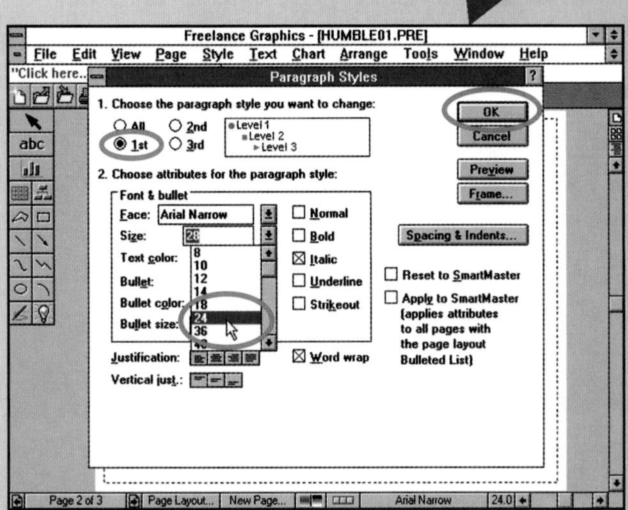

6 Choose **1st** in the first option group so you can change the size of level 1 text. In the Font & Bullet box, select **24** from the **Size** drop-down list; and then choose **OK**.

NOTE

Because levels 2 and 3 are already set at 24-point, changing level 1 to 24-point makes the bulleted list consistent.

TASK 24

Changing Bullet Attributes

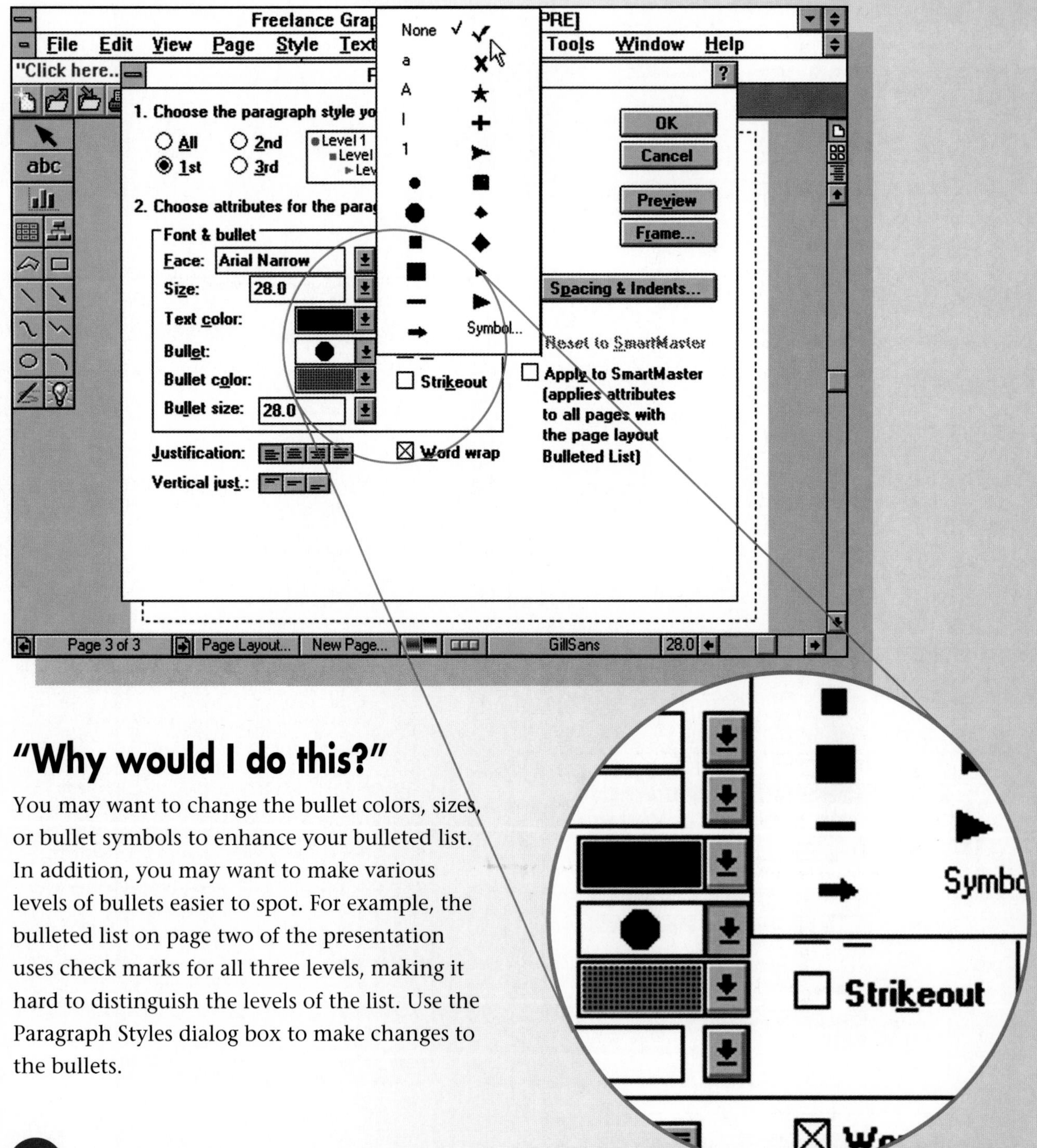

"Why would I do this?"

You may want to change the bullet colors, sizes, or bullet symbols to enhance your bulleted list. In addition, you may want to make various levels of bullets easier to spot. For example, the bulleted list on page two of the presentation uses check marks for all three levels, making it hard to distinguish the levels of the list. Use the Paragraph Styles dialog box to make changes to the bullets.

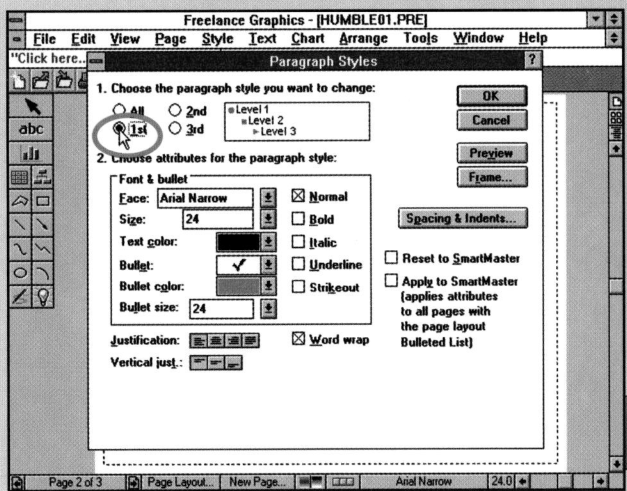

1 On page two of the presentation, double-click the bulleted list to display the Paragraph Styles dialog box. In the first option group, choose **1st** so you can change the bullet attributes of the first level.

2 To make the first-level bullets larger, select **48** in the **Bullet Size** drop-down list in the Font & Bullet box. This step makes the bullets twice as large as the text.

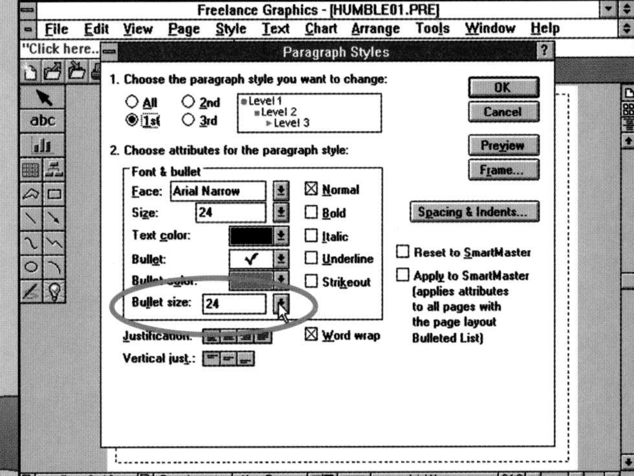

WHY WORRY?

If the size you want to use for your bullet is not listed in the drop-down list, position the cursor in the Bullet Size text box, delete the text, and enter the size you want for the bullet.

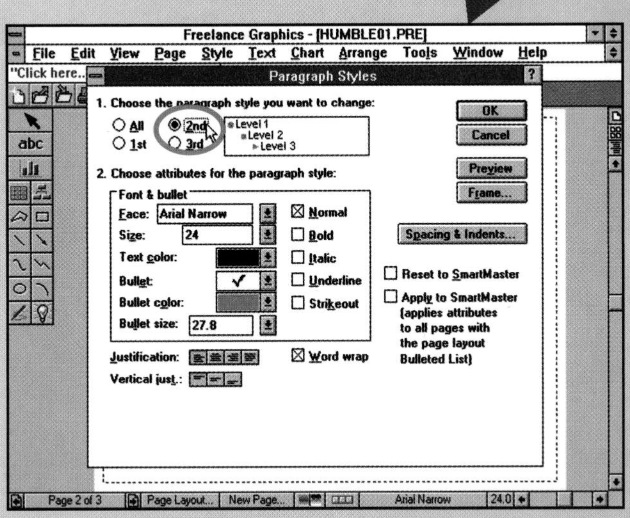

3 In the first option group, choose **2nd** to indicate that you want to modify the second level of the bulleted text.

Task 24: Changing Bullet Attributes

4 Choose **Bullet Color** to reveal the palette of color choices. Choose a green, or any color you want, for the bullet color of level 2. Repeat steps 3 and 4 to change the level 3 bullets to the same color as level 2.

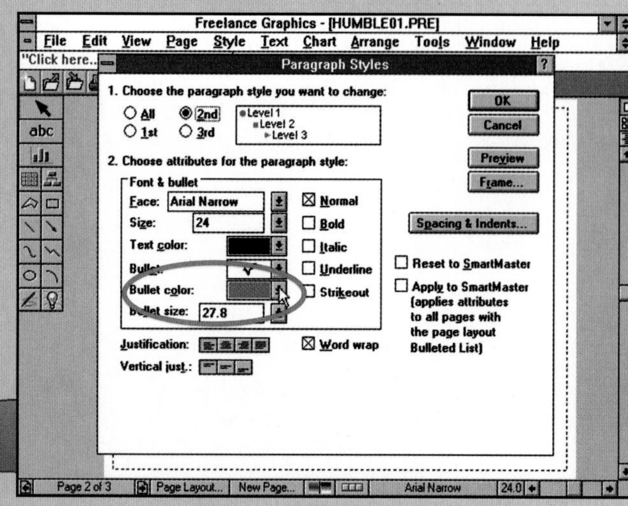

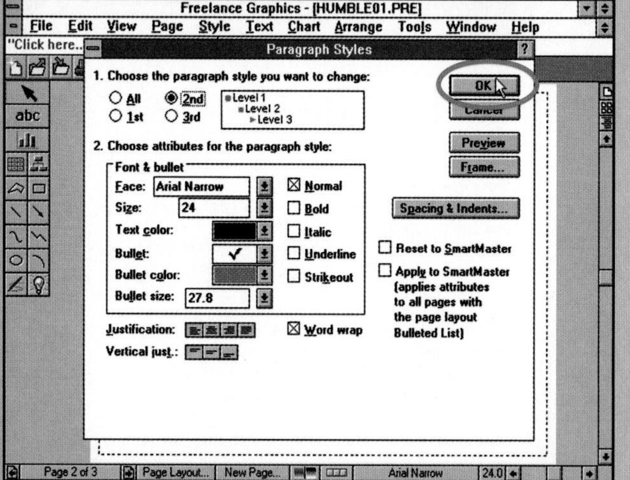

5 Choose **OK** to close the dialog box and accept the changes. Click outside the text block to hide the handles and view the modified document.

NOTE

It is a good idea to save your presentation periodically, in case of a power failure. To save, press Ctrl+S.

TASK 25

Aligning Text

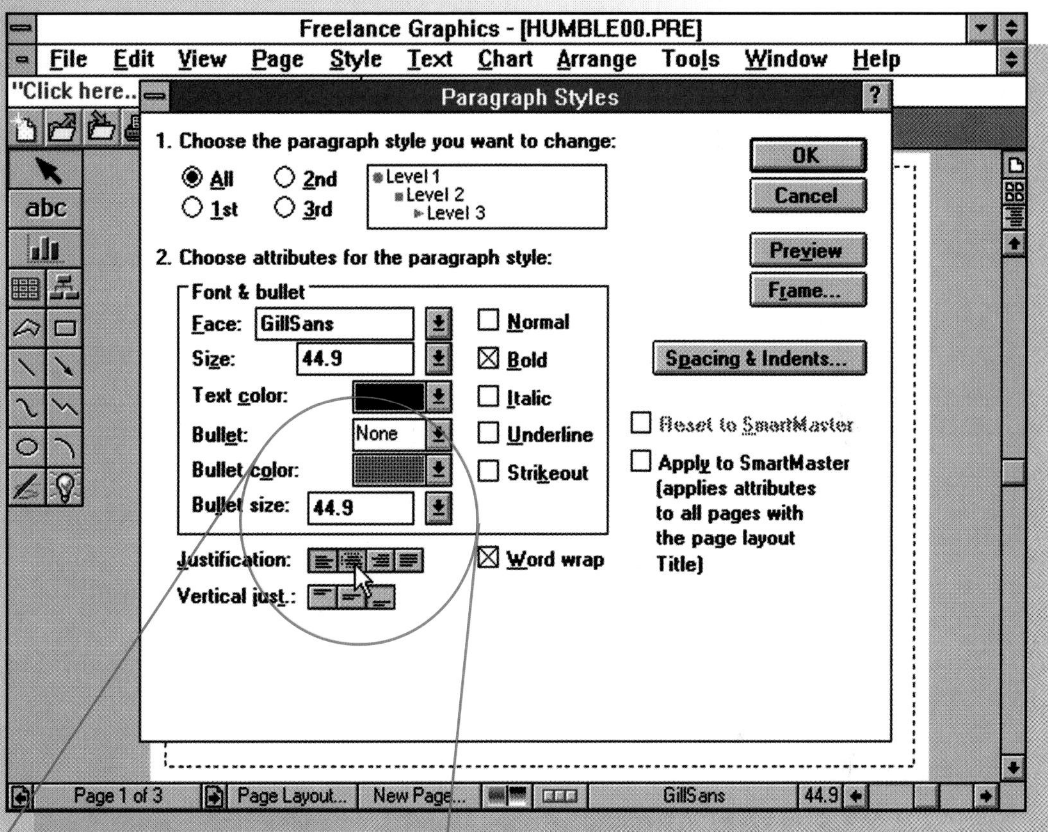

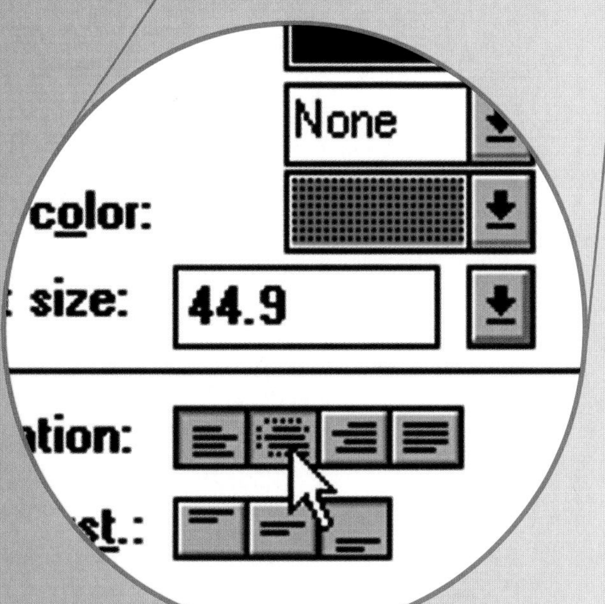

"Why would I do this?"

Alignment is a method of organizing paragraphs of text. You can choose to align the text in your presentation to the left, right, center, or justified. *Left-alignment* creates a flush-left edge and a ragged-right edge; *right-alignment* creates a flush-right edge with a ragged left. *Centered* text is ragged on both the right and left; *justified* text is flush on both the left and right edges. You can easily change the alignment using the Paragraph Styles dialog box.

Task 25: Aligning Text

1 On page one of your presentation, double-click the first text block, **Humble Opinions Corporation**, to reveal the Paragraph Styles dialog box.

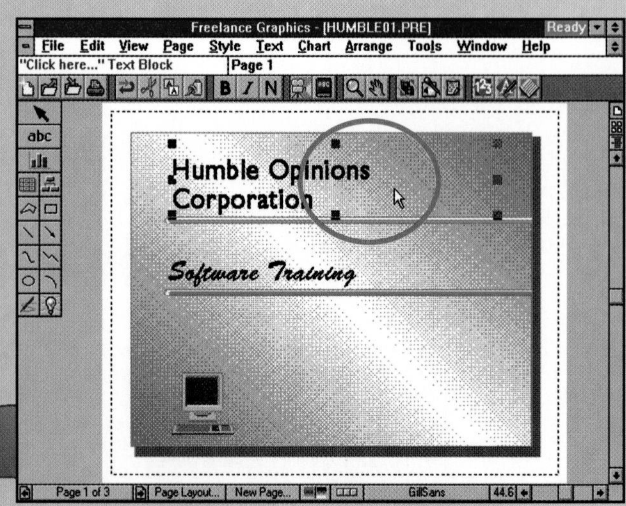

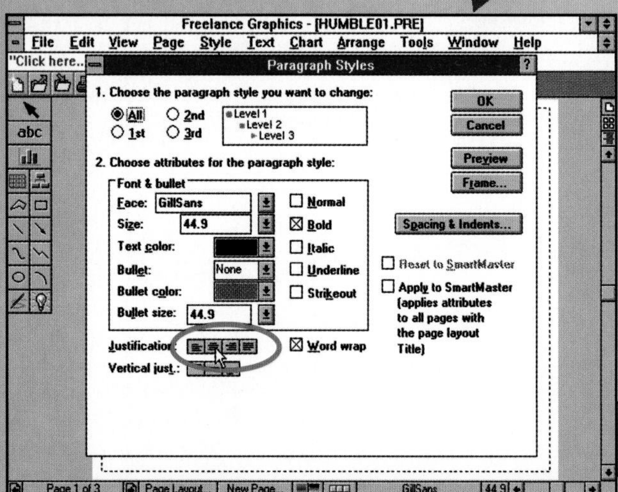

2 In the **Justification** area, choose the **Center** button, the second button from the left. This button represents center alignment. The buttons, from left to right, represent left-aligned, center-aligned, right-aligned, and justified text.

3 Choose **OK** to accept the change and close the dialog box. The selected text is centered.

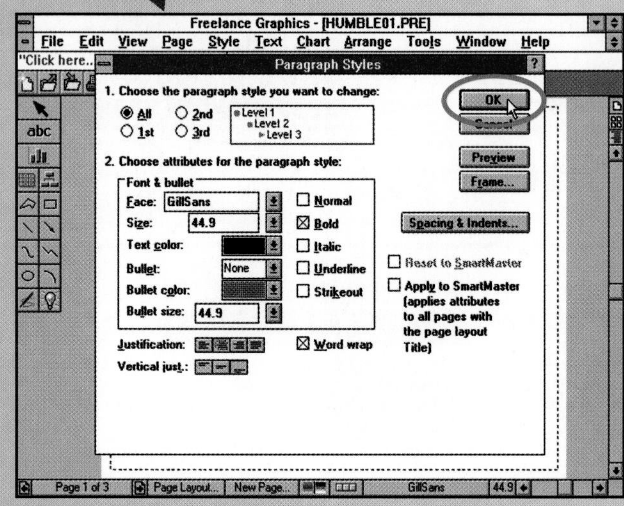

WHY WORRY?

Press Ctrl+S to save your presentation so if there is a power failure, you won't lose your work. Or, you can use the SmartIcon for Save the Current File (the third button from the left on the SmartIcon bar).

Freelance Graphics - [HUMBLE01.PRE]
File Edit View Page Style Text Chart Arrange Tools Window Help
Organization Chart Entry List
Edit View Gallery... Attributes...
Type all the entries you want in your chart:
Enter name here
Enter title here
Enter comment here
OK
Cancel
Preview
Tips
Press Enter to move to a new line or start a new entry.
Press:
Tab for a subordinate
Shift/Tab for a superior
Learn Lotus...
Freelance Graphics 2
Ami Pro 3.0
Lotus 1-2-3 Rel. 4
SmartSuite 2.1
Organizer 1.1
Organization Chart Staff
Type the entry for a staff position reporting to the person in the top box:
Name:
Title:
Comment:
Note: You can have one staff position per organization chart, and it always reports to the top box.
Remove
J. Smith
Purchasing
Enter comment here
Organization Chart Attributes
1. Choose what to change:
Text
Boxes
Connecting lines
Frame
Text line:
All lines
Font
Face
Arial MT
Size
10.3
Color
Justification
Normal
Bold
Italic
Underline
Strikeout
Edit Text...
Page Layout...
New Page...
GillSans

PART IV

Creating an Organization Chart

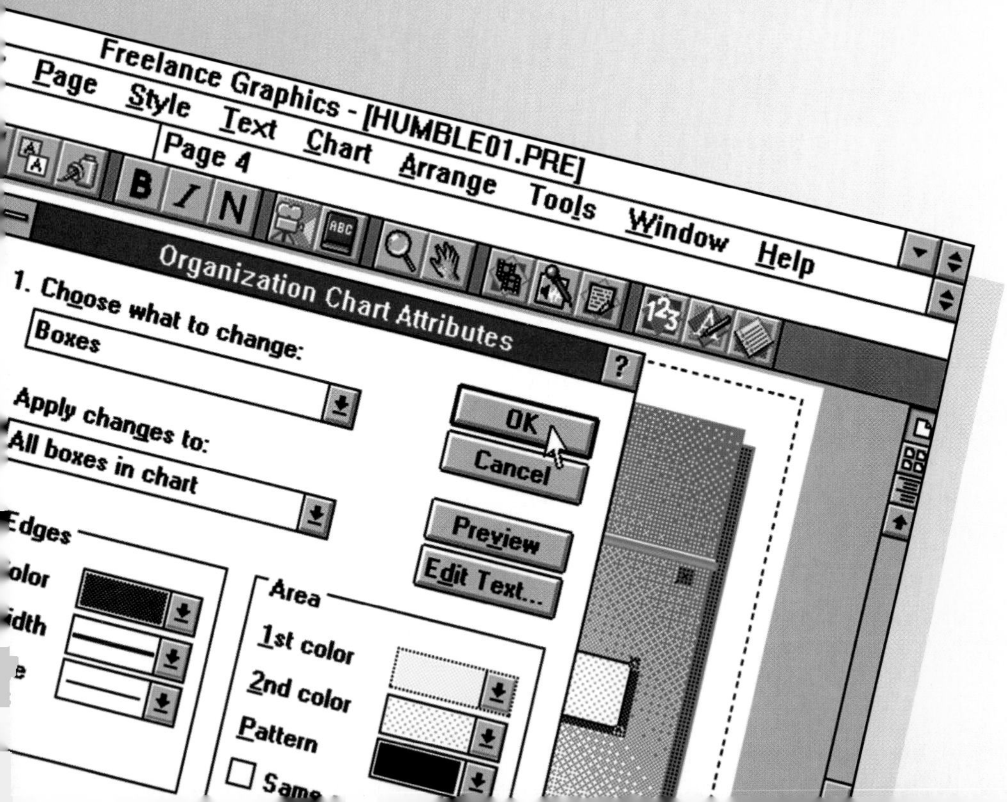

Part IV: Creating an Organization Chart

An *organization chart* shows the levels of a company's officers, managers, staff, and so on. At the top of each level is the highest ranking member of the company or department. Branching from the top level is a second level of members—usually two, three, or four people. Stemming from each of the members on the second level are those members directly beneath them. A fourth level may appear under the third level.

In one example of an organization chart, the top level contains the president of the company. The next level includes two vice presidents, and the third level shows the individuals who run each office location. Another example places the office manager at the top level, followed by managers for sales, manufacturing, and so on, on level two. Level three includes the department heads, and level four includes the support staff. The number of levels in an organization chart depends on the structure of the company.

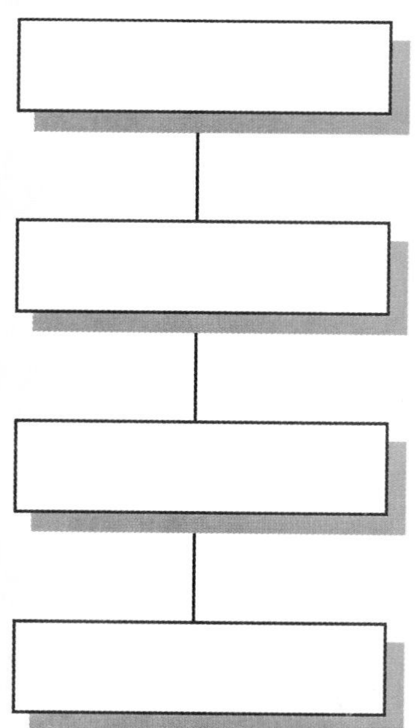

Freelance Graphics makes it easy to create an organization chart. In addition to "Click here..." text and symbol boxes, Freelance provides "Click here..." chart and table boxes. You can choose the Organization Chart page layout when adding a new page to your presentation, and Freelance provides a "Click here..." chart box. You can also choose to place a chart on any page by opening the Chart menu and choosing the Organization Chart command. Using the Organization Chart page layout, however, provides a consistent page design and font with the rest of the pages in your presentation.

When you create an organization chart, you first choose the chart style from a *Gallery*. The designs from which you choose consist of rectangles, ovals, rectangles with shadow boxes, and others. In addition, you can choose how to list the lower levels of the chart; for example, you can choose to box the names or just list them.

After you choose the style of chart, Freelance provides a dialog box in which you enter the names, titles, and comments for the chart. The Entry List dialog box guides you with instructions for entering the text and assigning levels to the entries. As you enter names, you can use shortcut keys to promote or demote the entry within the organization chart. You can preview the chart at any time.

In addition to providing easy entry of the chart contents, Freelance also preformats the text with styles that match the other pages in your presentation. You can, however, modify fonts, boxes, and even the connecting lines between levels. Freelance enables you to change attributes for the entire chart or for boxes within the chart, so you can create an organization chart that meets your needs.

TASK 26

Choosing a Chart Style

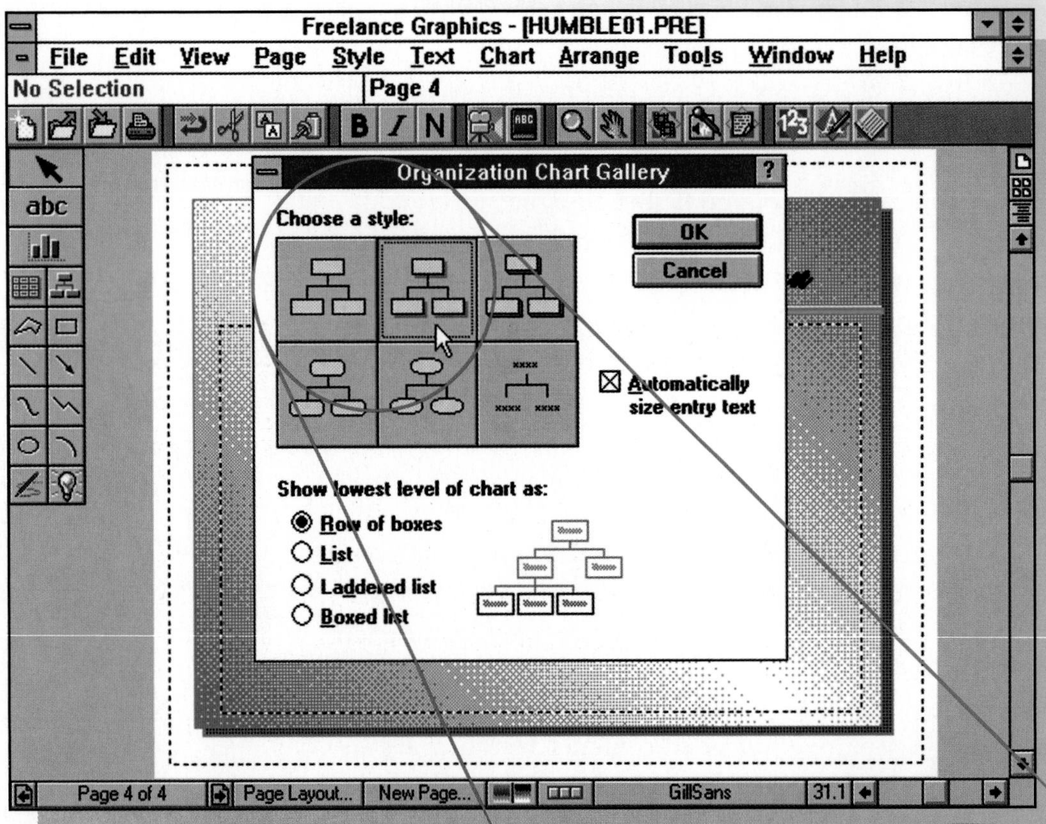

"Why would I do this?"

When you choose to create an organization chart, Freelance displays various *chart styles*, which consist of boxes to hold the names in the chart, lines to connect the boxes, fonts, and so on. You choose the style of chart you want and how you want to represent entries on the lower levels. A preview box within the Style dialog box displays the design before you accept it, but you can change the chart style at any time while creating the chart.

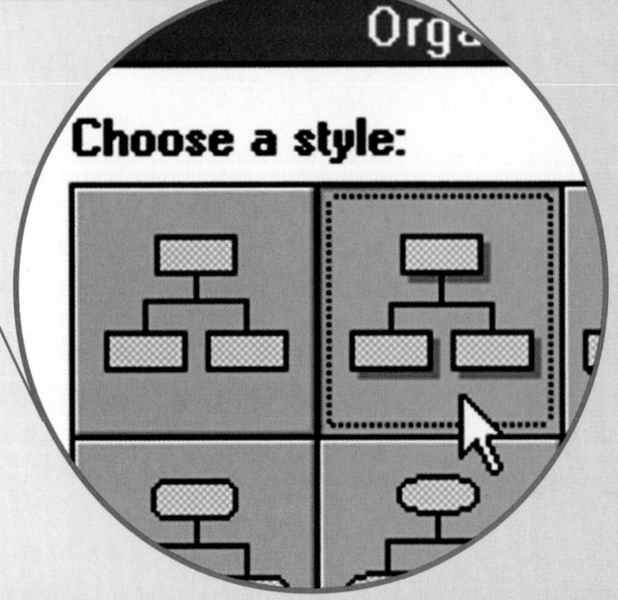

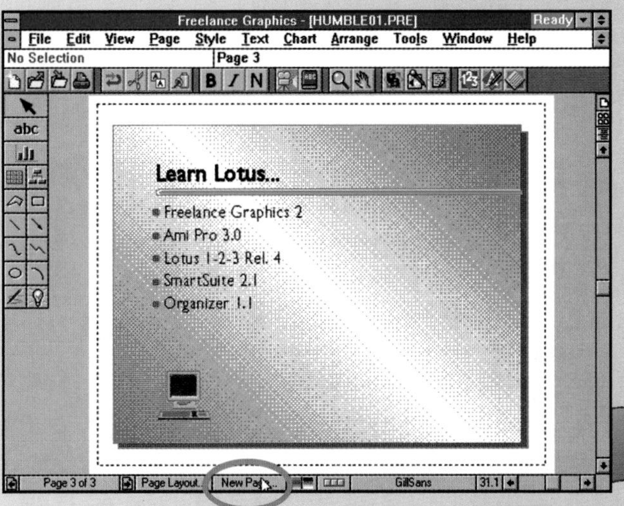

1 On page three of your presentation, click the **New Page** button in the status bar to display the New Page dialog box. From the Choose a Page Layout list box, select **Organization Chart**, and then choose **OK**. The new page appears.

2 The new page includes a "Click here to type page title" text area for the title and a "Click here to create organization chart" area for the chart. Click anywhere within the dotted chart box to display the Organization Chart Gallery dialog box.

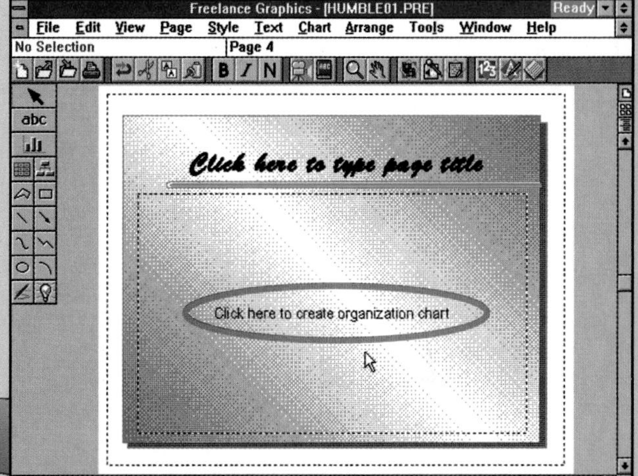

NOTE

You can fill in the "Click here..." title box with your own title or enter Humble Opinions Organization.

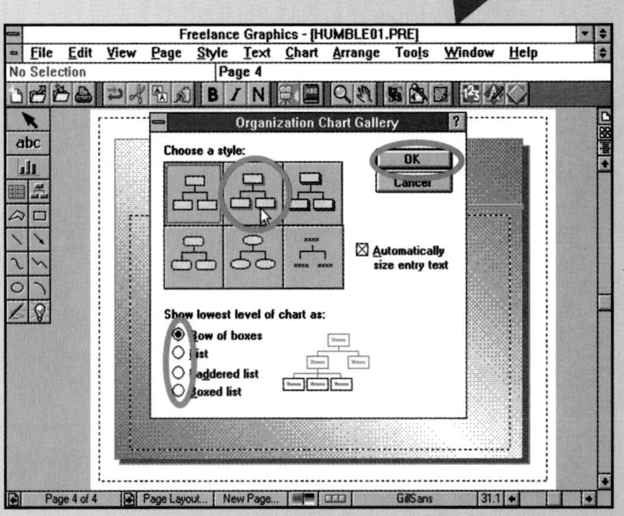

3 In the Choose a Style area, select the second style. In the Show Lowest Level of Chart As area, choose **List**. The preview chart in the lower right corner of the dialog box displays an example of the lowest level. Choose **OK**.

NOTE

For future reference, click each option in the Show Lowest Level of Chart As area to see each example.

TASK 27

Creating an Entry

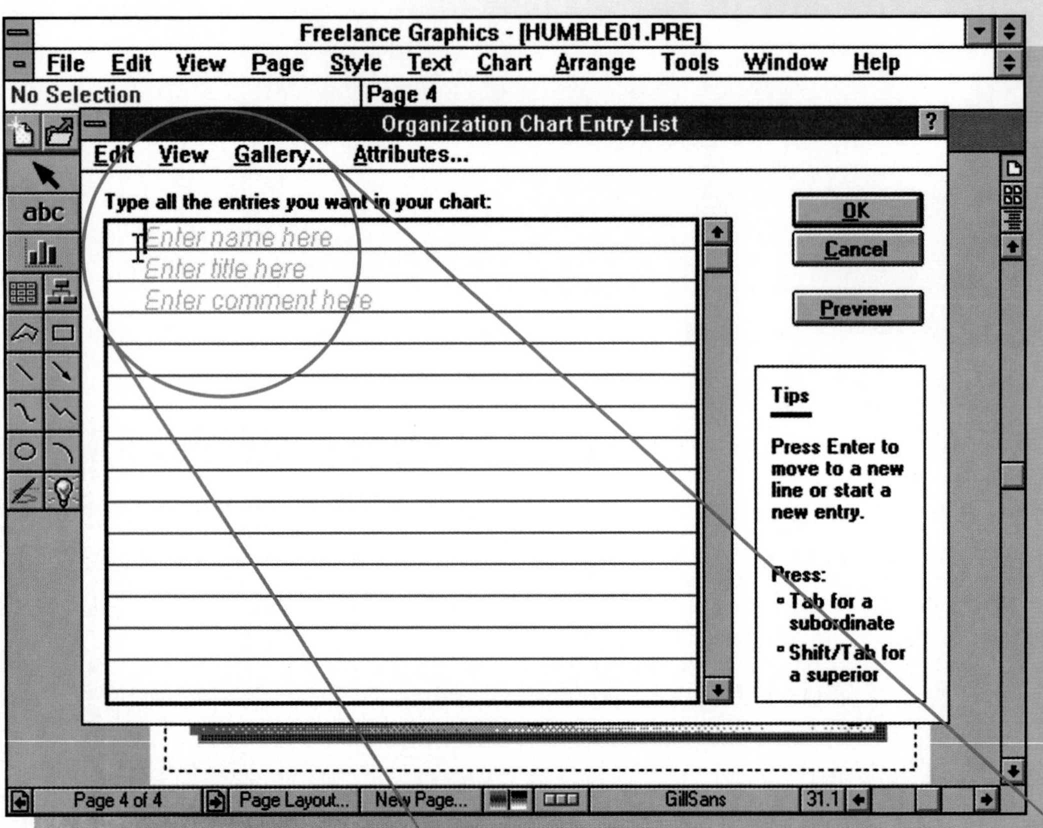

"Why would I do this?"

Freelance provides an Organization Chart Entry List. In this list, you can enter names, titles, and even comments for each box in the organization chart. Each entry represents a company member in the chart. Using Freelance's step-by-step help, you enter the information. The Entry List makes it easy to enter, edit, and rearrange names in the chart. When you are finished, Freelance creates the chart for you.

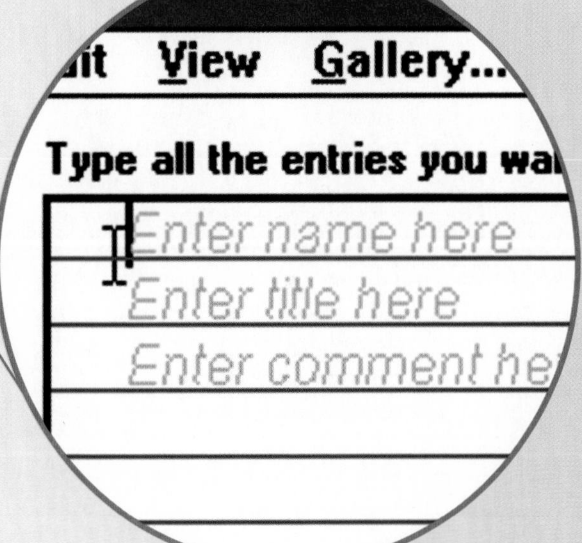

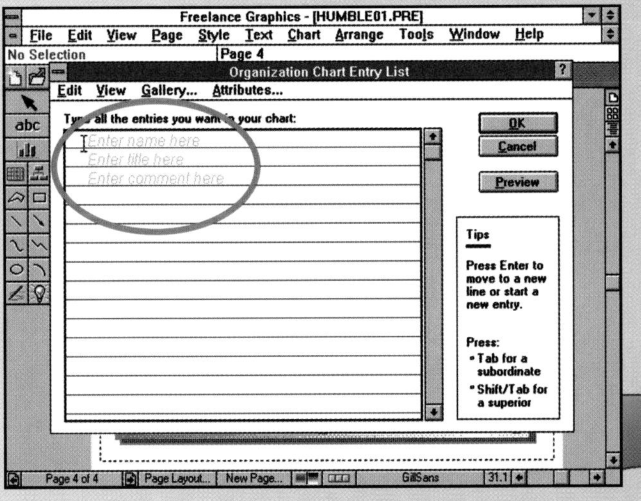

1 When you choose OK in the Organization Chart Gallery dialog box, the Organization Chart Entry List dialog box appears. Freelance supplies instructional text, screened in the background of the text area, as you type.

2 The insertion point is already positioned, type the person's name, press **Enter**, and then type the person's title. Use your own company information, or enter the text in the figure, and press **Enter** after each line of text.

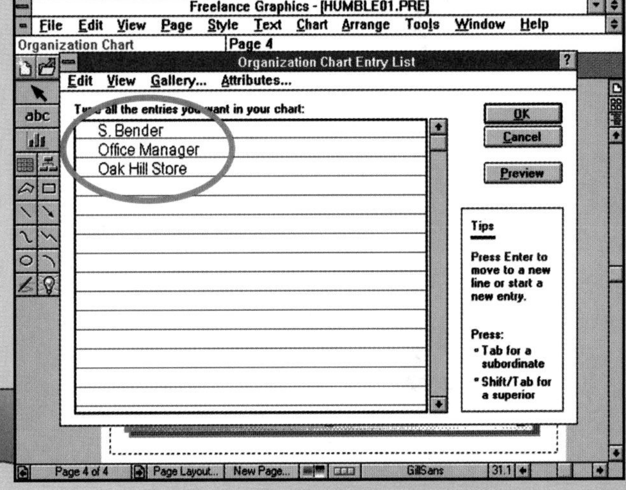

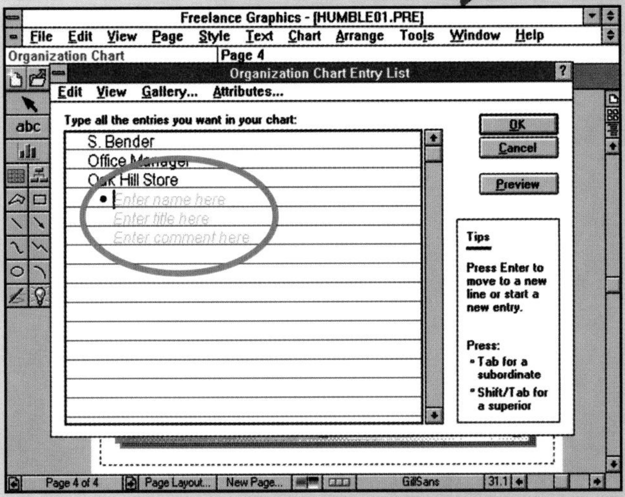

3 After you type the first three lines of text, press **Enter**. Freelance indents the text, adds a bullet, and provides more instructional text.

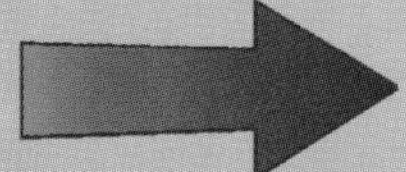

Task 27: Creating an Entry

4 Press **Tab** to create an entry for a subordinate or to demote a name, and press **Shift+Tab** for a superior or to promote a name on the list. Enter the following: **B. Crowder** (**Enter**), **Sales** (**Enter** twice, press **Tab**), **D. Alley** (**Enter**), **Secretary** (**Enter** twice), **J. Wallford** (**Enter**), **Assistant** (**Enter** twice, press **Shift+Tab**), **J. Smith** (**Enter**), **Purchasing** (**Enter** twice, press **Tab**), **W. Riner** (**Enter**), **C. Davis** (**Enter**) **Assistant.**

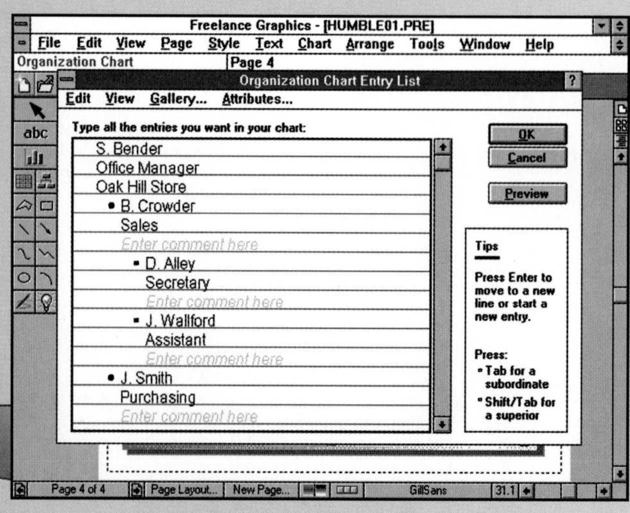

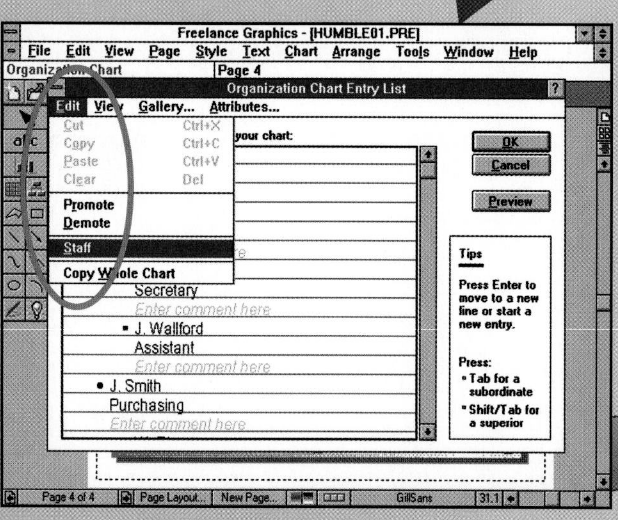

5 You can choose to add one staff person who reports directly to the person on the top level. You can have only one staff position per chart. To enter the information about the staff person, open the **Edit** menu and choose **Staff**.

6 The Organization Chart Staff dialog box appears. In the **Name** text box, type **D. E. Withrow**. Choose **OK** to close the dialog box; choose **OK** again to close the Organization Chart Entry List.

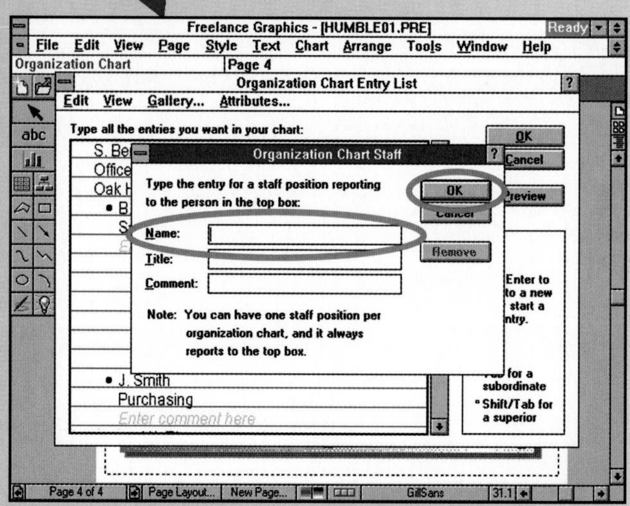

WHY WORRY?

To edit the text in the chart, double-click the chart frame on the presentation page, or select the chart and choose Chart Edit to display the Organization Chart Entry List dialog box.

TASK 28

Changing Chart Attributes

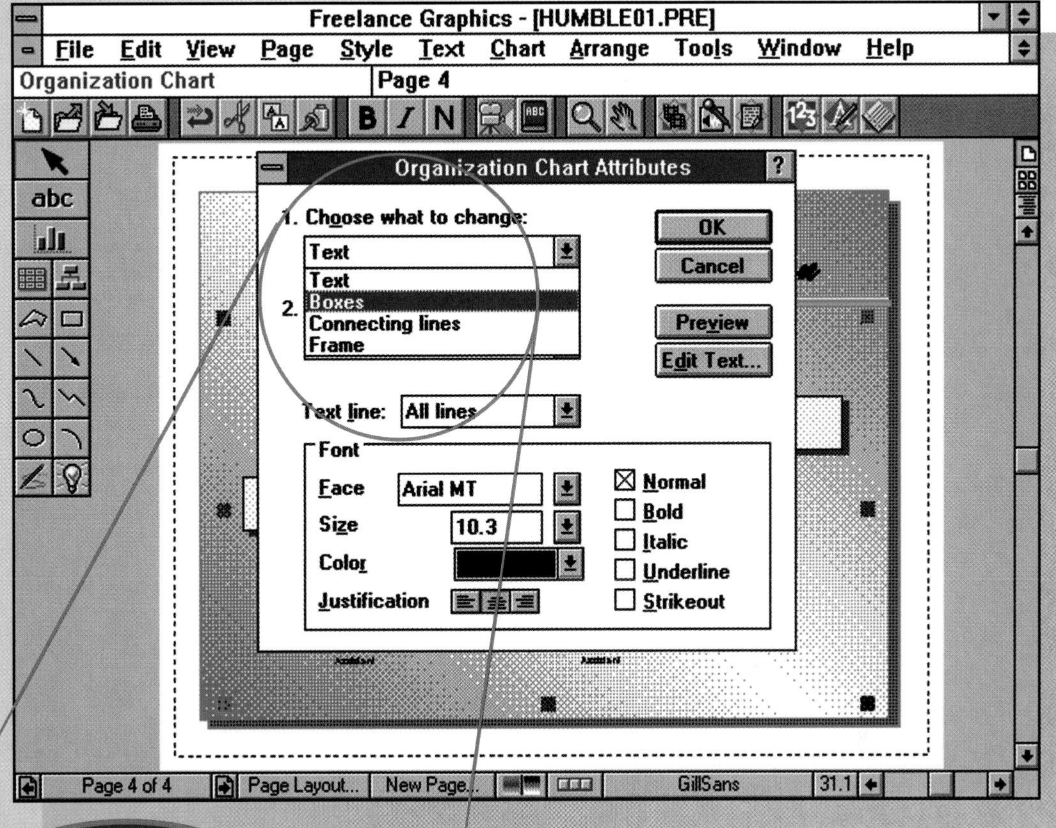

"Why would I do this?"

Chart attributes include text, boxes, the frame, and connecting lines. *Text attributes* include font, type size and color, and paragraph alignment. *Box attributes* include line color, width, and the style and color of the box background. With Freelance Graphics, you can change all of these attributes. Although Freelance provides a formatted organization chart for you, you can change the chart attributes to suit your presentation.

Task 28: Changing Chart Attributes

1 After creating the organization chart, you can modify the chart attributes, such as the text, colors, lines, and so on. To edit the chart attributes, open the **Chart** menu and choose **Attributes**. The Organization Chart Attributes dialog box appears.

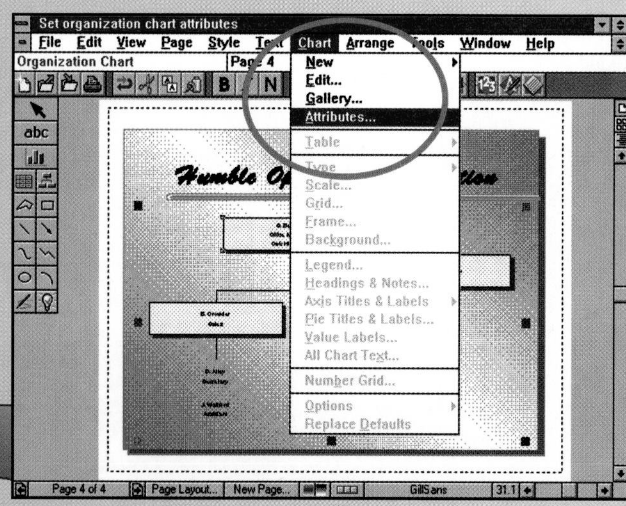

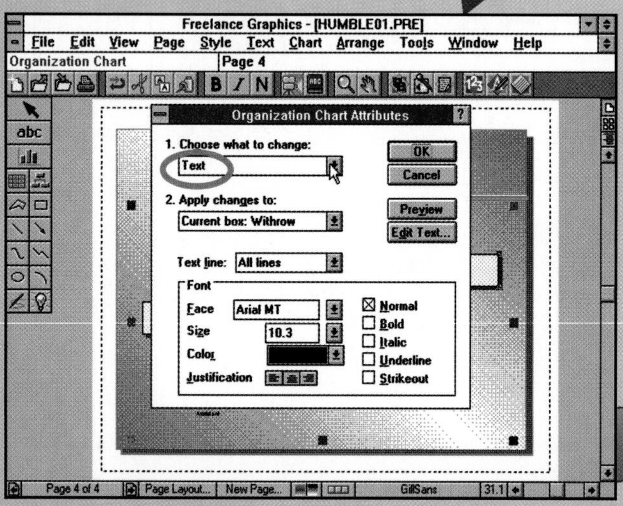

2 In the **Choose What to Change** drop-down list box, select **Text** if it is not already selected.

3 In the **Apply Changes To** drop-down list box, select **All Boxes in Chart**. In the **Font** area, choose **Size** and change the size to **12**. Freelance displays a message saying that changing the text size turns off the automatic sizing of the text. Choose **OK** to close the Changing Text Size message box.

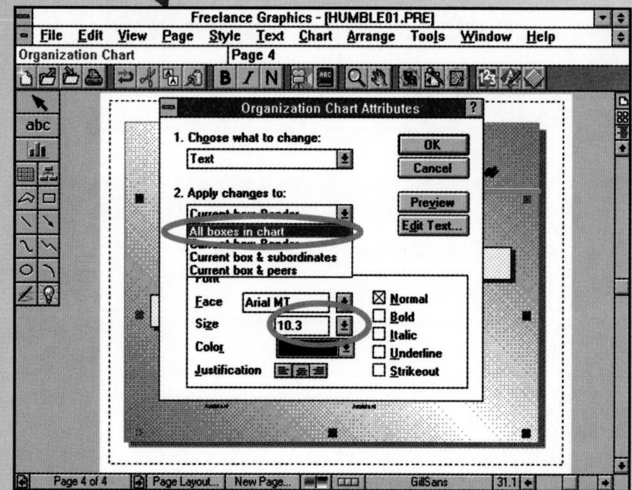

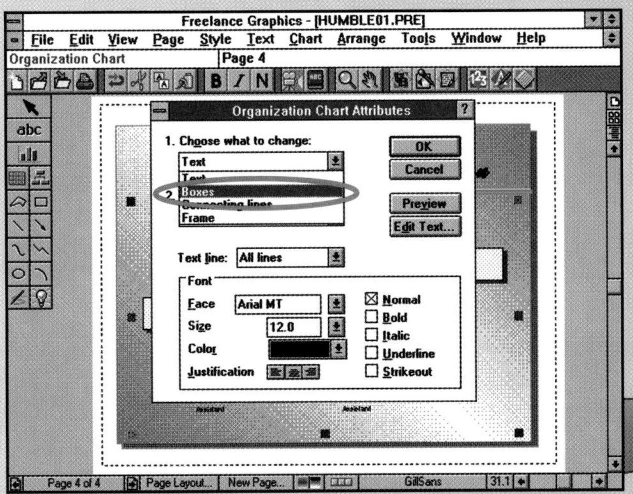

4 Open the **Chart** menu and choose **Attributes**. In the **Choose What to Change** drop-down list box, select **Boxes**. Again, in the **Apply Changes To** drop-down list box, select **All Boxes in Chart**.

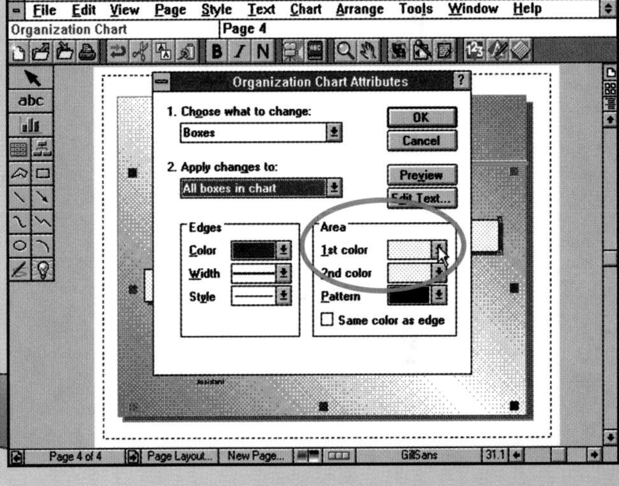

5 In the **Area** option group, choose **1st color**. The Palette color box appears; choose light yellow for the boxes. The Palette box closes.

NOTE

The Edges option group refers to the line and shadow around the box; the Area option group refers to the color and pattern of the box itself.

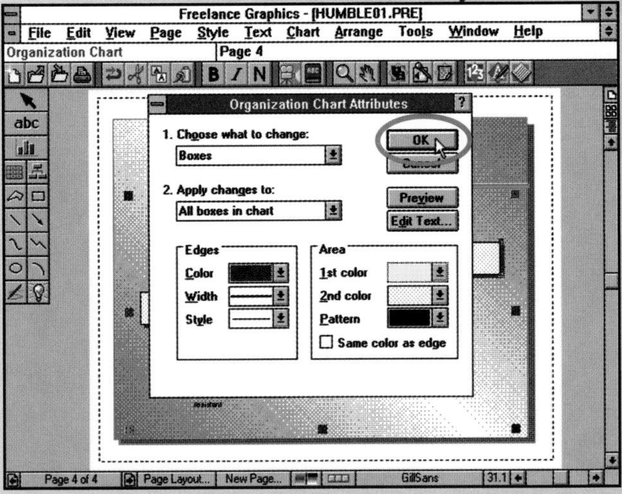

6 Choose **OK** to close the Organization Chart Attributes dialog box and accept the changes.

NOTE

You can choose the Preview button to see what the changes look like before you accept them. If you do not like the changes, return to the Organization Chart Attributes dialog box and change the attributes again.

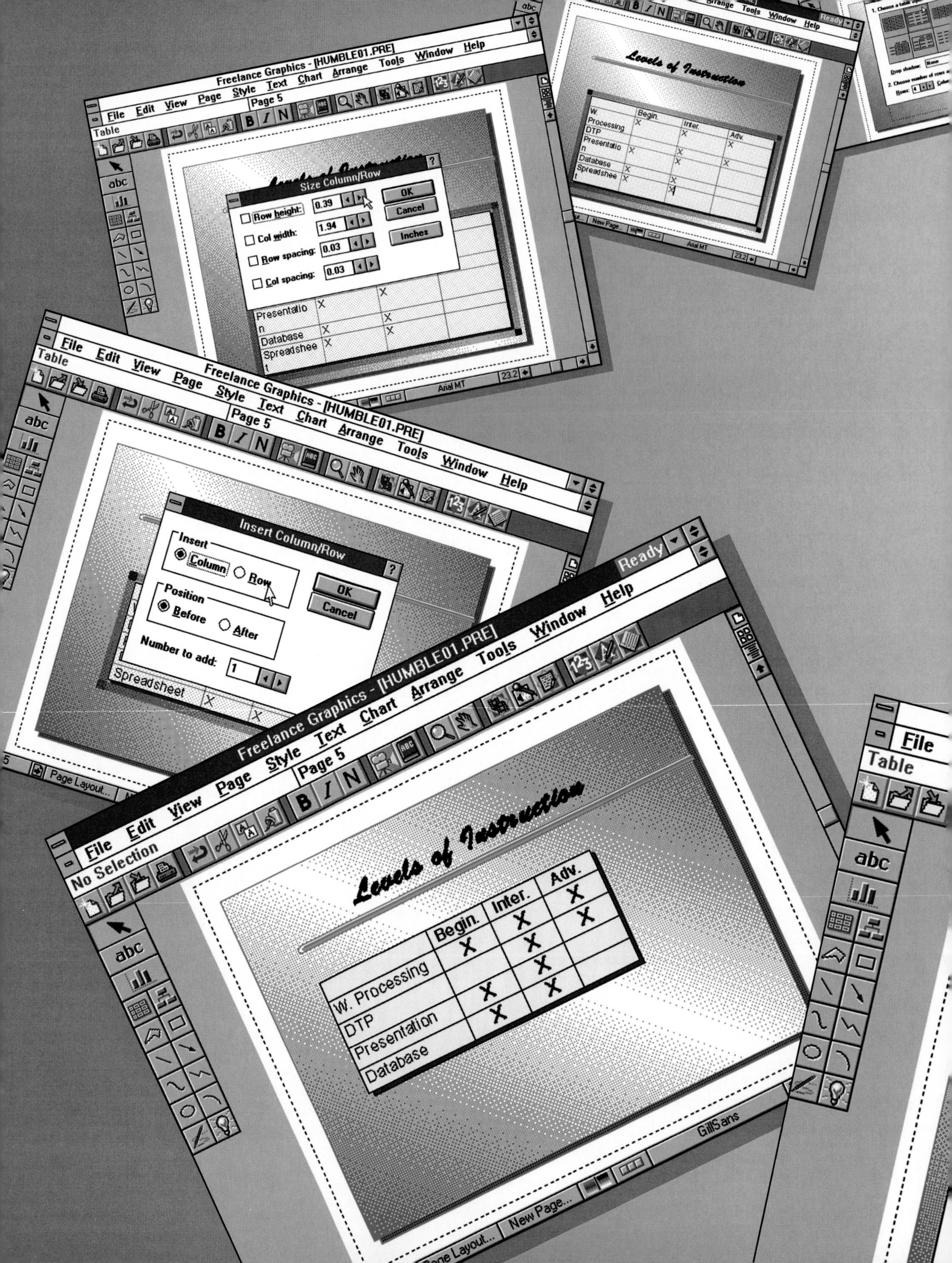

Freelance Graphics - [HUMBLE01.PRE]
File Edit View Page Style Text Chart Arrange Tools Window Help
Table
Page 5
Size Column/Row
Row height: 0.39
Col width: 1.94
Row spacing: 0.03
Col spacing: 0.03
OK
Cancel
Inches
Presentatio n
Database
Spreadshee t
Arial MT
23.2
Levels of Instruction
W. Processing
DTP
Begin.
Inter.
Adv.
New Page...
Insert Column/Row
Insert
Column
Row
Position
Before
After
Number to add: 1
Spreadsheet
Page Layout...
Ready
No Selection
Presentation
GillSans

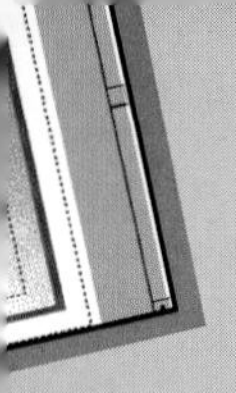

PART V

Creating a Table

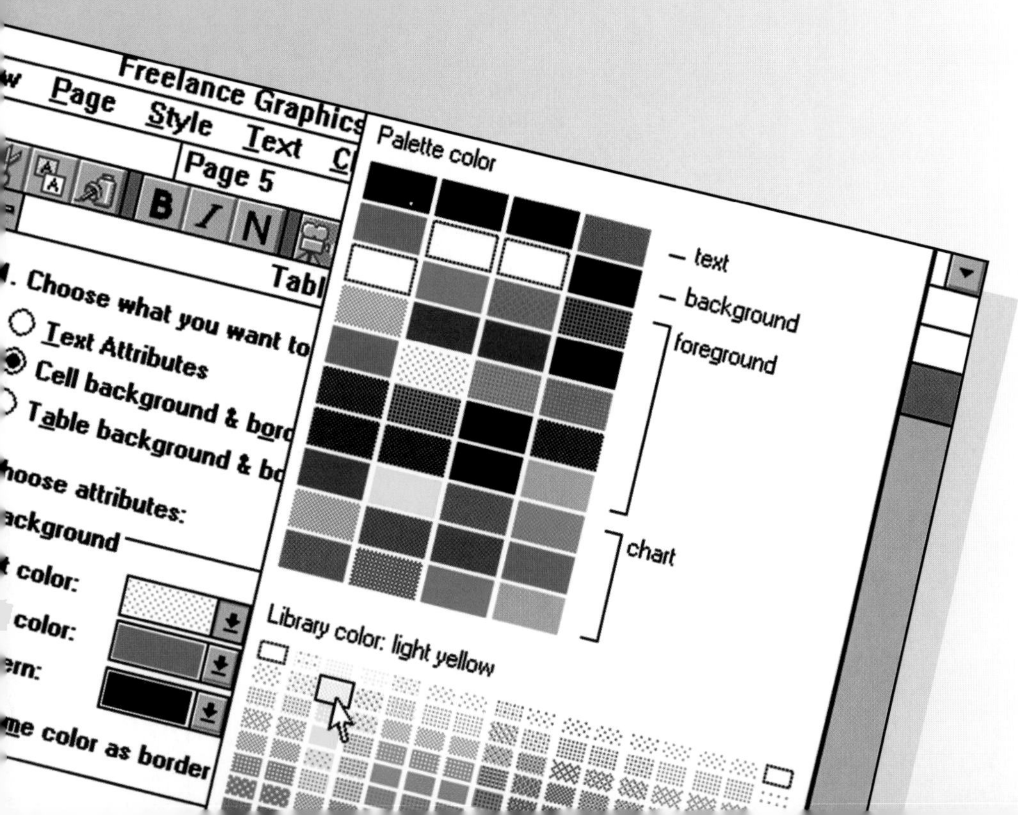

With Freelance Graphics, you can create tables to use in your presentations. Tables organize information or data so that it is easy to read and understand. You can enter columns of numbers in a table to illustrate sales, purchases, profits, and so on, or to organize information such as names, products, or services.

Freelance provides a Table page layout you can use to create a table. The page design includes a "Click here..." text block for the table title and a "Click here..." box for the table. Or, you can choose to create a table on a page other than the Table page layout.

After choosing to insert a table in your presentation, you choose a table style from the Table Gallery. Choose the design that best suits your data and your presentation. Next, you enter the number of rows and number of columns; you can include as many as 30 rows and 30 columns.

To select the table, you click it; small black handles appear on the corners and sides. You can move, size, or change the table attributes when the table is selected. Move the table by positioning the mouse pointer inside the table and dragging the table to a new location. Size the table by positioning the mouse pointer over any handle until you see the double-headed arrow; drag the arrow in the direction you want to size the table. *Table attributes* include background colors and borders; line width, style, and color; and text attributes such as font, size, and color.

If you click a selected table, you can enter text into the table—this is *text editing mode.* Use the mouse to move the pointer around in the table; click to place the insertion point. You can also move around in the table by using the keyboard. Press Tab to move to the beginning of the next cell, from column to column, and from row to row. Press Shift+Tab to move to the beginning of the previous cell. The arrow keys also enable you to move around the table.

Freelance includes several shortcut items that help you as you create and edit the table. When the table is in text editing mode, click the Table icon in the toolbox to display the Table Choices dialog box. Using the options in this dialog box, you can quickly and easily insert, delete, size, and move columns and rows. Additionally, you can choose to change table styles and attributes with this shortcut.

Similarly, you can press the right mouse button, while pointing at the selected table, to reveal a quick menu of common table commands: Edit, Gallery, Attributes, and Size Column/Row. If the table is in edit mode, pressing the right mouse button reveals a more detailed menu that includes insert, delete, size, and move columns or rows commands.

You also can change column width and row height by entering values in a dialog box; or you can choose the easier method of dragging the column and row lines with the mouse pointer. Position the pointer over the line until you see a double-headed arrow, and then drag the arrow and the line to the new position. You can resize rows and columns only in text editing mode.

Freelance's "Click here..." boxes and accessible features and commands make creating a table for your presentation quick and painless.

TASK 29

Choosing a Table Style

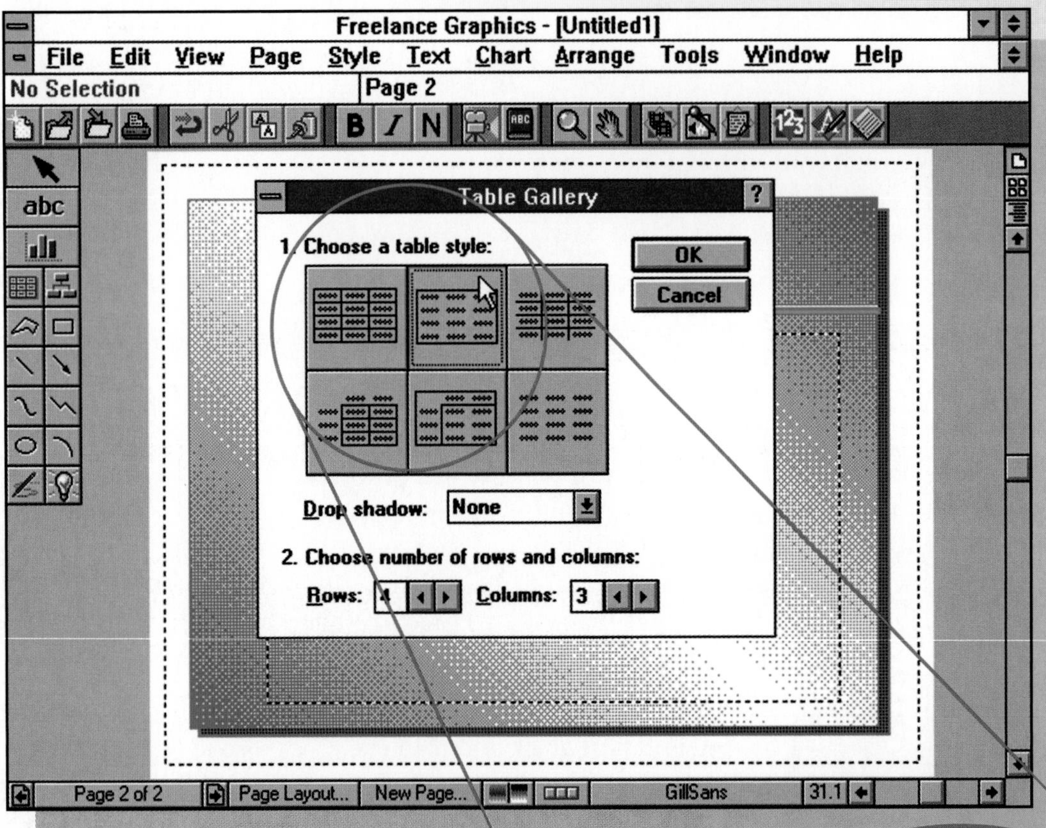

"Why would I do this?"

When you choose to add a table to your presentation, Freelance Graphics displays the Table Gallery from which you choose a *table style*. The style you choose should conform to the data you plan to enter. You can choose a style with border and grid lines, border lines only, grid lines only, or even no lines at all.

You can also enter the number of rows and columns you want to use, and you can add a decorative drop shadow, if you like.

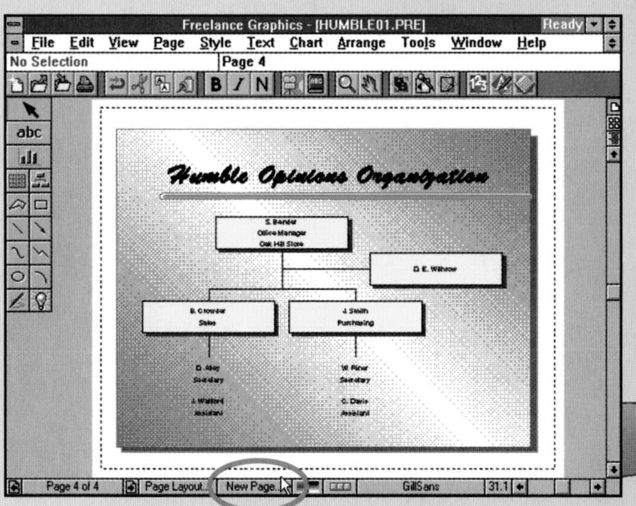

1 On page four of your presentation, choose the **New Page** button in the status bar.

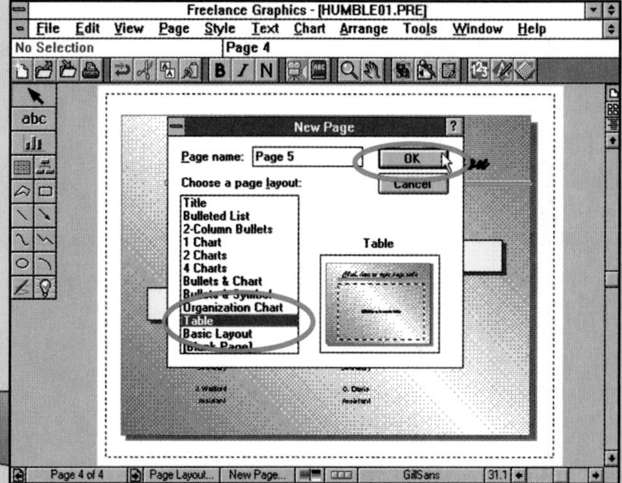

2 In the New Page dialog box, choose the **Table** page layout and choose **OK**.

WHY WORRY?

If you want to create a table on a page other than a Table page layout, choose the Chart New Table command. Freelance displays the Table Gallery.

3 Click in the title **Click here to type page title** text block and type **Levels of Instruction.** When you are finished entering the title, click in the **Click here to create table** box to display the Table Gallery.

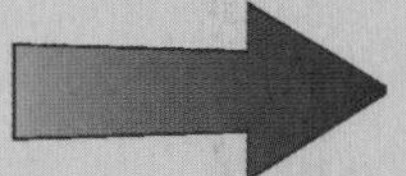

Task 29: Choosing a Table Style

4 In the Table Gallery, the first option group, Choose a Table Style, enables you to select the style for your table. For this exercise, use the first style, which is selected by default. From the **Drop Shadow** drop-down list, select **Bottom Right**.

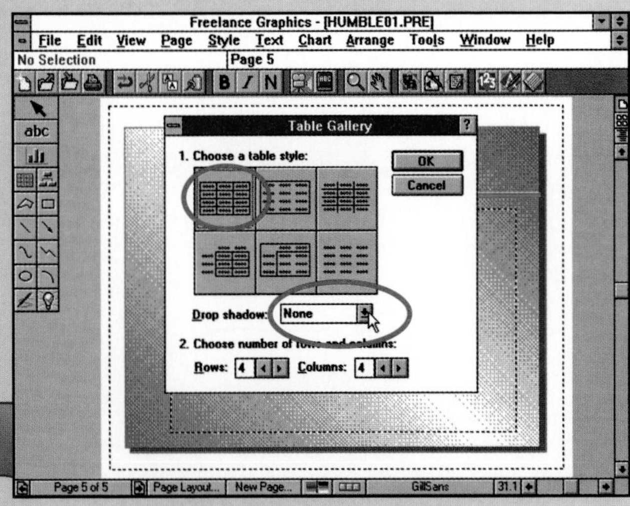

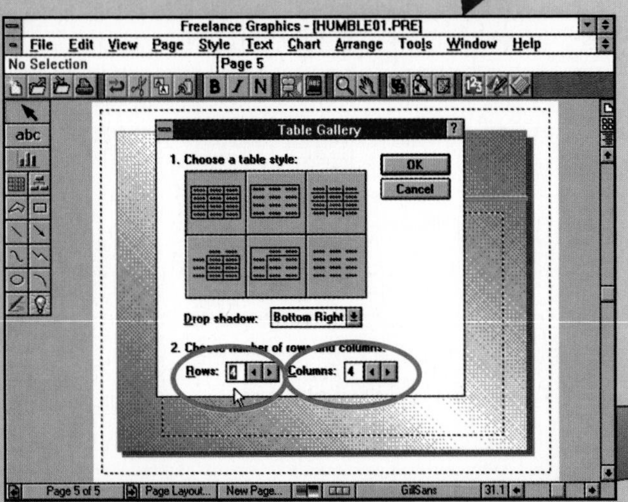

5 In the second option group, Choose Number of Rows and Columns, enter **6** in the **Rows** text box and **4** in the **Columns** text box.

NOTE

You can delete the numbers in the Rows and Columns text boxes, and then enter a new number; or you can use the arrows beside the text boxes to change the numbers.

6 Choose **OK** to create the table.

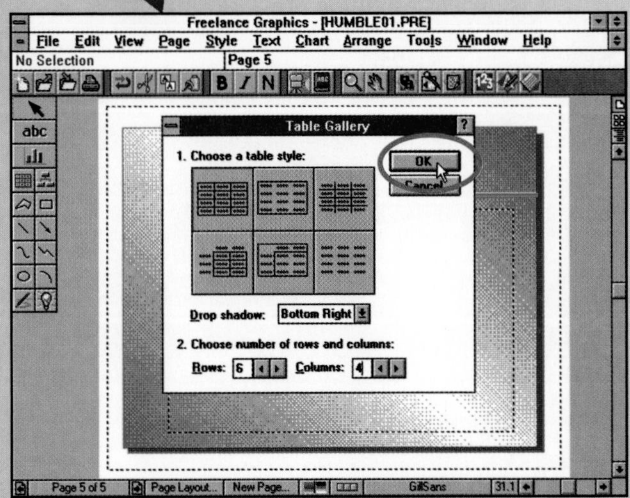

TASK 30

Entering Data

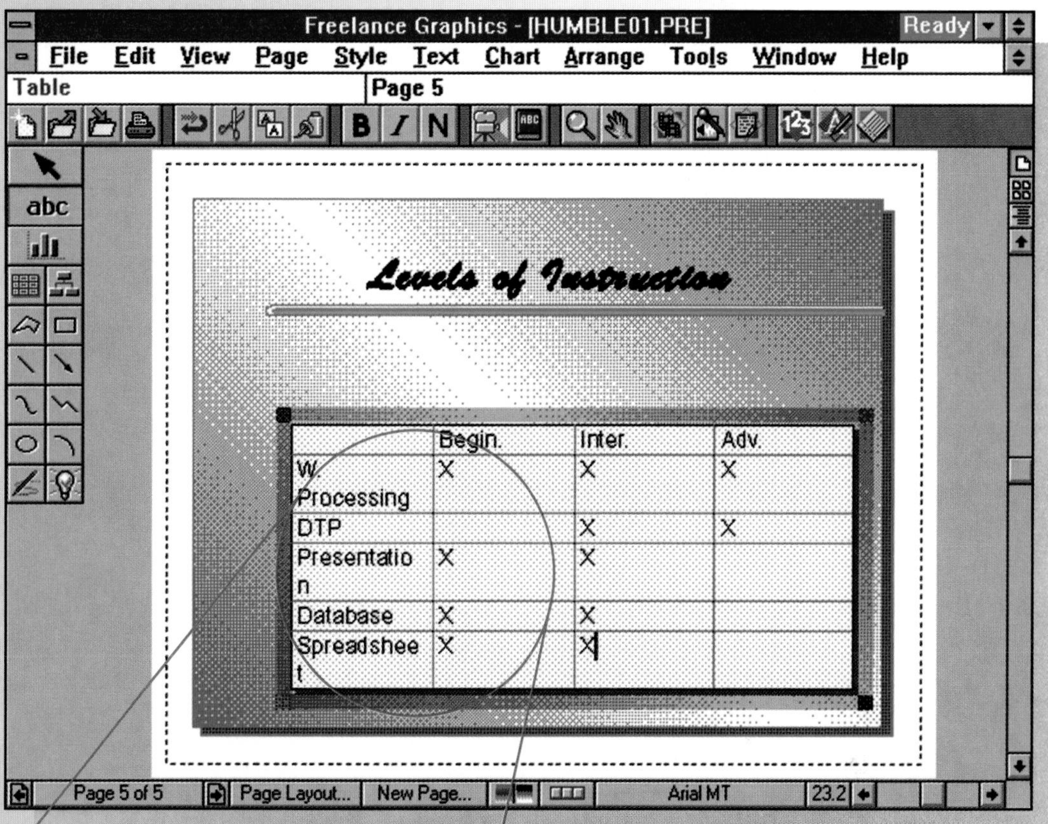

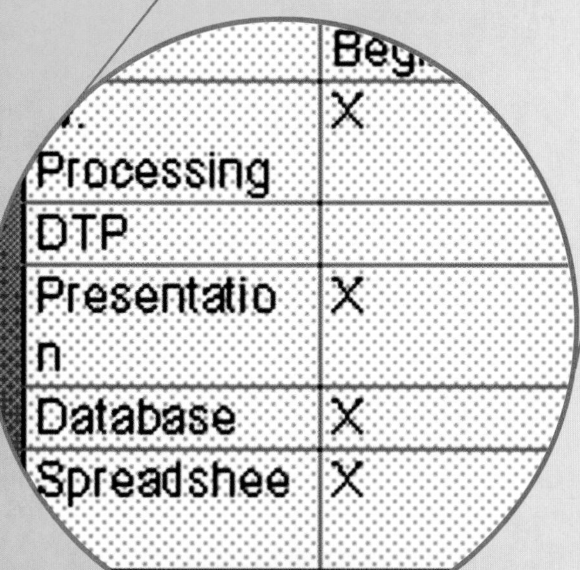

"Why would I do this?"

A table is an excellent way to organize data. It makes reading data faster and easier than reading paragraphs of information. When creating a presentation, you want the client to quickly read and understand the information displayed on each page; if that information is in table format, it can be quickly read and understood. You can label rows and columns to identify the data in each cell and remove any extra text that might distract the reader.

Task 30: Entering Data

1 Click anywhere in the table to select it. Handles appear on the corners and the sides. You can move, size, or change table attributes when the table is selected.

WHY WORRY?

If you accidentally double-click the table, Freelance displays the Table Attributes dialog box. Choose Cancel and try again.

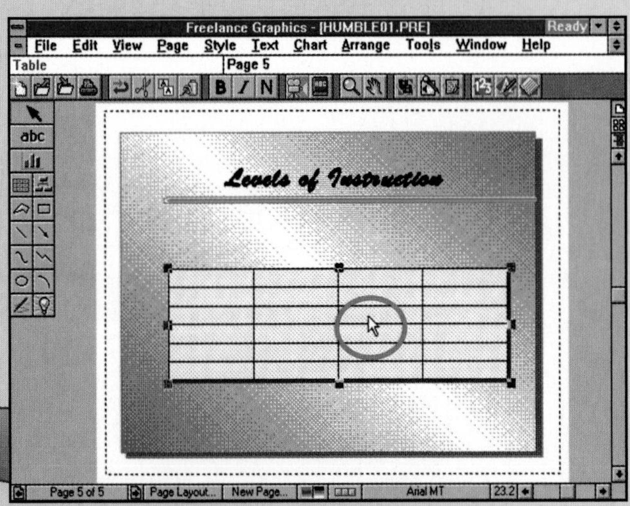

2 Click the table again to change to text editing mode. The insertion point appears in one of the cells, and a gray border appears around the table.

NOTE

You can move the table on the page by clicking in the screened border of the table in text editing mode; a four-headed arrow appears. Drag the table to a new position on the page.

3 Position the insertion point in the first cell and press **Tab**. The insertion point moves to the second column. Enter the following text: **Begin.** (**Tab**), **Inter.** (**Tab**), **Adv.** (**Tab**), **W. Processing** (↓), **DTP** (↓), **Presentation** (↓), **Database** (↓), **Spreadsheet**. Enter an **X** in the cells as shown in the figure.

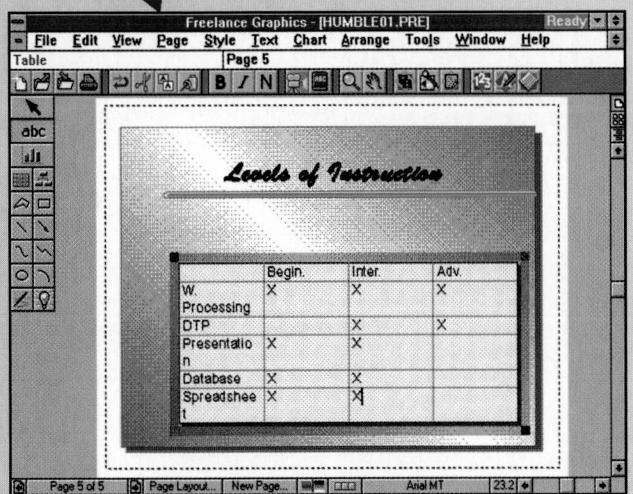

TASK 31

Changing Column and Row Size

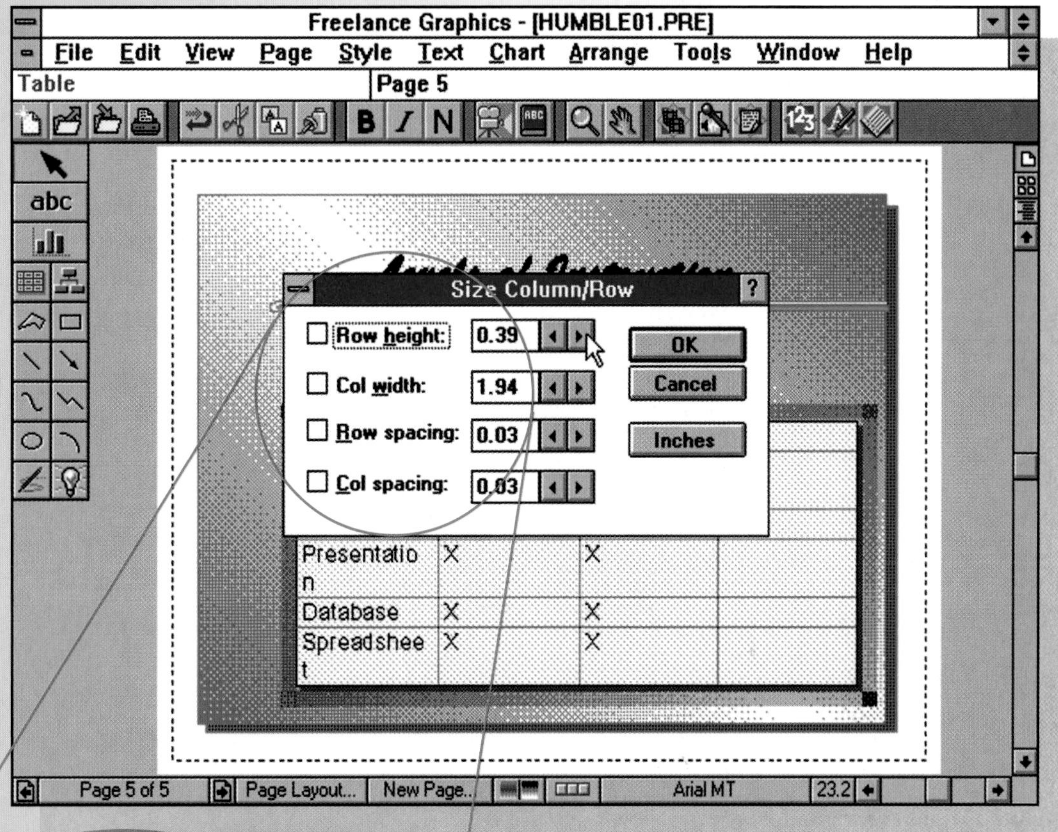

"Why would I do this?"

You can alter the size of the columns and rows in your table to better fit the text. With Freelance Graphics, you can change the column width to wider or narrower columns and adjust row height so that you have more or less space between row lines. In addition, you can make all rows the same height and all columns the same width, or you can vary the size of the columns and rows within the table.

Task 31: Changing Column and Row Size

1 To adjust the column width so that all text fits within the column, position the mouse pointer on the first column line. The pointer changes to a double-headed arrow—if not, you may not be in text editing mode. Click and drag to the right until each word fits on one line. Use the same method to adjust the next column (`Begin.`), and then adjust the last two columns so that they are close in width to the second column.

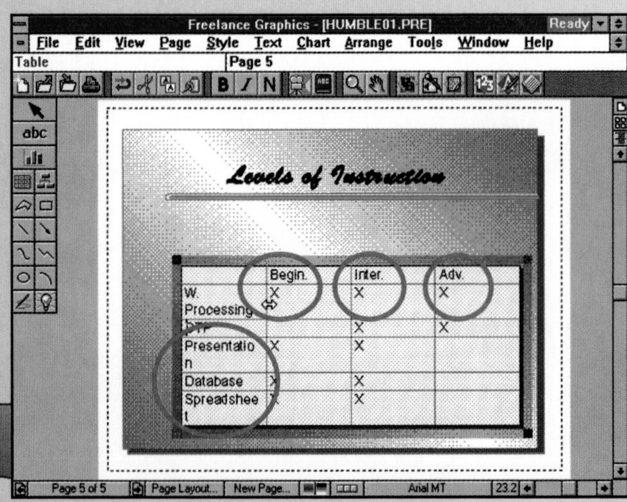

2 As an alternative to step 1, use the Size Column/Row dialog box to adjust several columns or rows at one time. In text editing mode, select the text in the first column. Click the table, using the right mouse button to display the Table quick menu. Next, choose **Size Column/Row**. Use this method for more precise measurements. The Size Column/Row dialog box appears.

3 Click the **Row Height** check box, and then enter **.33** in the text box to the right of the option. Make sure the measurement command button is "Inches"; if it is not, click the command button until `Inches` appears on the button. Choose **OK**.

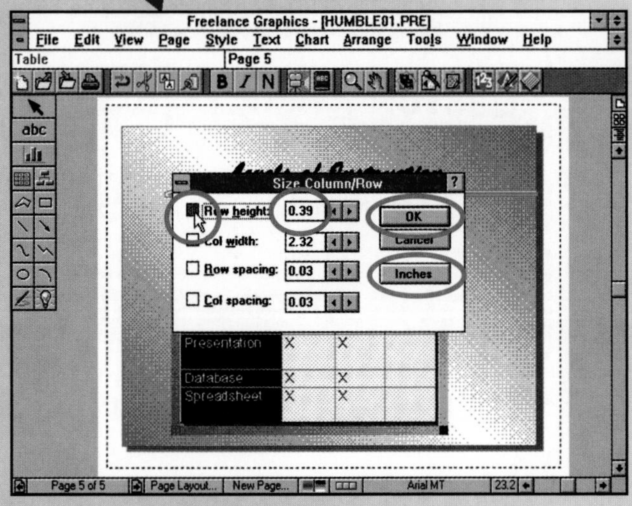

NOTE

You can also change Row and Col spacing in this dialog box to prevent text in a cell from running up against the column or row lines.

TASK 32

Inserting and Deleting Columns and Rows

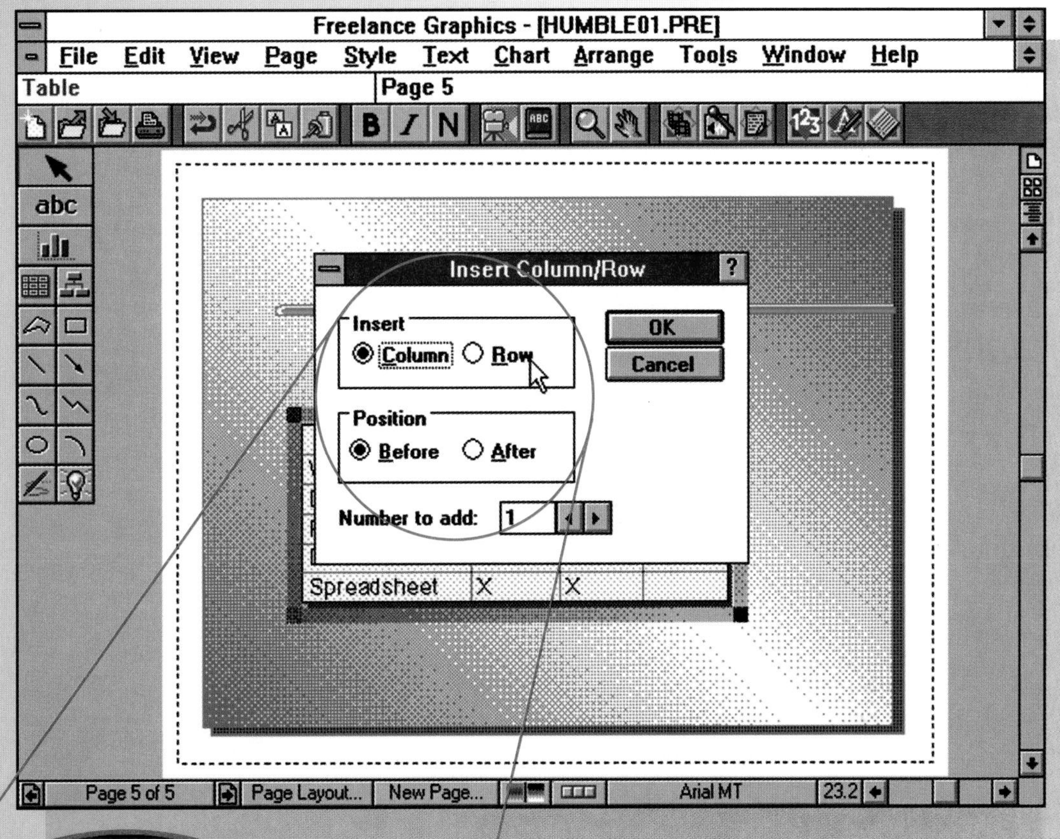

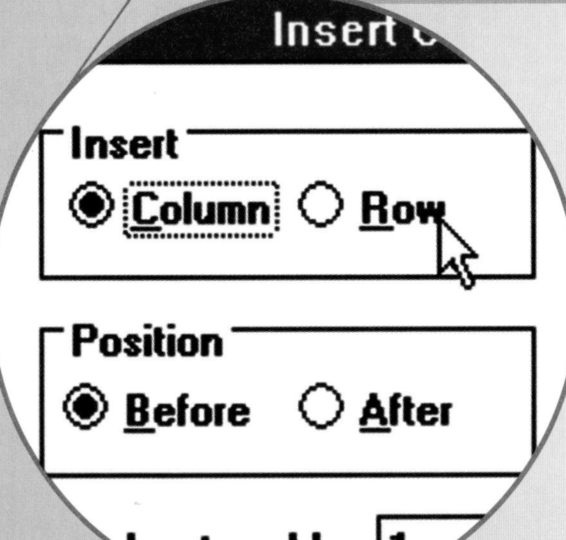

"Why would I do this?"

It's not always easy to decide how many columns and rows you need when planning a table. After you create the table, you may decide you have too many columns or discover you do not have enough rows. You can insert or delete as many columns and rows as you need to make the table fit your data. In addition, you can choose the exact position in which you want to insert the new column or row.

Task 32: Inserting and Deleting Columns and Rows

1 To insert a row at the end of the table, position the insertion point in the last row—the Spreadsheet row—and press the right mouse button to display the Table quick menu.

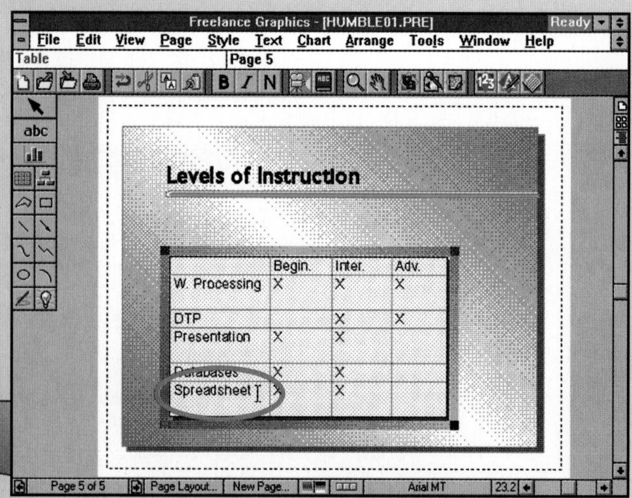

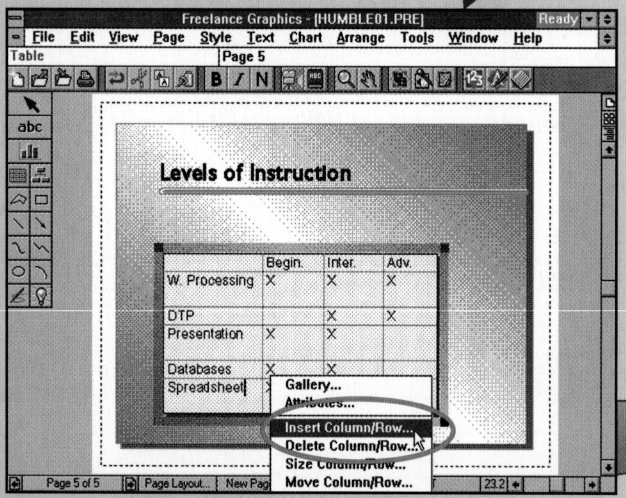

2 Choose **Insert Column/Row** from the Table quick menu to display the Insert Column/Row dialog box.

3 In the Insert area, select **Row**; in the Position area, select **After**. Choose **OK** to close the dialog box and insert the row.

NOTE

You can add more than one column or row at a time by choosing Number to Add in the Insert Column/Row dialog box.

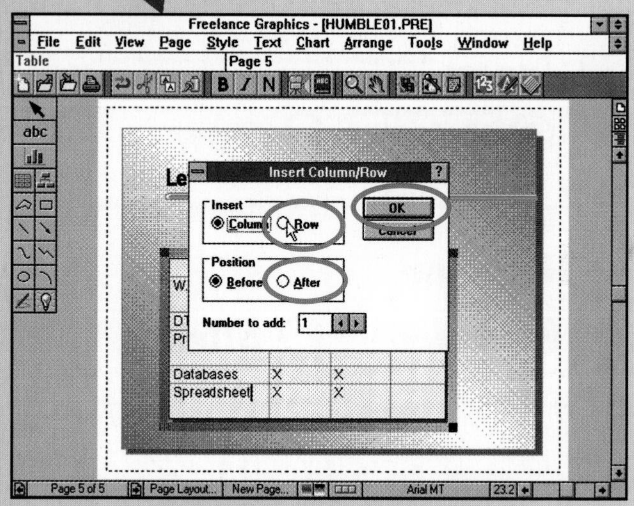

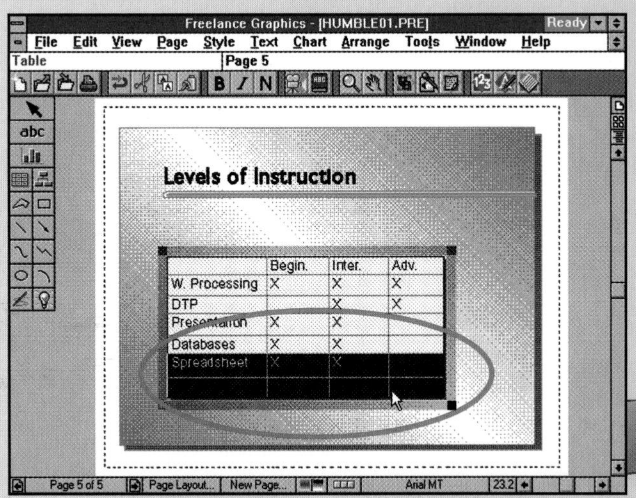

4 To delete a column or row, make sure you are in text editing mode. Select the Spreadsheet row and the newly added row to delete the two rows.

5 Click the table, using the right mouse button to display the Table quick menu. Choose **Delete Column/Row** to display the Delete Column/Row dialog box.

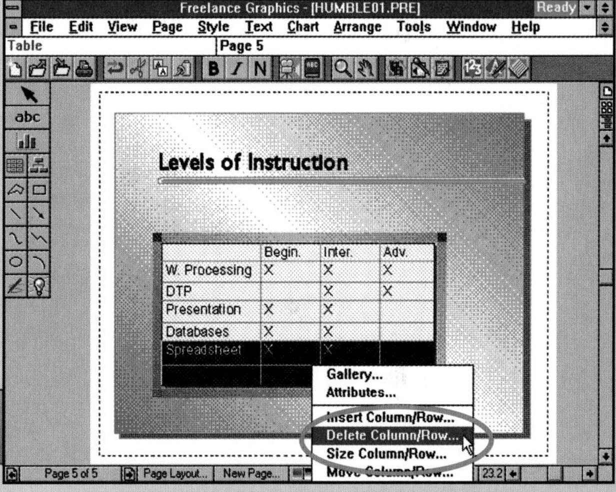

6 Select **Row** and choose **OK**; Freelance deletes the selected rows.

TASK 33

Changing Table Attributes

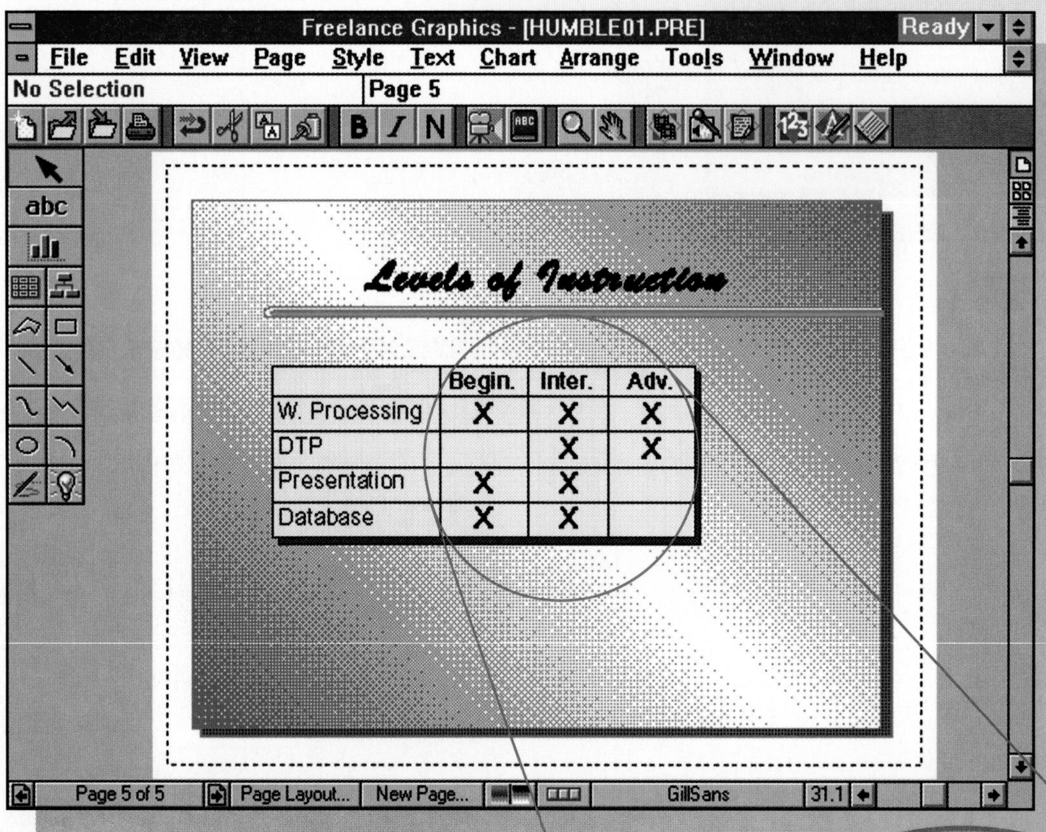

"Why would I do this?"

You can change the table's attributes—including font, type size, text alignment, table color, and border line style—to make the table more attractive or easier to read, or to match your presentation design. Changing the table's text attributes is similar to changing any text attributes in Freelance Graphics. You can control the table attributes in the Table Attributes dialog box.

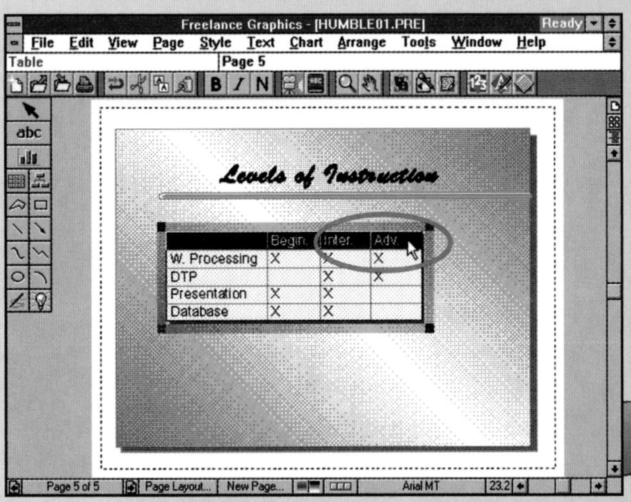

1 When changing the table attributes, you can apply the changes to one cell or one character, to one row or column, or to the entire table. To change the text attributes in the first row, in text editing mode select the first row of text.

2 Click the table, using the right mouse button to display the Table quick menu. Choose **Attributes** to display the Table Attributes dialog box.

NOTE

Or, you can choose the Table button on the toolbar to display the Table Choices dialog box. Choose Change Attributes and OK to display the Table Attributes dialog box.

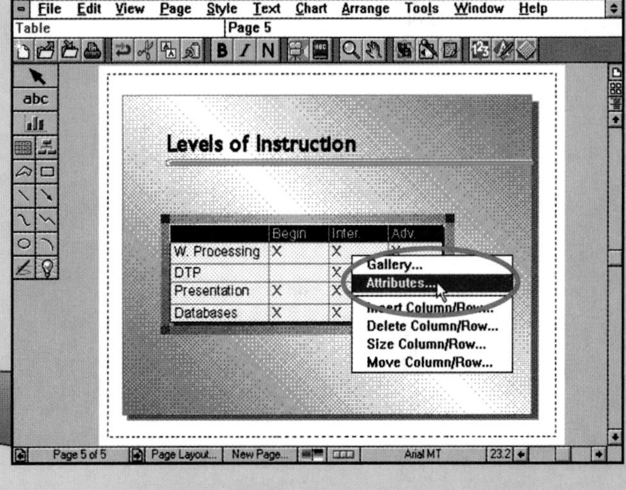

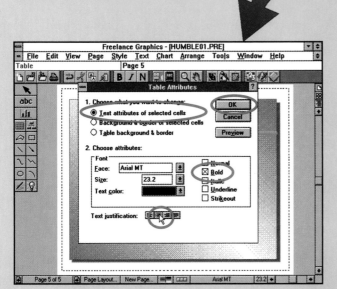

3 In the Table Attributes dialog box, the default option in the first group, Choose What You Want to Change, is **Text Attributes of Selected Cells**. In the second group, Choose Attributes, select **Bold**. By Text Justification, choose the **Center** button. Choose **OK**.

Task 33: Changing Table Attributes

4 To change the text formatting of the ×'s, select all the cells with an × in them—from column 2, row 2 to column 4, row 5. Point to the table and press the right mouse button. Choose **Attributes** to display the Table Attributes dialog box.

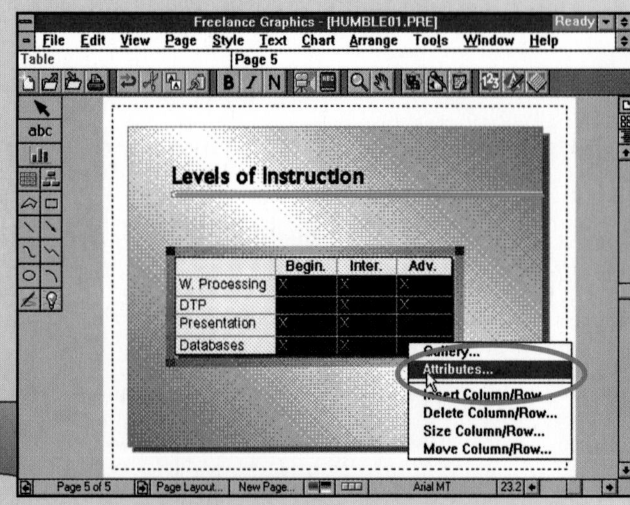

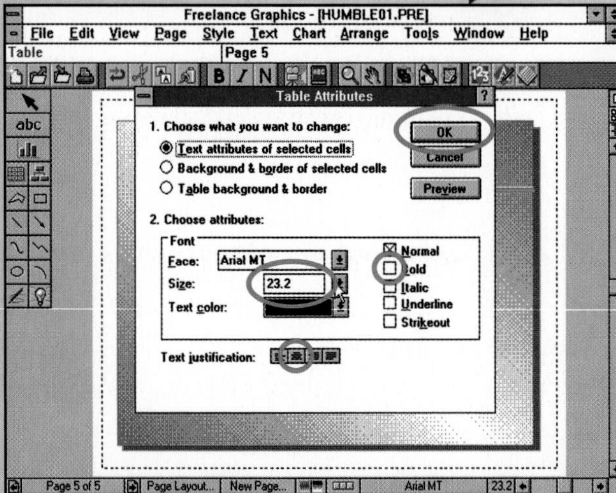

5 In the Table Attributes dialog box, in the second group of options, Choose Attributes, enter **28** for the size, and then select the **Bold** check box. By Text Justification, choose the **Center** button. Choose **OK** to close the dialog box.

6 Click outside the table to get out of text editing mode, and then click the table to select it. Double-click the table. This step opens the Table Attributes dialog box and applies all changes to the entire table.

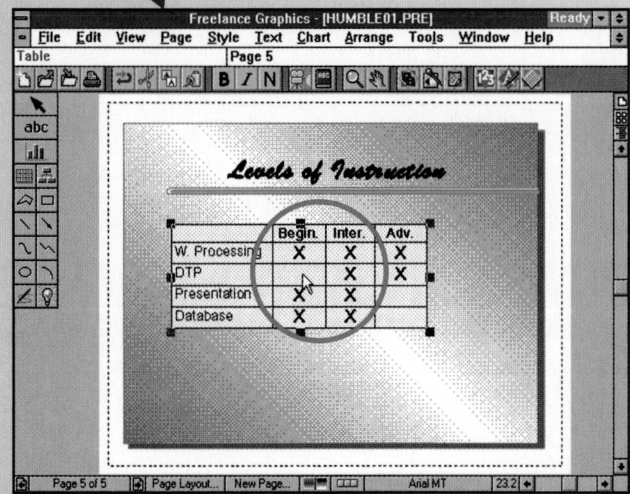

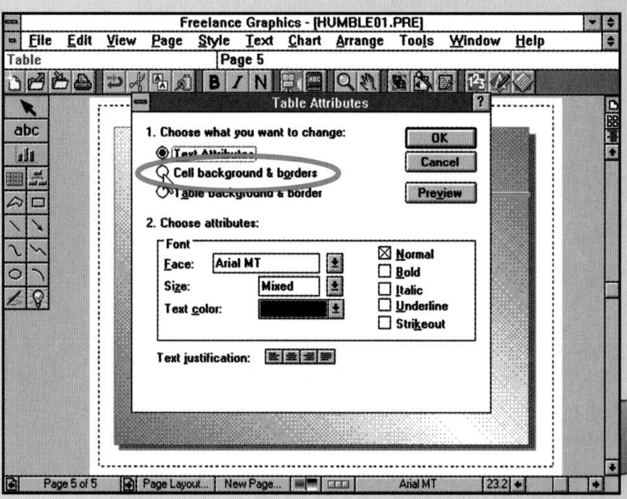

7 In the first group of options, Choose What You Want to Change, choose **Cell Background & Borders**.

8 In the second group of options, Choose Attributes, choose **1st color** in the Background option group to display the Palette.

NOTE

The 2nd color choice in the Background option group is for use with the Pattern option. If you select a pattern to fill a table, you choose a color for the pattern and a color for the background.

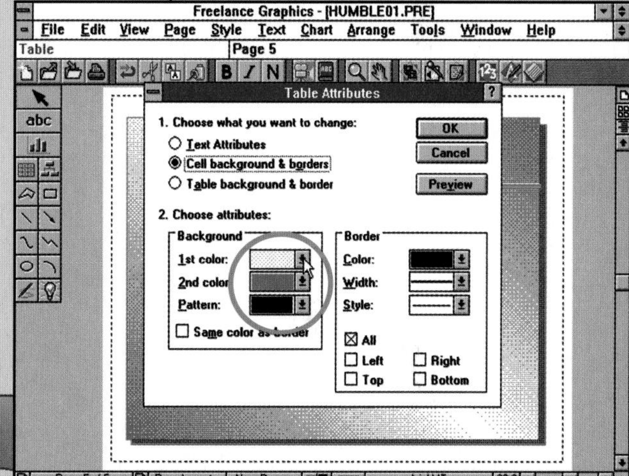

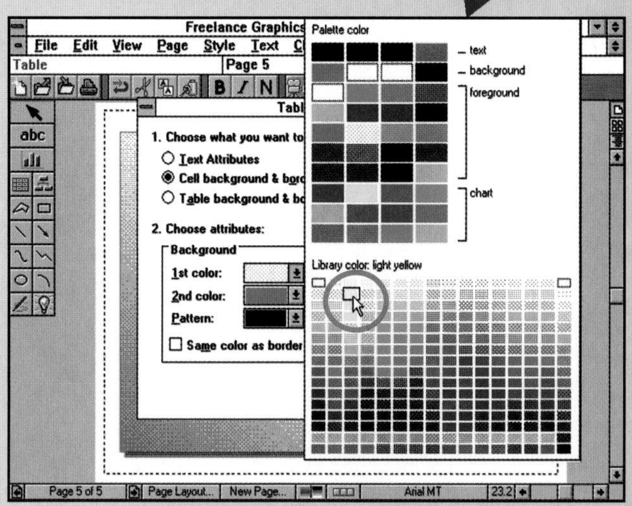

9 In the Palette, choose a light yellow (to match the color of the organizational chart). The Palette closes and returns to the Table Attributes dialog box. Choose **OK** to close the dialog box and return to the presentation.

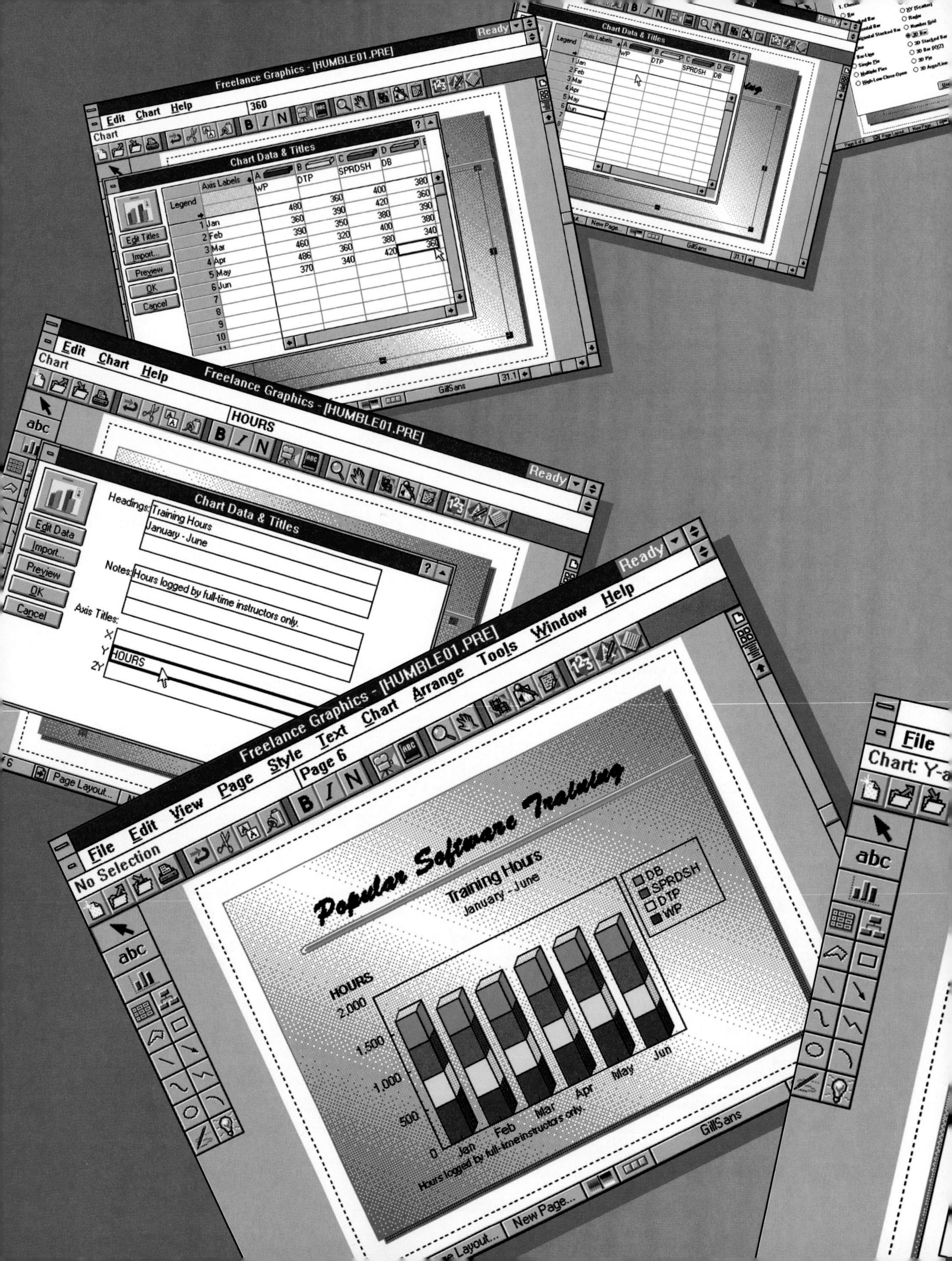

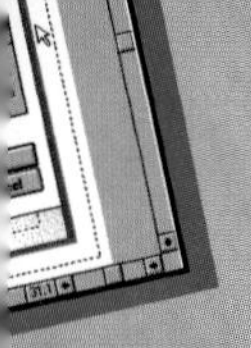

PART VI

Creating a Chart

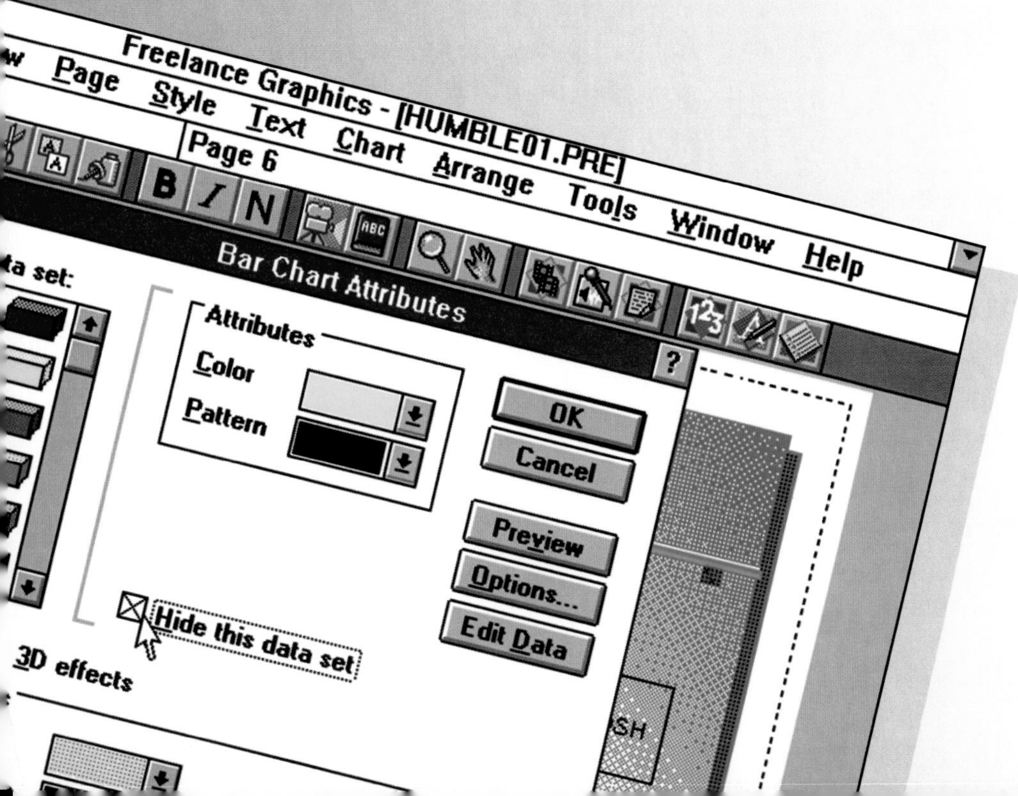

Part VI: Creating a Chart

A chart (or graph) is a visual representation of data that makes the data easy to understand. You can use charts to compare and contrast data or see trends over a period of time. You can, for example, show your company's product sales over the last year, or you can illustrate how one person's sales compare to another's. Freelance Graphics supplies a variety of chart types and options for you to use.

The chart type you choose depends on the data and how you want to represent it. To compare similar sets of data over time, for example, you use a bar chart or a stacked bar chart. Suppose, for example, you want to compare the sales of two products over the last three quarters; you can use a bar, stacked bar, or horizontal bar chart to illustrate this data.

Stacked bar charts can also show the relationship of parts to the whole. Data for a stacked bar chart might consist of figures comparing the sales of three products for each quarter. Therefore, you can see how each product sold compared to the other two products in one quarter and how a product's sales did over the period of time.

A pie chart also compares parts to the whole; however, with a pie chart, the data is limited to one period in time. You can, for example, compare the sales of each sales person in your company. Each wedge in the pie represents one person's sales. You can, therefore, compare the wedges to each other and each wedge to the whole.

To show trends or patterns over a period of time, choose the line chart. You can plot one, two, three, or more products' sales over a year, for example. You can tell the direction of sales as well as compare two or more products' sales. Similarly, an area chart shows the fluctuations in data over time, perhaps emphasizing the totals more than a line chart.

In addition to selecting the type of chart you want to represent your data, you have many other options from which to choose. Freelance provides features you can add to a chart to help the viewer understand the data. You can add axis labels, legend labels, a heading, notes, and axis titles to your chart.

Most charts have two axes. An axis is a vertical or horizontal reference line in a chart. The x-axis is the horizontal line, and the y-axis is the vertical line. If you choose a 3D (three-dimensional) chart, you will notice there is also a z-axis. The z-axis marks the depth of the 3D chart.

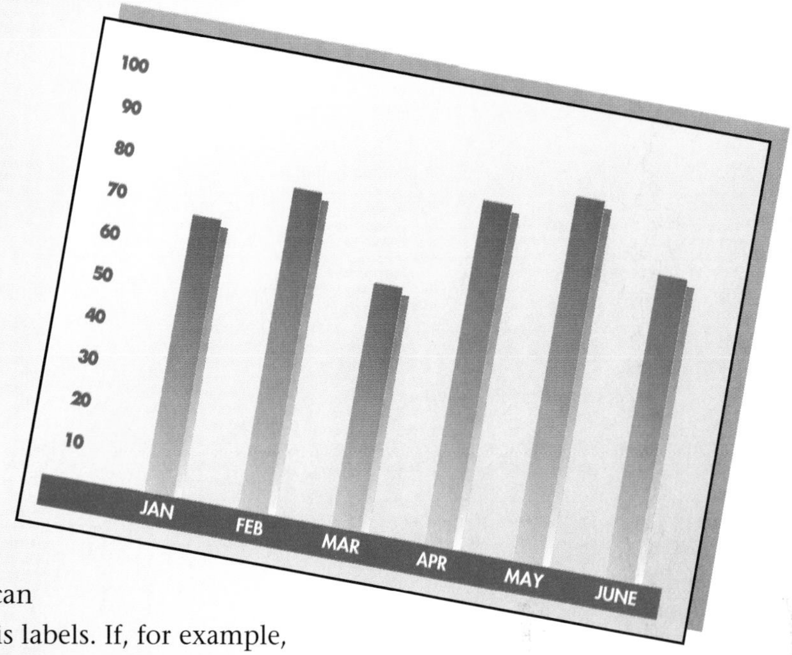

You can add to a chart by entering labels for each axis. A label identifies points on the axis. Depending on the chart, the label could be a year, a value, a percentage, or another identifier. In addition to axis labels, you can enter axis titles. The titles describe the axis labels. If, for example, the y-axis has labels consisting of values such as 10, 20, 30, and so on, the title for the y-axis may be "in thousands" or "in millions." Titles for the x-axis could be "Years" or "Quarters."

In addition to labels, a chart usually has a legend. A legend, usually contained in a box, describes which data a pattern, symbol, or color represents. The legend box contains markers that show samples of the pattern or color and identifying labels. A legend label is an identifier for each data set. A data set is one group of data; for example, sales listed in one month or products sold in one year.

Last in the group of labels, titles, and so on, are headings and notes. You can add a heading, or name, to your chart, such as "3rd Quarter Sales" or "1994 Profits." Freelance places headings above the chart. Finally, you can add notes, or annotations, to your charts to note special circumstances, resources, and so on. Freelance adds any notes in small type below the axis titles.

Now that you know the basic chart terms, you can create your own chart for your presentation.

TASK 34

Choosing a Chart Type

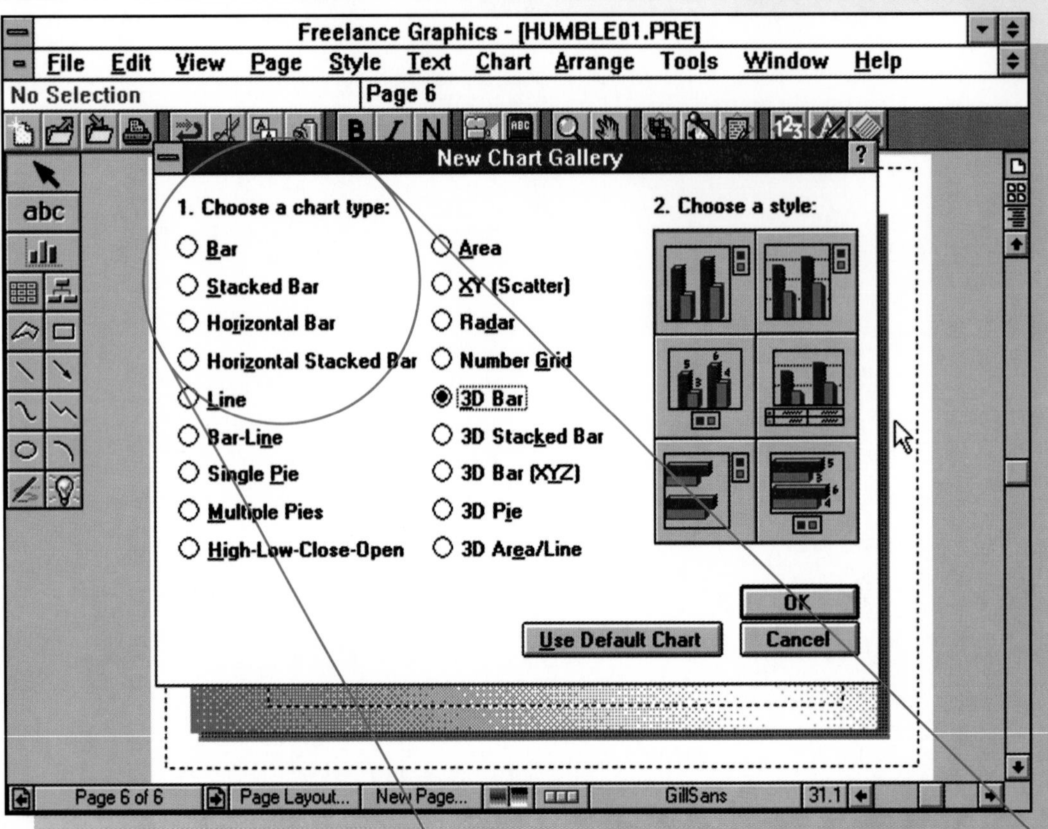

"Why would I do this?"

When choosing a chart type, consider the data and what you want to communicate. Some chart types may show the data as profitable or advantageous to the company; whereas other chart types may make the exact same data look less than favorable. Study the representation carefully, and then change the chart type if you think another would better represent the data.

Task 34: Choosing a Chart Type

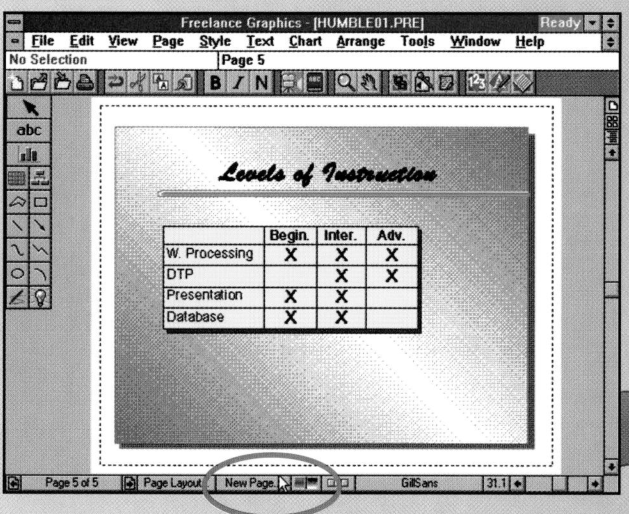

1 On page five of the presentation, choose the **New Page** button in the status bar.

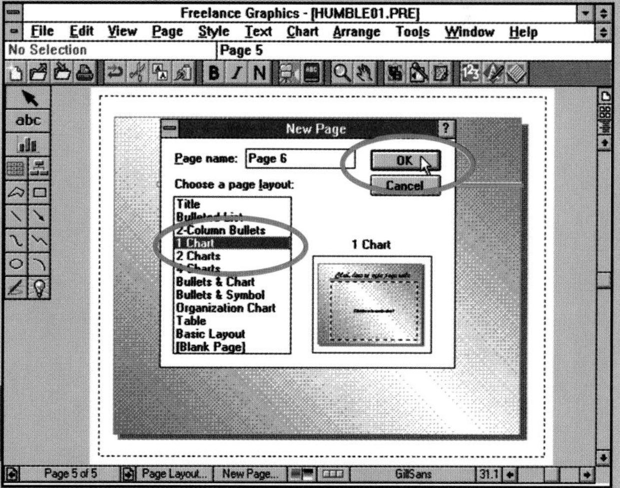

2 In the New Page dialog box, choose **1 Chart**, and then choose **OK**.

> **NOTE**
>
> Notice that you can add various page layouts that contain a chart or charts. When creating your own presentations, you may need a page design containing a chart and a bulleted list or one containing two or three charts. Freelance offers variety in page designs.

3 On page six, enter the title **Popular Software Training** in the "Click here..." text block. Click in the **Click here to create chart** box to display the New Chart Gallery dialog box.

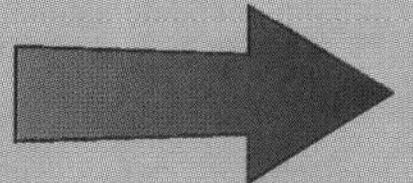

Task 34: Choosing a Chart Type

4 In the first group of options, **Choose a Chart Type**, select **3D Bar**.

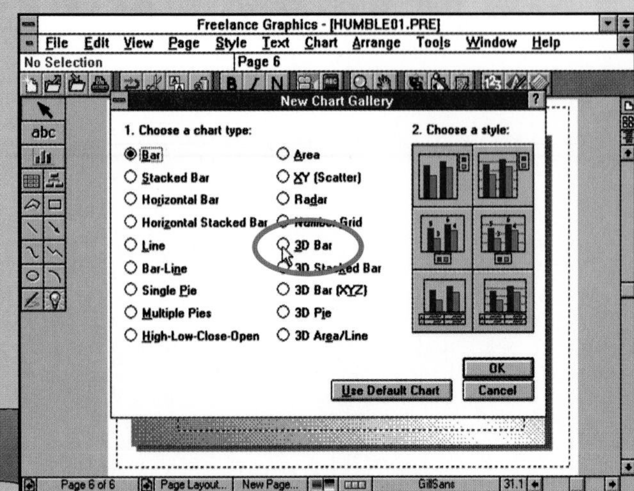

5 In the second group of options, **Choose a Style**, click the first chart style.

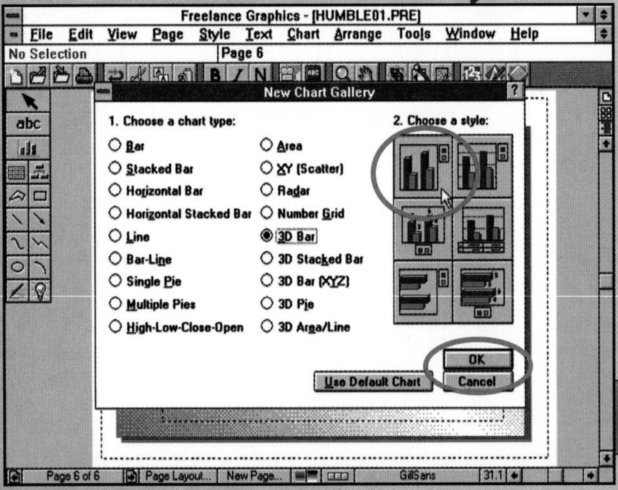

6 Choose **OK**. The Chart Data & Titles dialog box appears.

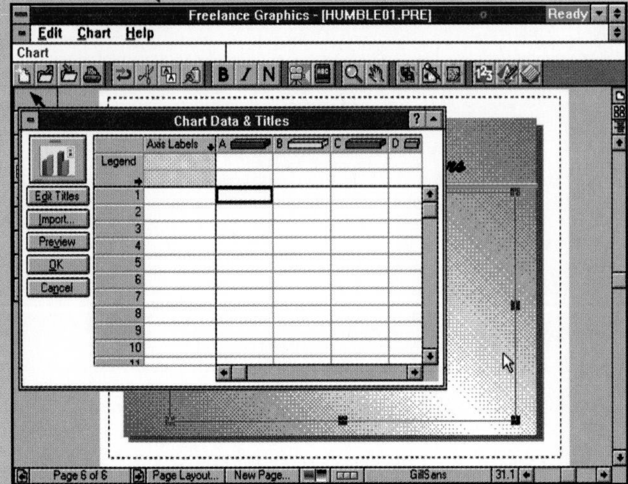

TASK 35

Entering Axis Labels and Legends

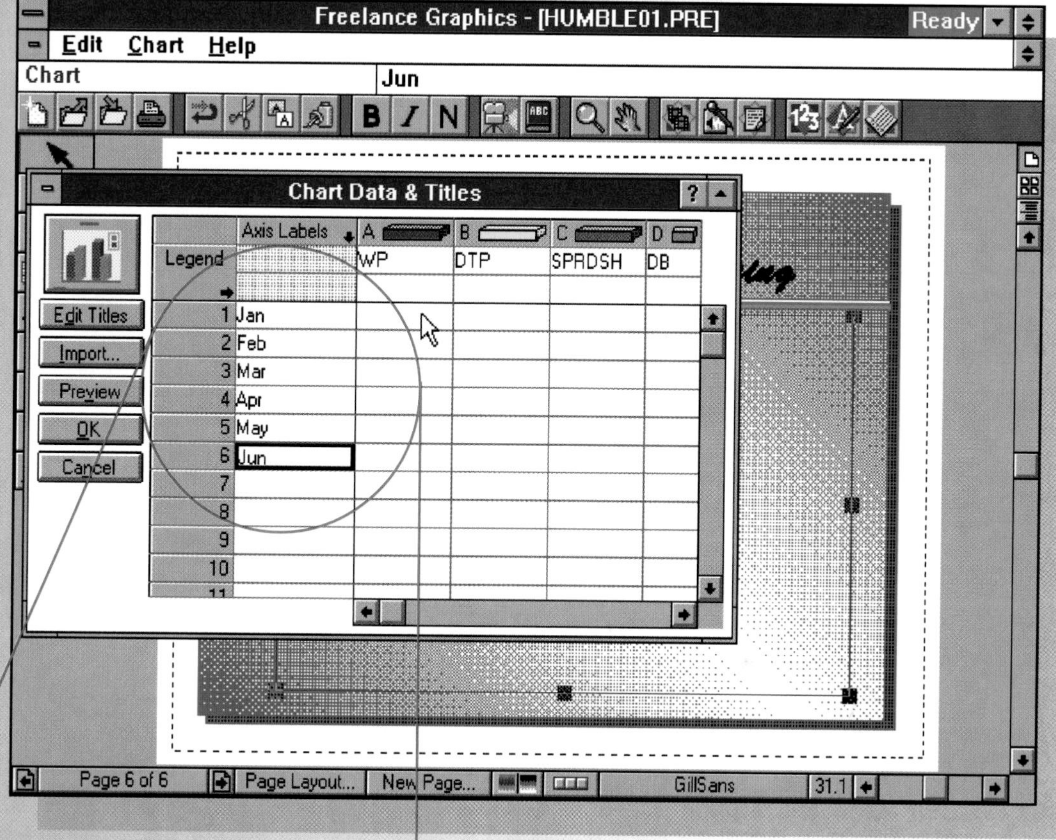

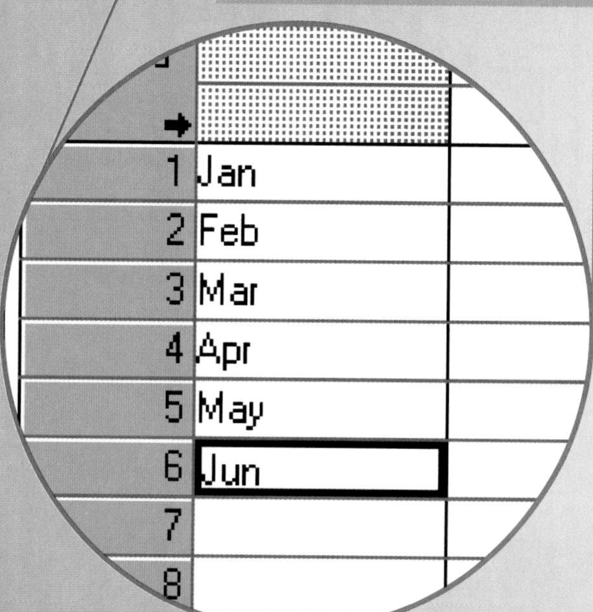

"Why would I do this?"

Axis labels identify the points on the chart, and legends identify the chart elements, such as the bars on the bar chart. The identifiers can be either values or text that you enter in the Chart Data & Titles dialog box. The dialog box looks like a worksheet in a spreadsheet program and, in fact, is very similar. To display the Chart Data & Titles dialog box, choose OK in the New Chart Gallery dialog box.

Task 35: Entering Axis Labels and Legends

1 To enter the legends in the Chart Data & Titles dialog box, click the first cell in column A. The dark outline moves to the cell, and you can now enter text. Type **WP** and press the right-arrow key →; type **DTP** (→); type **SPRDSH** (→); type **DB**.

NOTE

You can supply one- or two-line legends. To enter the second legend line, click the second cell in column A.

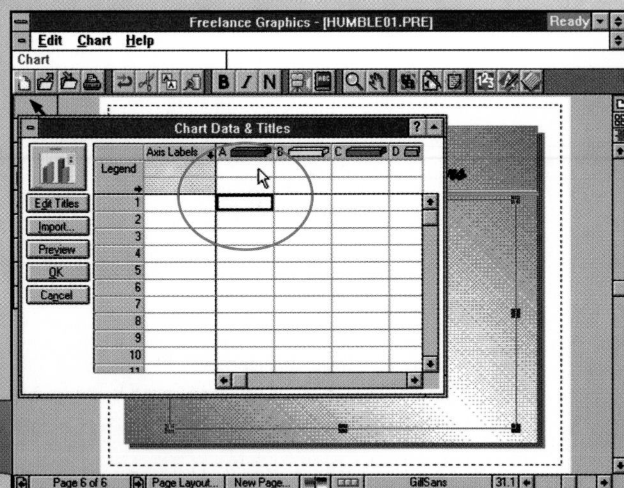

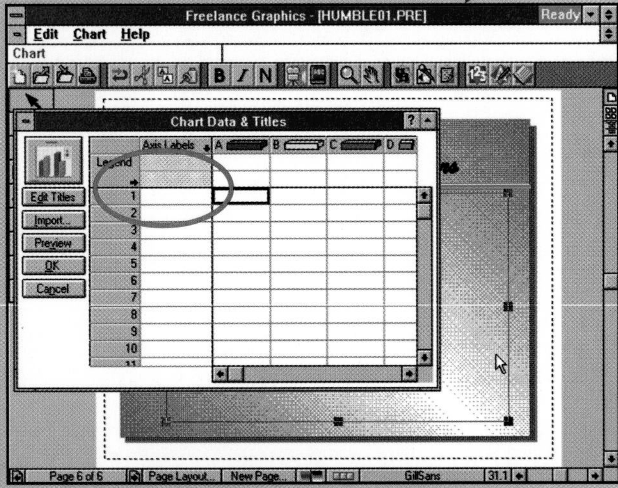

2 Click the cell in column one, row one to enter the horizontal axis labels (x-axis).

NOTE

You can edit the data in a chart at any time, even after closing the Chart Data & Titles dialog box, by selecting the chart and choosing the Chart Edit command.

3 Type **Jan** and press the down-arrow key (↓); type **Feb** and press ↓. Continue entering the months as shown in the figure.

NOTE

You can use the Tab key to move the cursor to the beginning of the next cell; press Shift+Tab to move the cursor to the next cell to the right.

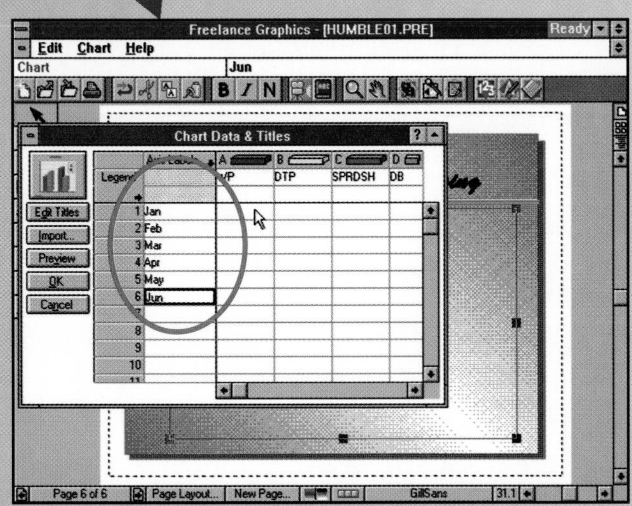

TASK 36

Entering Data

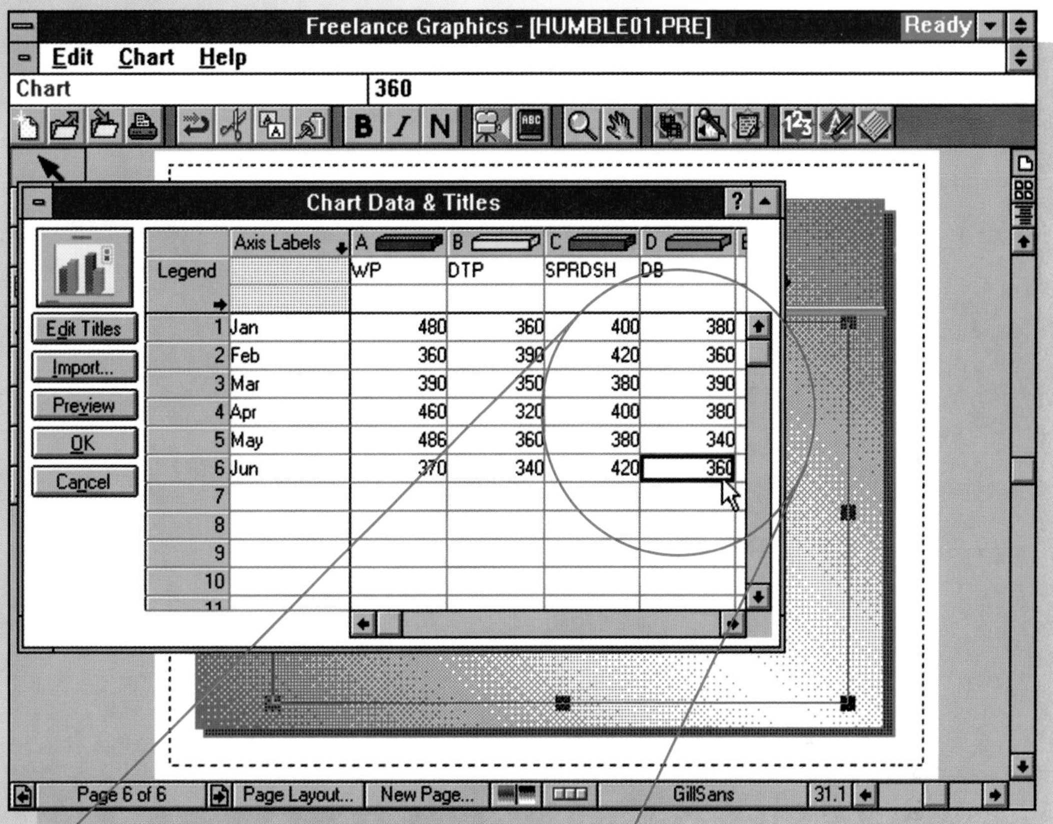

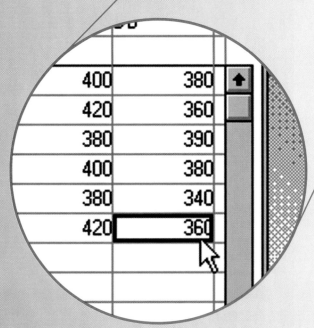

"Why would I do this?"

The data you enter into the table determines the size of the graph elements, such as the bars in a bar chart or the wedges in a pie chart. In the example chart, the value you enter for January in the WP column represents the number of hours word processing was taught in that month by the company.

From this chart, you can identify which classes were taught the most in any one month, and you can compare the hours of training between class types.

Task 36: Entering Data

1 Click the cell created by column A intersecting with row 1. Type the following values, pressing the down-arrow key (↓) between each value: **480**, **360**, **390**, **460**, **486**, **370**.

WHY WORRY?

If you need to edit or delete text in a cell, click in the cell and type the text or number. The original text is replaced.

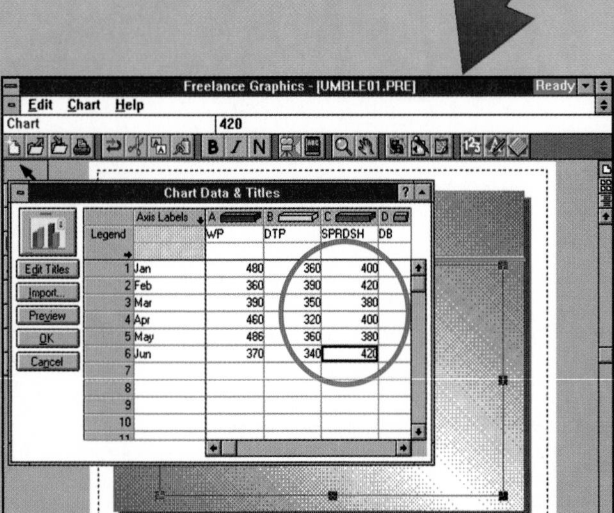

2 Click the cell created by column B intersecting row 1, and enter the following values: **360**, **390**, **350**, **320**, **360**, **340**. Move to column C, row 1 and enter these values: **400**, **420**, **380**, **400**, **380**, **420**.

3 Move within the worksheet so that you can see the entire DB column, column D, by using the horizontal scroll bar. Move the cursor to column D row 1, and enter the following values: **380**, **360**, **390**, **380**, **340**, **360**.

NOTE

Alternatively, position the mouse pointer on the right window border until you see a double-headed arrow. Drag the arrow to the right to enlarge the window.

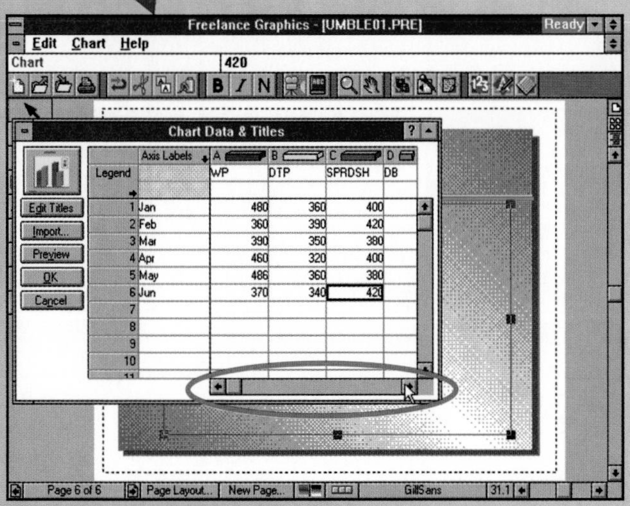

TASK 37

Adding Titles

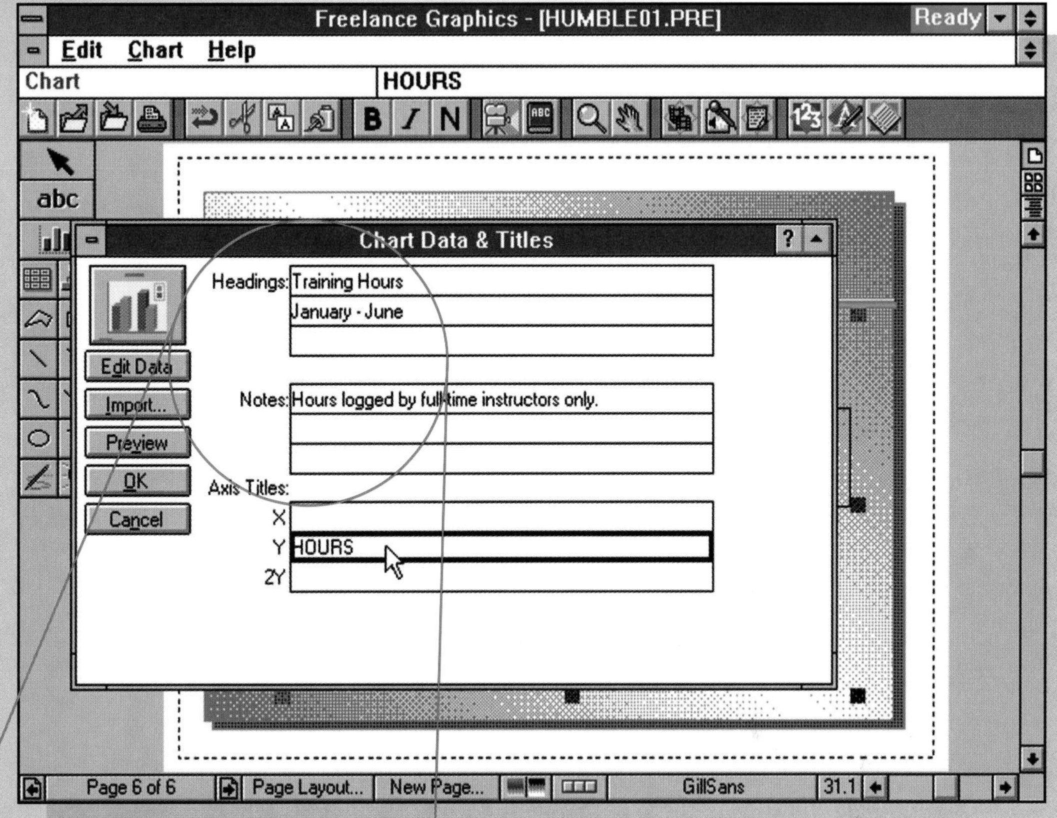

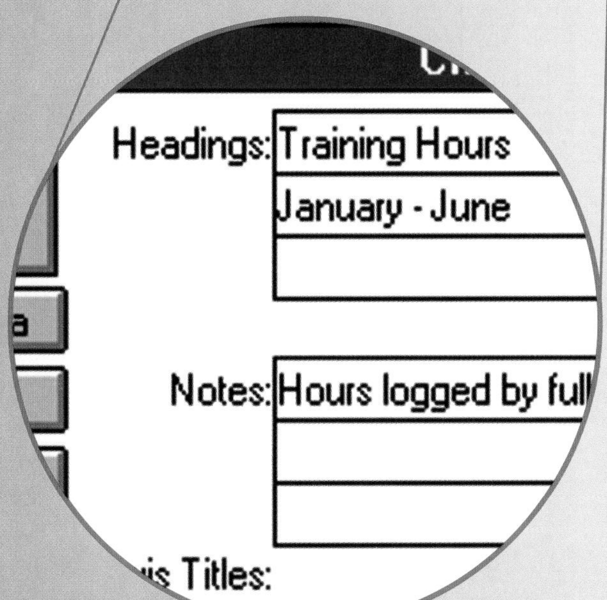

"Why would I do this?"

You can enter various titles and notes to your chart to further explain the information. You can, for example, add a chart title that describes the data shown. Freelance Graphics displays the title at the top of the chart. You can also add axis titles, such as "Months," "Training," or "Classes." Finally, you can add up to three lines of notes to the chart. The notes appear below the horizontal axis title.

Task 37: Adding Titles

1 Click the **Edit Titles** command button to display the Headings, Notes, and Axis Titles text boxes.

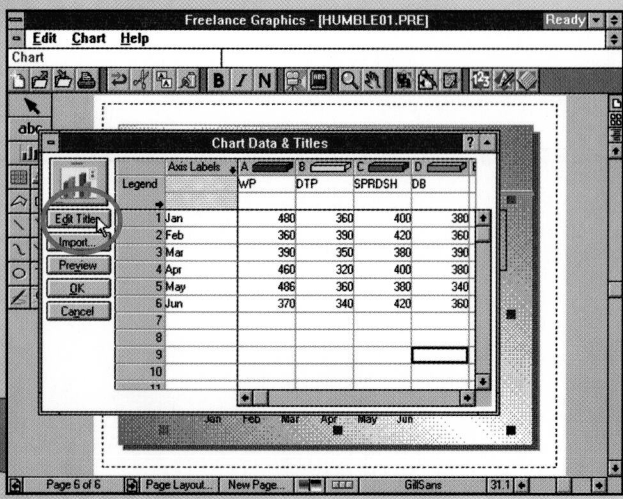

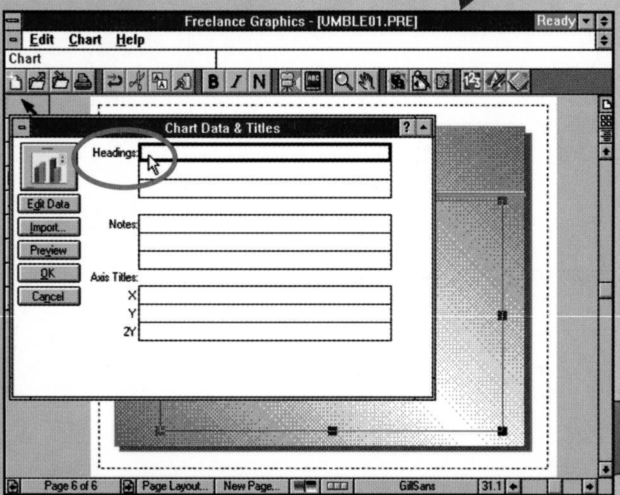

2 In the **Headings** text box, type **Training Hours**. Press the down-arrow key (↓) once and enter **January - June**.

NOTE

You can enter as many as three heading lines as well as three lines for notes. Additionally, you can enter over 70 characters on each line.

3 Click the first **Notes** text box and enter the following: **Hours logged by full-time instructors only.**

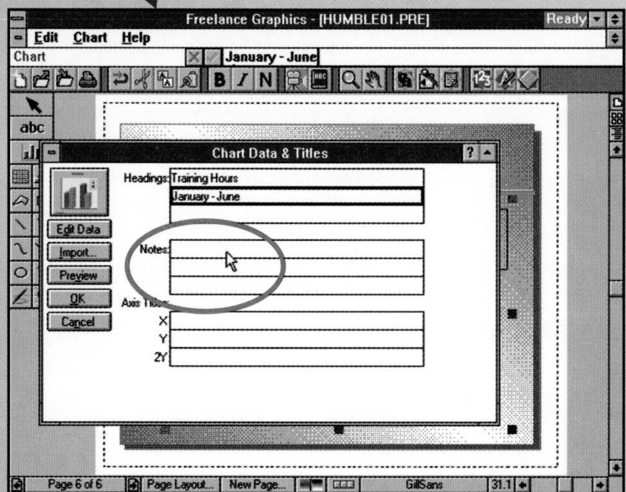

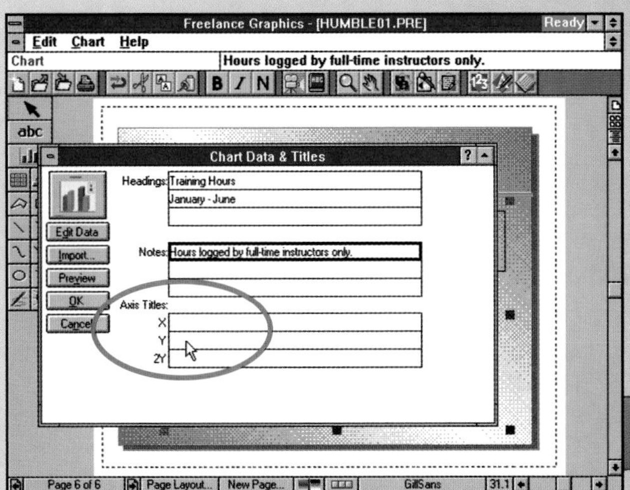

4 Click the **y-axis** text box. Type **HOURS**.

WHY WORRY?

You can add or edit titles and notes at any time by selecting the chart and clicking the Chart button on the toolbar.

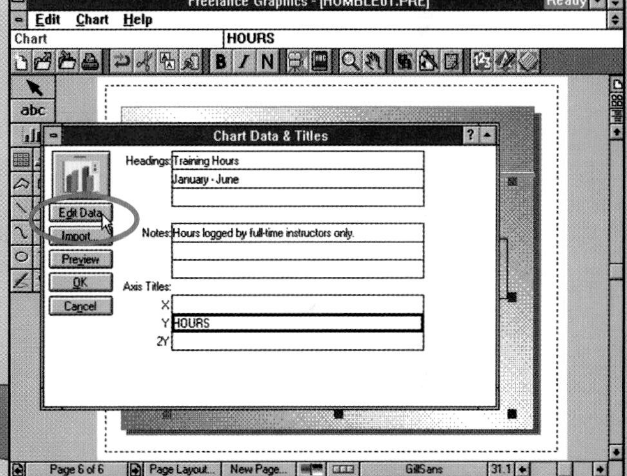

5 Click the **Edit Data** command button to return to the chart data; the Edit Data button changes back to Edit Titles.

6 Click and hold the **Preview** command button to view the chart. Click **OK** to close the Chart Data & Titles dialog box.

TASK 38

Changing the Chart Type

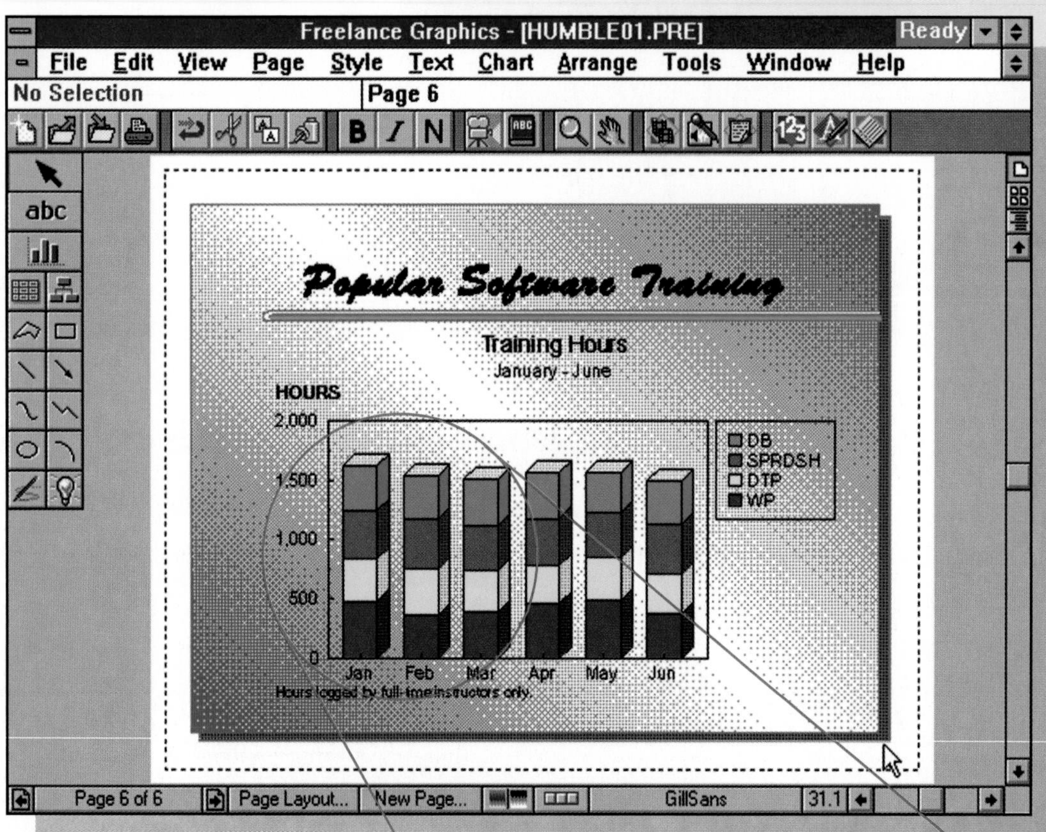

"Why would I do this?"

After you enter the chart data, titles, and notes, you may decide the chart does not depict the data the way you want. Changing the chart type changes the representation of the data. In the example, the bars representing each type of training show that word processing is the leader of the four classes. However, by changing to a stacked bar chart, the noticeable message is that January was the month with the most training hours in these four areas. The chart type you choose depends on the message you want to relate.

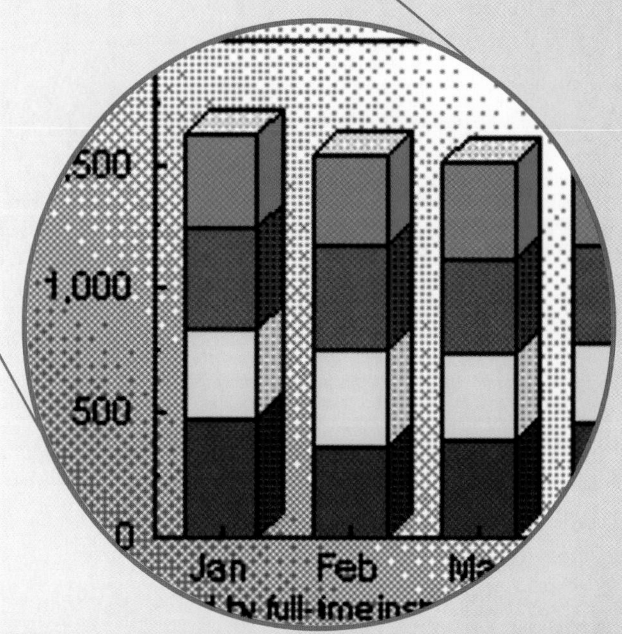

Task 38: Changing the Chart Type

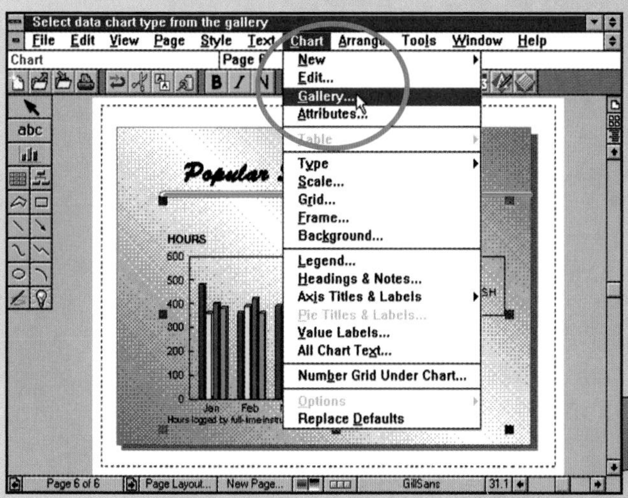

1 To change the chart type, select the chart, open the **Chart** menu, and choose **Gallery**. The Chart Gallery dialog box appears.

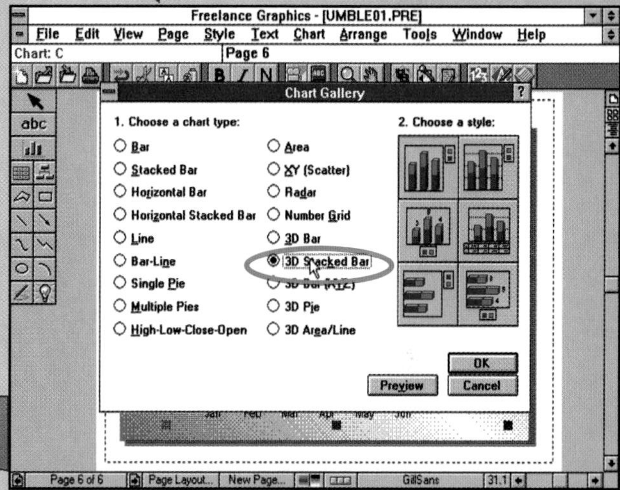

2 In the first group of options, select **3D Stacked Bar**. The default style in the second group of options, Choose a Style, is the top left button.

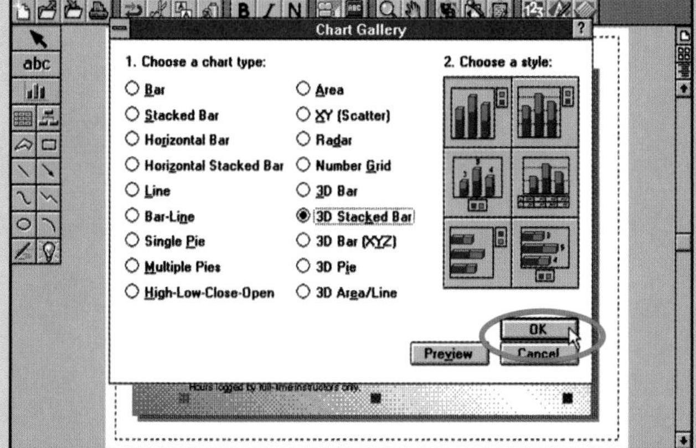

3 Choose **OK** to close the dialog box and return to the chart.

WHY WORRY?

If you want to change back to the previous chart type, choose the Edit Undo Chart Gallery command; or press the Undo keyboard shortcut Ctrl+Z.

TASK 39

Changing Chart Attributes

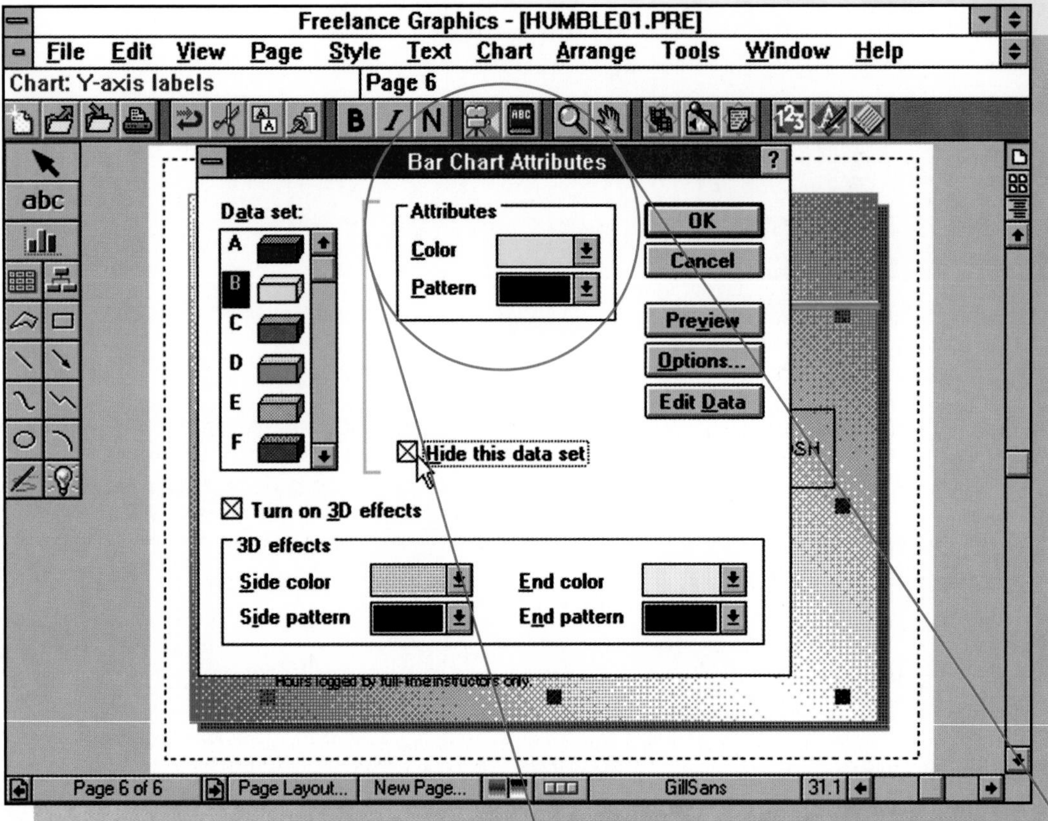

"Why would I do this?"

Chart attributes include the color of the bars, wedges, lines, or other representatives of the chart data. If you are using a 3D chart, you can also choose the color of the sides and tops of the bars or wedges. Another important part of the attributes is that you can choose to hide one or more data sets. By hiding a data set, you can further alter the chart to better suit your purposes.

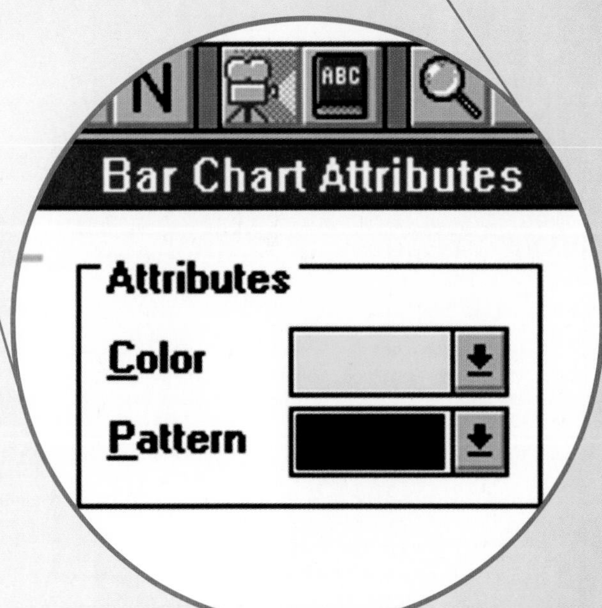

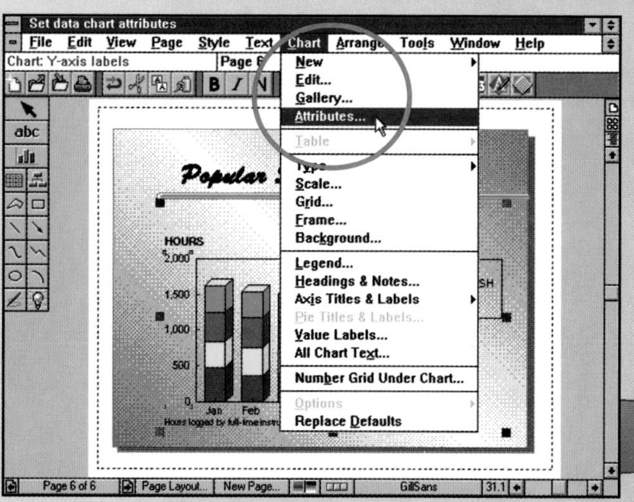

1 To change the attributes of a chart, select the chart, open the **Chart** menu, and choose **Attributes**. The Bar Chart Attributes dialog box appears.

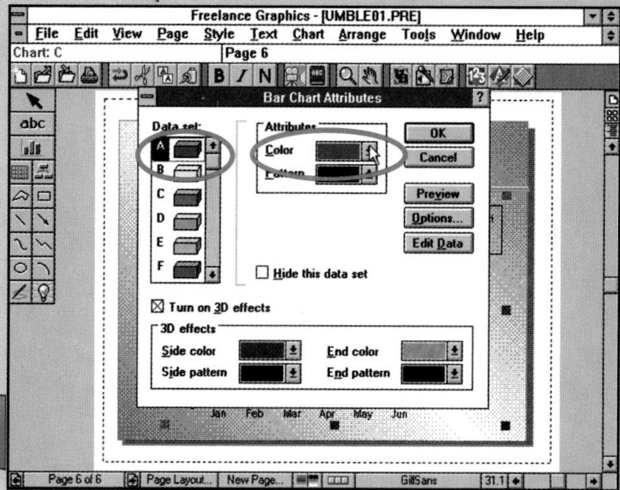

2 In the **Data Set** area, A is selected by default. The A data set represents the data in column 1, which is also Word Processing. In the **Attributes** area, choose **Color**.

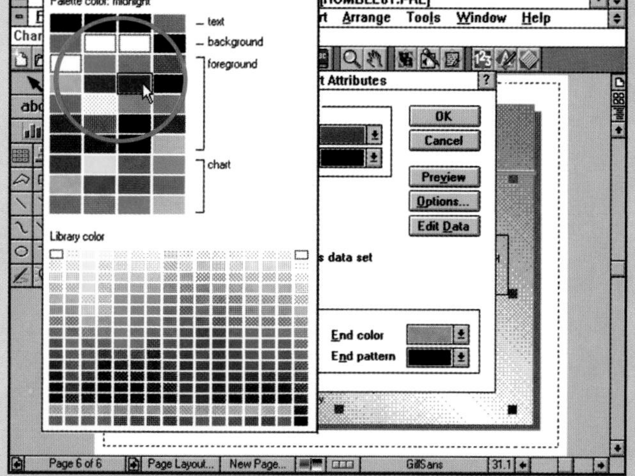

3 The Palette appears. Choose another color to represent the front of the 3D bar in data set A.

NOTE

Choose the side color or end color in the 3D Effects option group, and change the colors of the entire bar by choosing a color from the Palette.

Task 39: Changing Chart Attributes

4 In the Data Set area, choose **B**, which represents DTP, Desktop Publishing, in the chart.

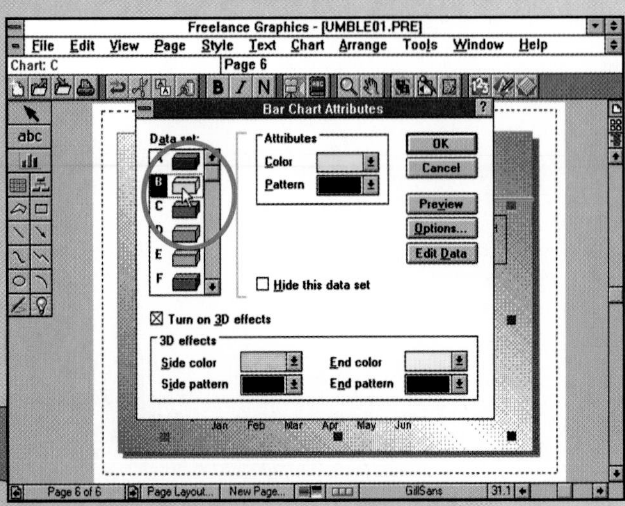

5 Select the **Hide This Data Set** check box.

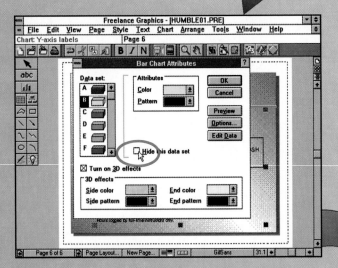

6 Choose **Preview** to view the chart without column B, DTP, represented. Choose **OK** to return to the chart page.

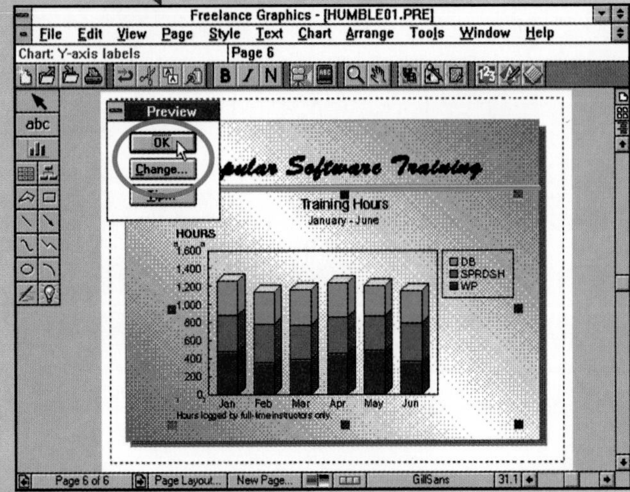

TASK 40

Changing Type in the Chart

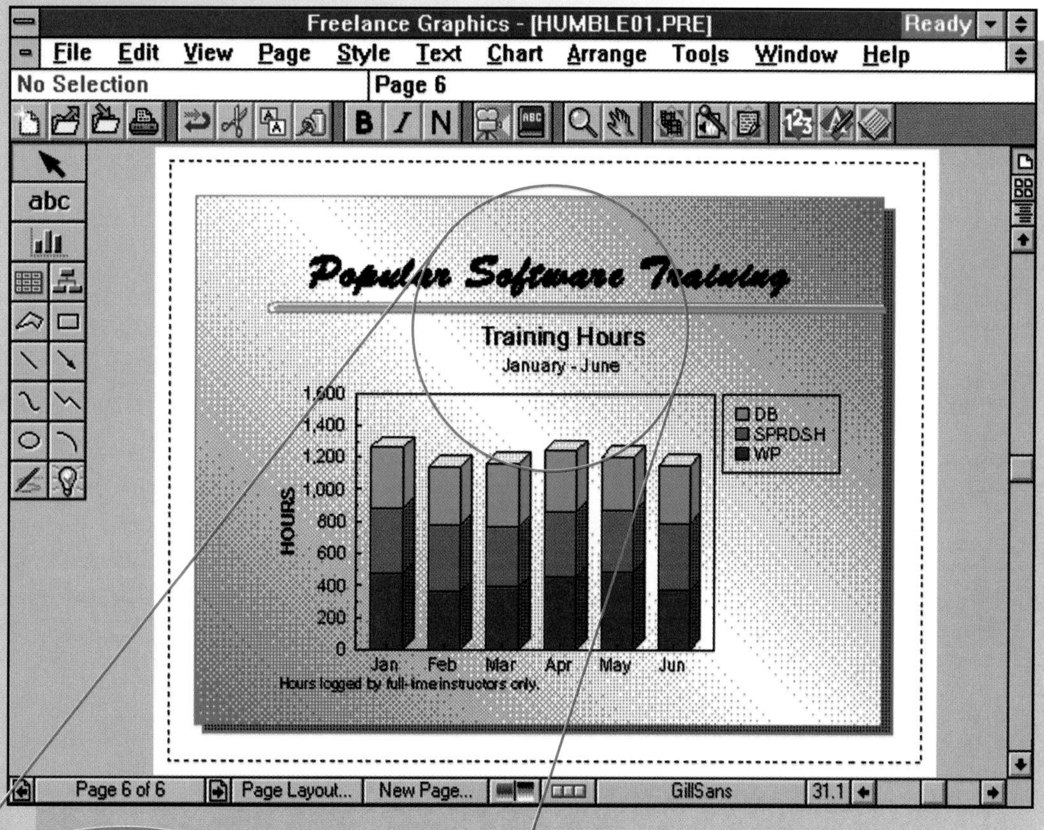

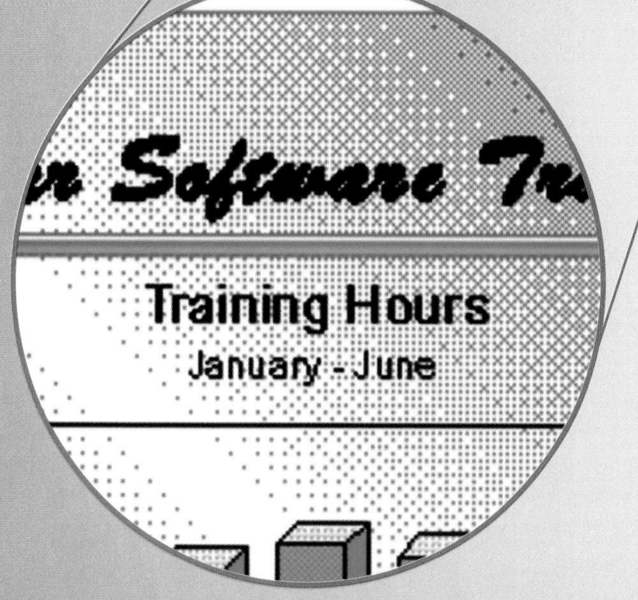

"Why would I do this?"

In most cases, the face and size of the type in a chart work well with the design of the presentation. However, you may need to make changes to Freelance Graphics' preformatted styles. Suppose some text is too small to really show up against the background; you can enlarge it or make it bold.

All you have to do to change the typefaces and type sizes in a chart is double-click the text you want to change to display a dialog box.

Task 40: Changing Type in the Chart

1 Select the chart and place the mouse pointer on **Training Hours**, the title of the chart. Double-click to display the Chart Headings & Notes dialog box.

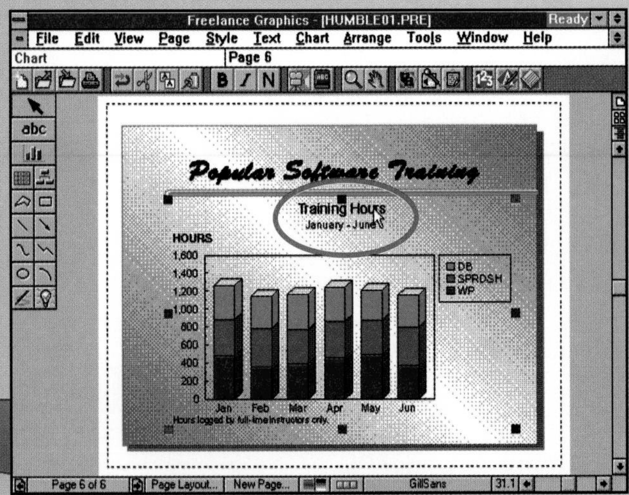

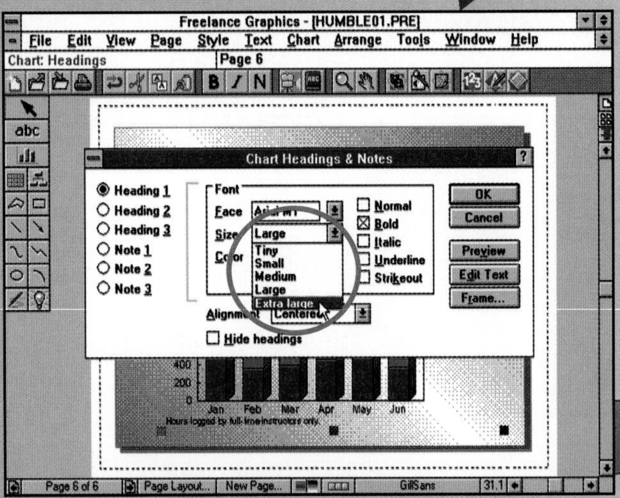

2 In the left side of the dialog box, notice that the Heading 1 option is already selected; Heading 1 is "Training Hours." In the **Font** area, click the **Size** drop-down list and select **Extra Large**.

NOTE

You can also change the face or color of the selected heading or note, as well as change the alignment or hide the selected text altogether.

3 Choose **OK** to close the dialog box.

WHY WORRY?

You can also change the type size and typeface for Heading lines 2 and 3 as well as the type for Notes 1, 2, and 3 in this same dialog box.

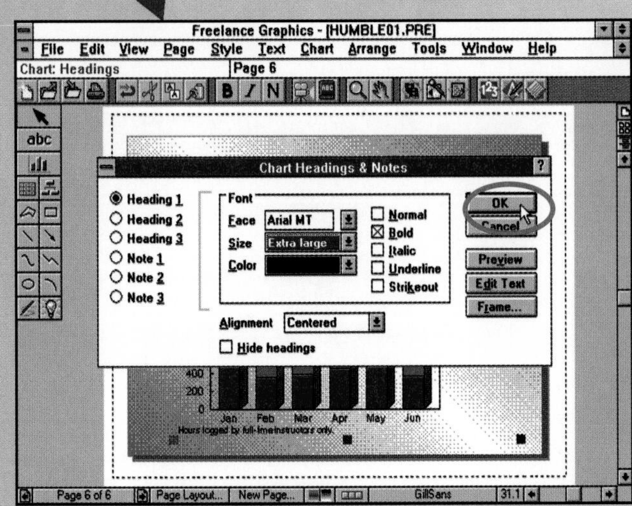

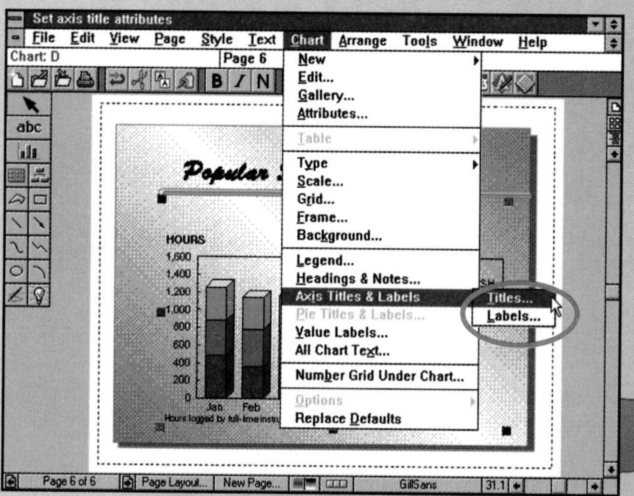

4 You can also change the type by opening the **Chart** menu and choosing **Axis Titles & Labels**. From the secondary menu, choose **Titles** to display the Chart Axis Titles dialog box.

NOTE

You also can change typeface, type size, and so on, of axis titles and labels by double-clicking the title or label. The Chart Axis Titles or Chart Axis Labels dialog box appears.

5 In the **Axis to Modify** area, choose **Y**.

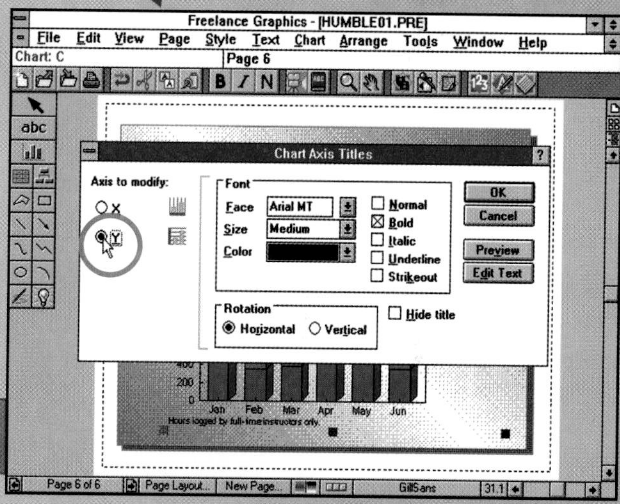

6 In the **Rotation** area, choose **Vertical**, and then choose **OK**.

NOTE

You can also change the typeface, size, or color of the selected text in this dialog box.

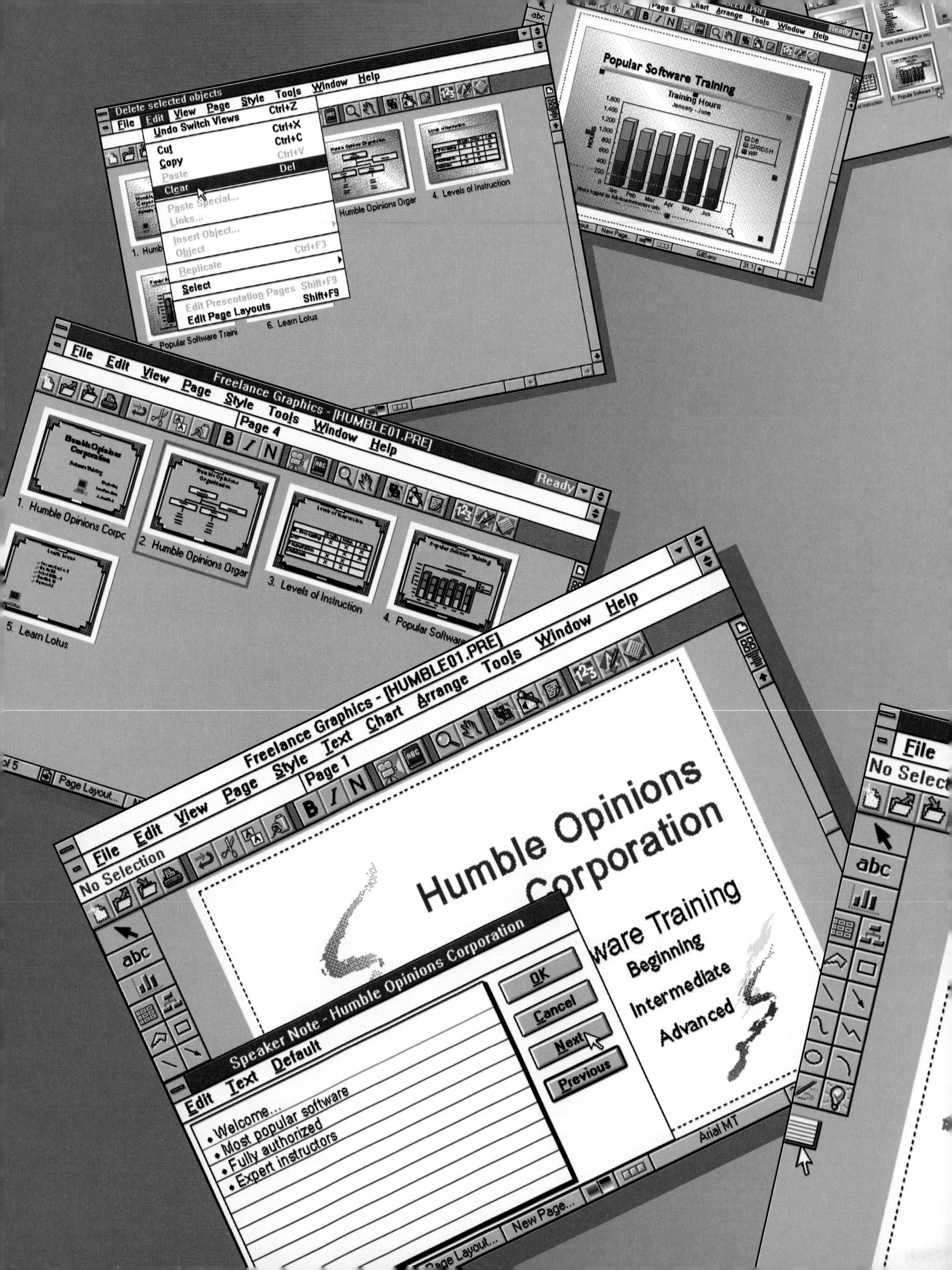

Delete selected objects
File Edit View Page Style Tools Window Help
Undo Switch Views Ctrl+Z
Cut Ctrl+X
Copy Ctrl+C
Paste Ctrl+V
Clear Del
Paste Special...
Links...
Insert Object...
Object Ctrl+F3
Replicate
Select
Edit Presentation Pages Shift+F9
Edit Page Layouts Shift+F9
Humble Opinions Orgar
4. Levels of Instruction
6. Learn Lotus
Popular Software Traini
Popular Software Training
Training Hours
January - June
Jan Feb Mar Apr May Jun
DB
SPRDSH
WP
Freelance Graphics - [HUMBLE01.PRE]
File Edit View Page Style Tools Window Help
Page 4
Ready
1. Humble Opinions Corpo
2. Humble Opinions Orgar
3. Levels of Instruction
4. Popular Software
5. Learn Lotus
Freelance Graphics - [HUMBLE01.PRE]
File Edit View Page Style Text Chart Arrange Tools Window Help
No Selection
Page 1
Humble Opinions
Corporation
ware Training
Beginning
Intermediate
Advanced
Speaker Note - Humble Opinions Corporation
OK
Cancel
Next
Previous
Speaker Note Text Default
Edit
• Welcome...
• Most popular software
• Fully authorized
• Expert instructors
Arial MT
Page Layout...
New Page...

PART VII

Viewing and Editing the Presentation

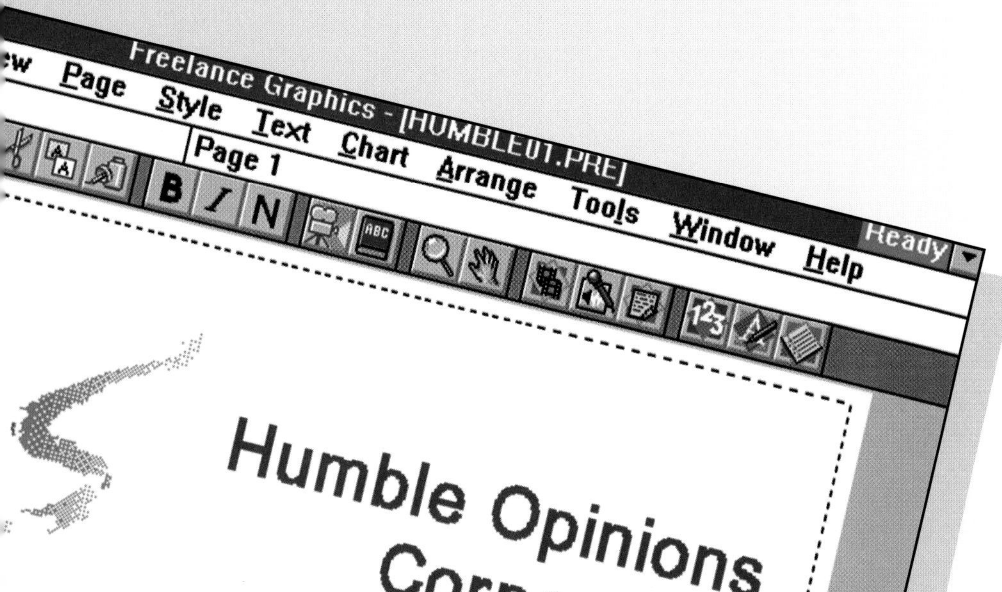

Before you print or show your presentation to a client, you may want to make some changes. As you have already seen, Freelance Graphics enables you to edit text, tables, charts, and other objects in your presentation by changing colors, modifying fonts, moving or deleting objects, changing styles, and so on. In addition, you can change the look of the overall presentation.

With the *Page Sorter* view, you can view 12 pages of the presentation at one time by displaying them as *thumbnails*, or small pages. Using Page Sorter view, you can see if the page designs are consistent, view the order in which the pages appear, and even rearrange the page order, if you want.

To change the page order, for example, you can simply drag a page to a new location in Page Sorter view. In addition, you can move more than one page at a time by holding down the Shift key when selecting the pages you want to move. With a drag of the mouse, you can arrange all the pages on-screen and then rearrange them, if necessary.

You can also use Page Sorter view to add or delete pages. While viewing and sorting your presentation pages, you may decide you have too many pages or you just want to delete one page. You can remove pages within the presentation and you can add pages, as well.

Additionally, you may want to magnify a page to edit some text or just to review the contents. You can enlarge and reduce the view of each presentation page using the View menu or a shortcut button. Freelance supplies several viewing options from which you can choose, including Full Page, Zoom In, and Zoom Out.

In addition to viewing and sorting the presentation, you can also change the look of the presentation. When you first began the presentation, you chose a SmartMaster set to use as a color and design for your presentation pages. You can choose a different SmartMaster set and apply a different design to the pages.

Choose any of over 50 SmartMaster set backgrounds, including symbols, scenes, and gradations in color. You can even change the colors used in the SmartMaster set. View the set to see if it is what you want and change it again, if you like. You can even view the different SmartMaster sets in Page Sorter view so that you can see the overall effect on the presentation.

Finally, Freelance provides a useful feature you may want to use with your presentation: speaker notes. Speaker notes are comments or annotations you may want to remember when showing your presentation. Speaker notes are not shown as part of the presentation; you view the notes only when you open the Speaker Notes dialog box. Freelance does, however, display a small icon below the toolbox to indicate presentation pages with speaker notes.

After you create your speaker notes, you can print them. Freelance prints speaker notes on the bottom half of the page with the reduced printed presentation page on top to help you during an on-screen or projected presentation.

This part shows you how to make sure your presentation is perfect before you show it to your client.

TASK 41

Sorting Pages

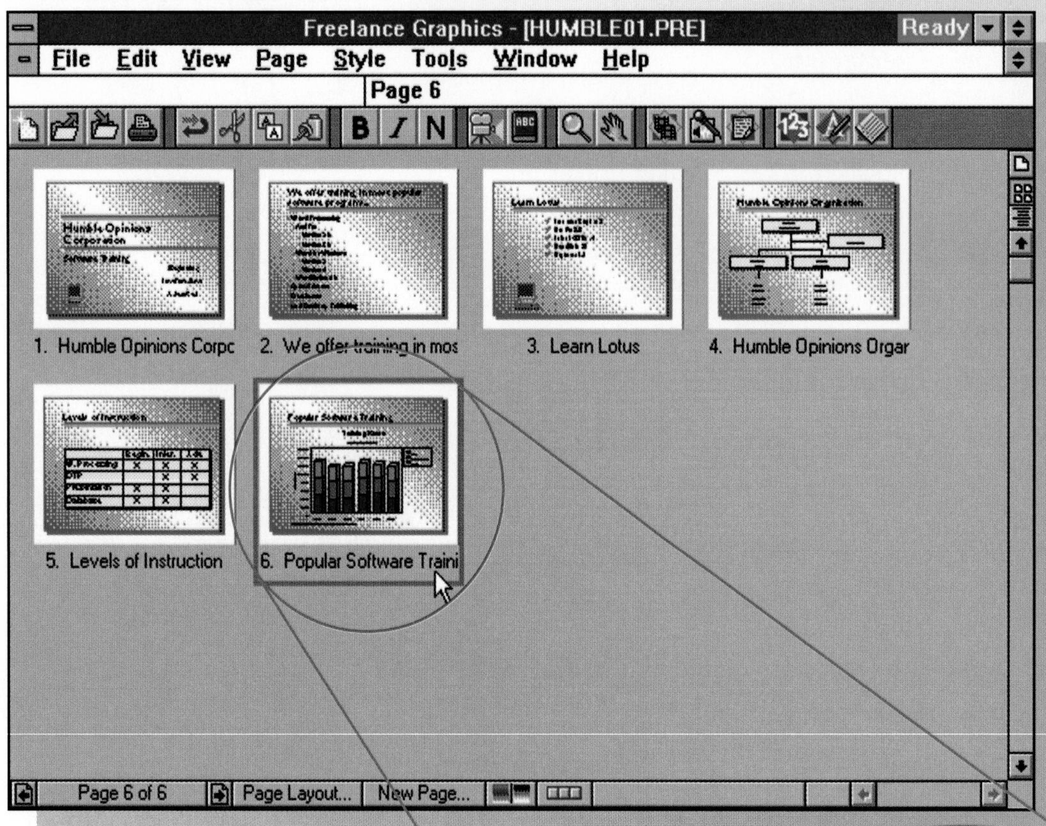

"Why would I do this?"

You use Page Sorter view to see the overall look of your presentation. You can compare the pages, check the consistency of the page designs, and so on, by viewing the presentation in Page Sorter view.

You can also sort— or rearrange— the order of the pages in this view. If you want to move page three to the end of the presentation, you can drag that page to any location within the presentation when you are in Page Sorter view.

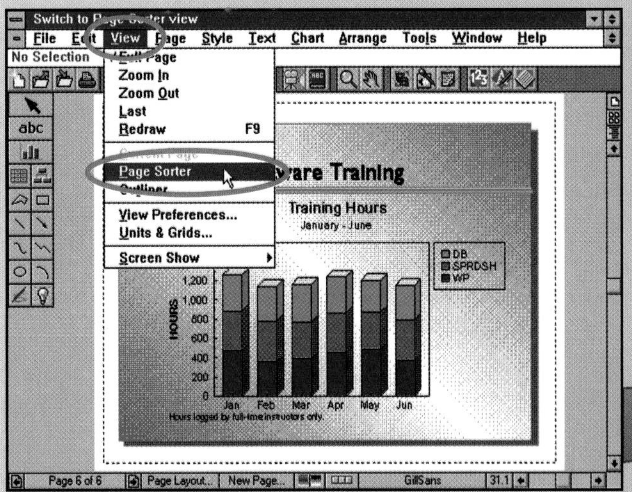

1 To change to Page Sorter view, open the **View** menu and choose **Page Sorter**.

NOTE

You can quickly switch to Page Sorter view by clicking the Page Sorter button located above the vertical scroll bar. The Page Sorter button is the second button from the top and looks like four small pages.

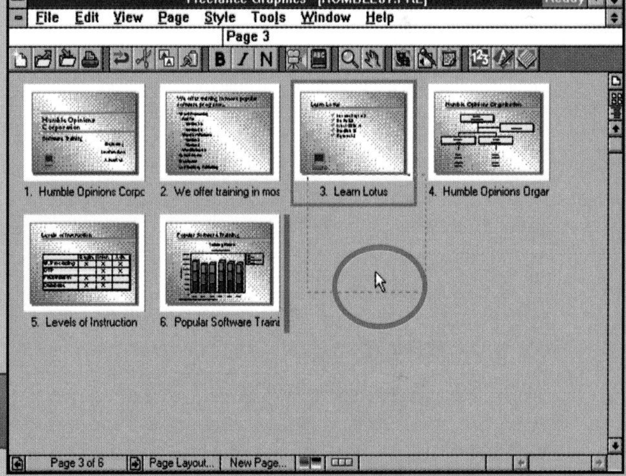

2 Page Sorter view displays the pages of your presentation. To move page three to the end of the presentation, click **page three** to select it and then drag the mouse to the right of page six. As you drag the page icon, you see a dotted rectangular border move with the mouse. When the page gets close to the new position, a gray vertical bar appears to mark the new position; the page is placed to the right of the vertical bar.

3 To return to the full page view, select the page you want to view. Open the **View** menu and choose **Current Page**. Freelance displays a full page view of the selected page.

NOTE

You can, alternatively, choose the Full Page button at the top of the vertical scroll bar. Clicking the button changes the view from Page Sorter to Full Page.

TASK 42

Viewing Pages

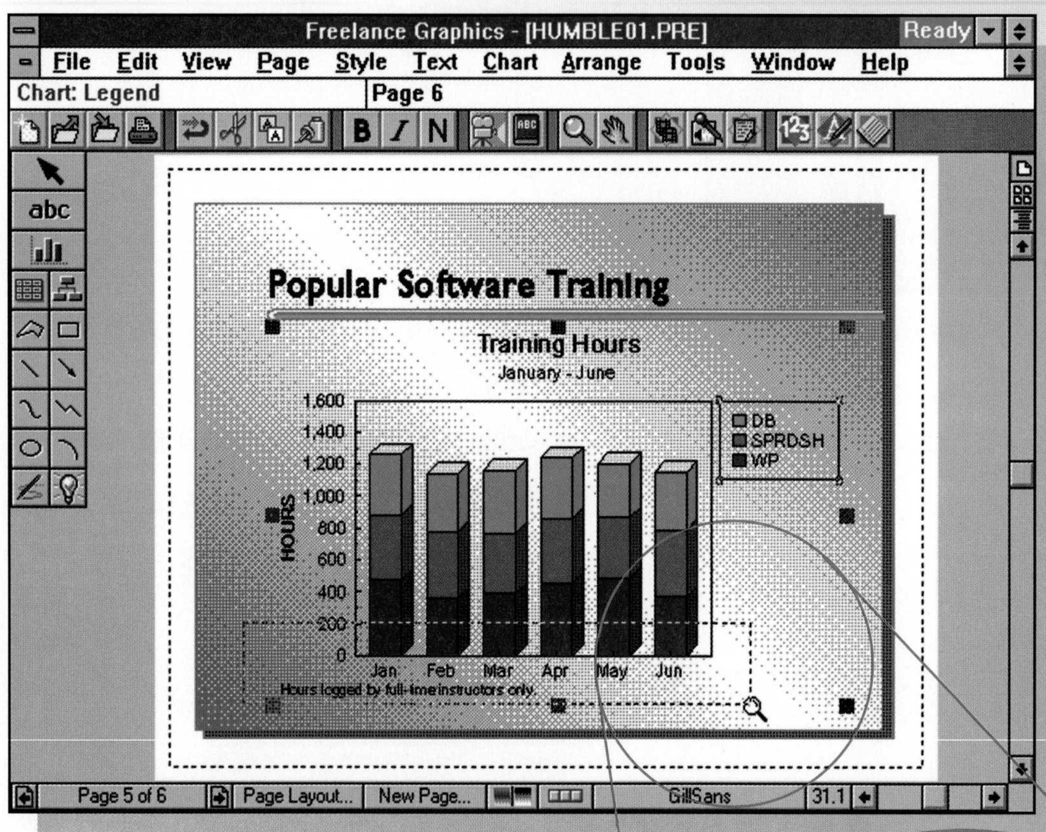

"Why would I do this?"

You can enlarge the view of a page so that you can study, and perhaps edit, the details of the page. Suppose you can't read the note text in a chart; you can enlarge the view to see the text better. You also can reduce the view of the page so that you can see the overall effect of the page design and placement of the text and graphics. Freelance Graphics provides a Zoom tool and three view commands you can use to magnify and reduce the view.

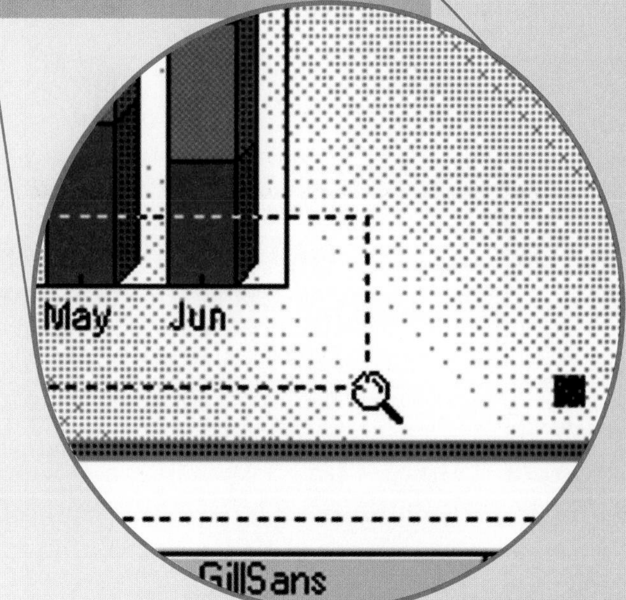

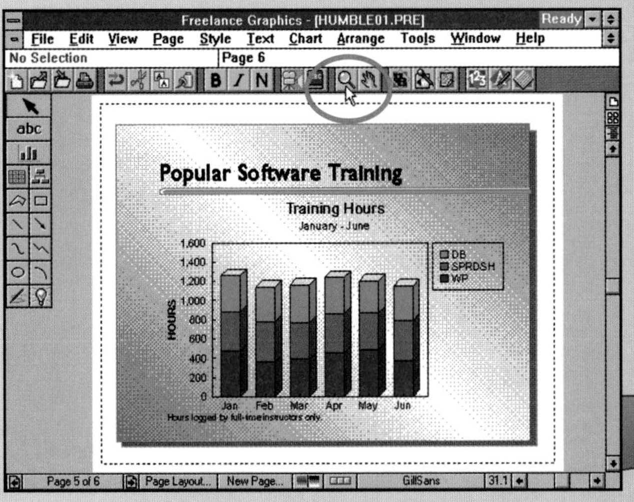

1 On page five of your presentation, click the **Zoom Page** button in the SmartIcons. The Zoom Page button contains a magnifying glass.

WHY WORRY?

Use the SmartIcons to view a description of the tool by placing the mouse pointer on the icon and holding down the right mouse button. Freelance displays a description of the tool in the title bar.

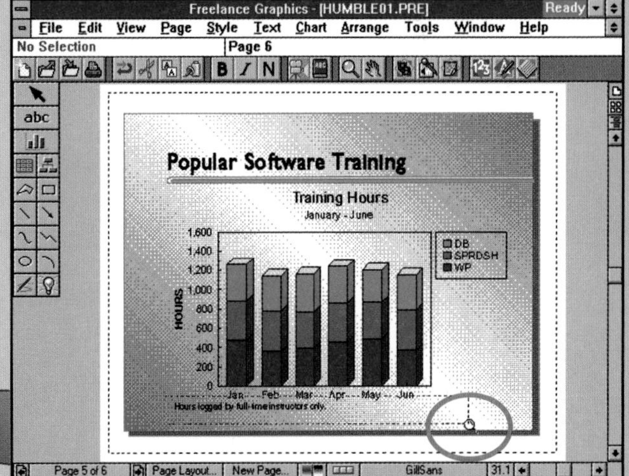

2 Use the tool to drag a *marquee*—or rectangular guide—around the entire note at the bottom of the chart. The smaller the marquee, the more Freelance magnifies the view.

WHY WORRY?

To view a part of the page that is not in the window, use the scroll bars.

3 To reduce the view, open the **View** menu and choose **Zoom Out**.

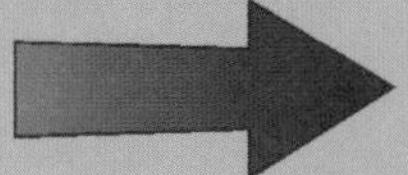

Task 42: Viewing Pages

4 Open the **View** menu and choose **Full Page** to change the view back to Full Page view.

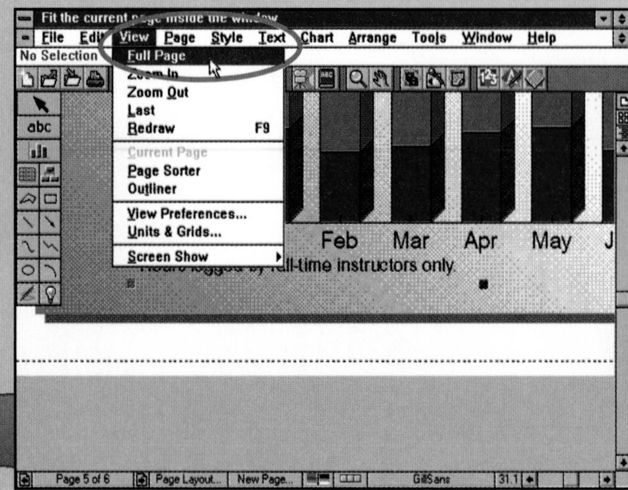

5 Open the **View** menu and choose **Last** to view the previous magnified or reduced view; in this case, choosing the Last command enlarges the view again.

6 Open the **View** menu and choose **Zoom In** to view the page at a slightly enlarged setting.

NOTE

When you move to another page or another view, the magnified view automatically changes back to Full Page view.

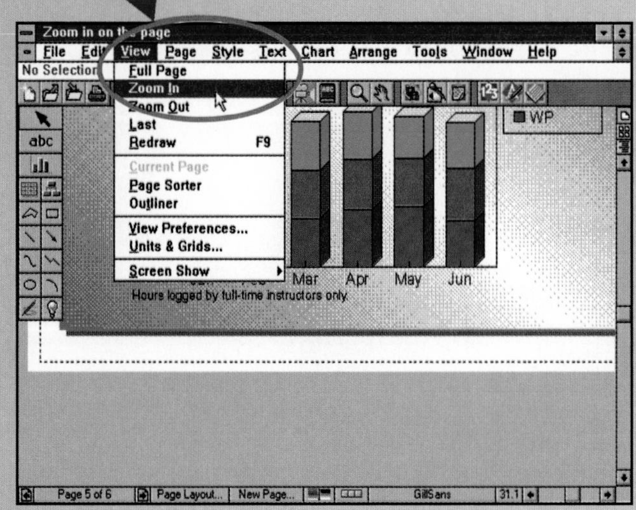

TASK 43

Removing Pages

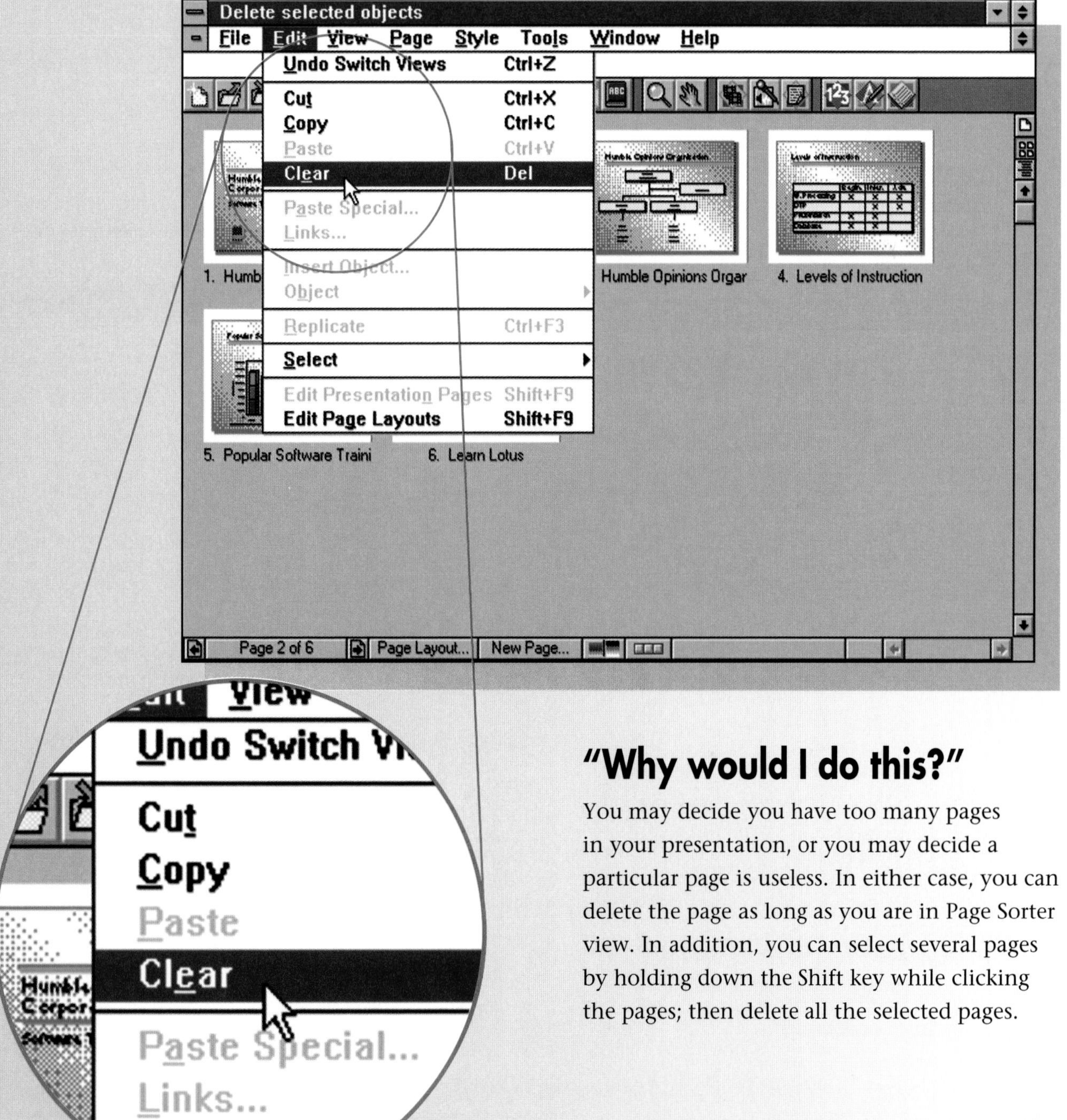

"Why would I do this?"

You may decide you have too many pages in your presentation, or you may decide a particular page is useless. In either case, you can delete the page as long as you are in Page Sorter view. In addition, you can select several pages by holding down the Shift key while clicking the pages; then delete all the selected pages.

Task 43: Removing Pages

1 Click the **Page Sorter** button— the second icon from the top in the vertical scroll bar— to change to Page Sorter view.

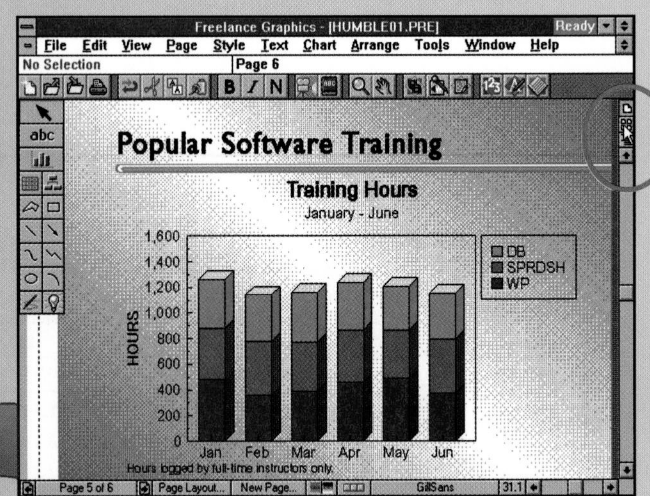

2 Select page 2, "We offer training in...," by clicking the page icon.

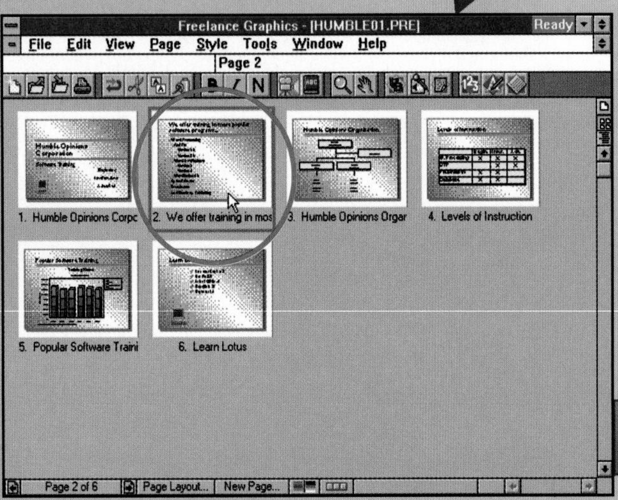

3 Open the **Edit** menu and choose **Clear** to remove the page. Or, press **Delete.** Freelance removes the page without a warning or confirmation box.

WHY WORRY?

If you change your mind, choose Edit Undo Delete Page(s) before performing any other task.

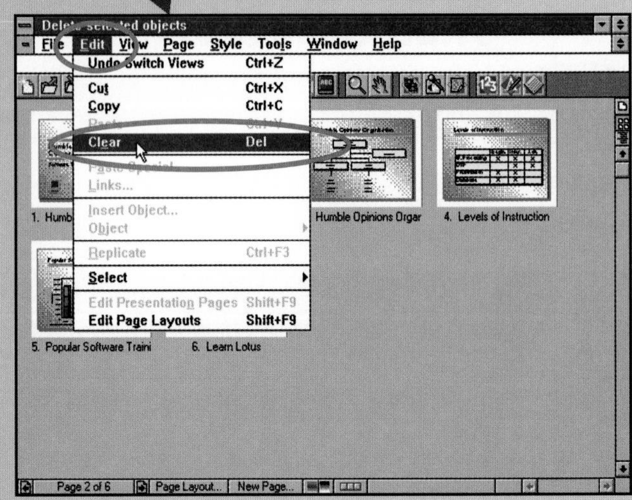

TASK 44

Changing the Look of the Presentation

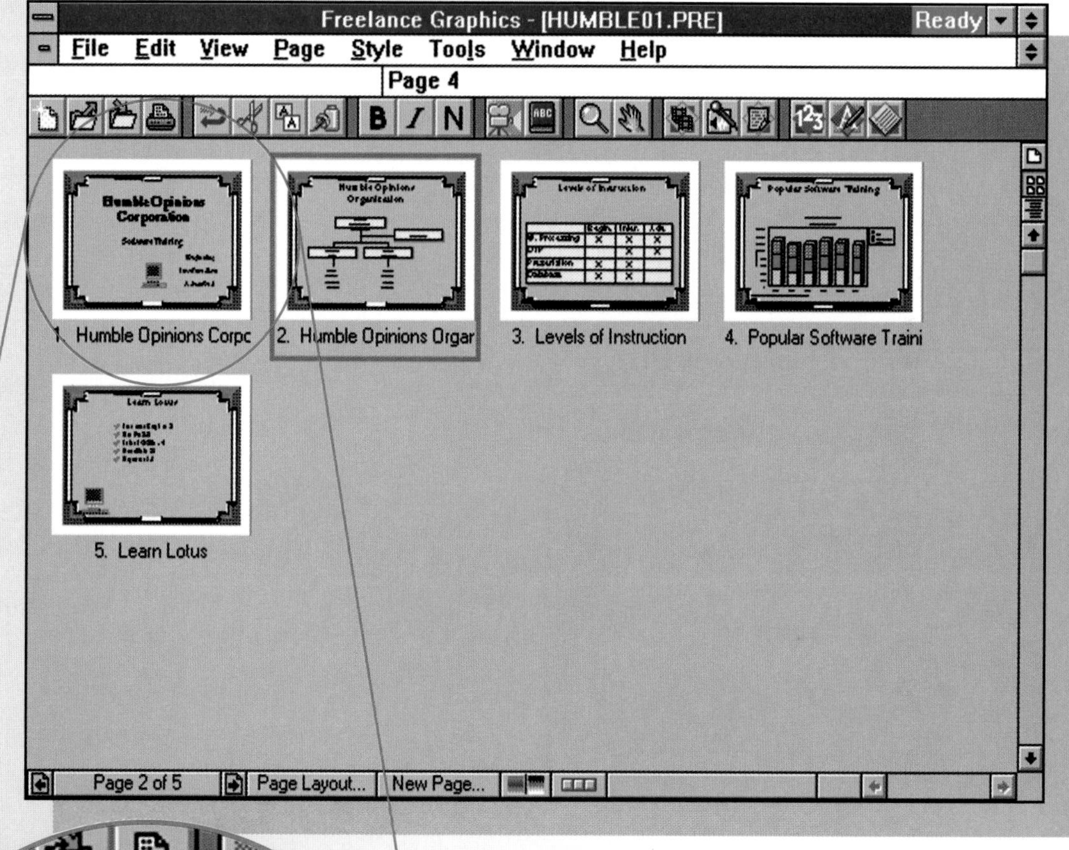

"Why would I do this?"

You can change the SmartMaster set for the pages of your presentation. You may want a white background, for example, for a presentation with colorful graphics and charts. On the other hand, you may want to use a distinctive design for your presentation; you may use the forest.mas set, for example, for a presentation on recycling. With Freelance Graphics, you can easily change the SmartMaster set for all the pages and view them in the Page Sorter or Full Page view.

Task 44: Changing the Look of the Presentation

1 In Full Page view, move to page one of the presentation. Open the **Style** menu and choose **Choose SmartMaster Set**. The Choose SmartMaster Set dialog box appears.

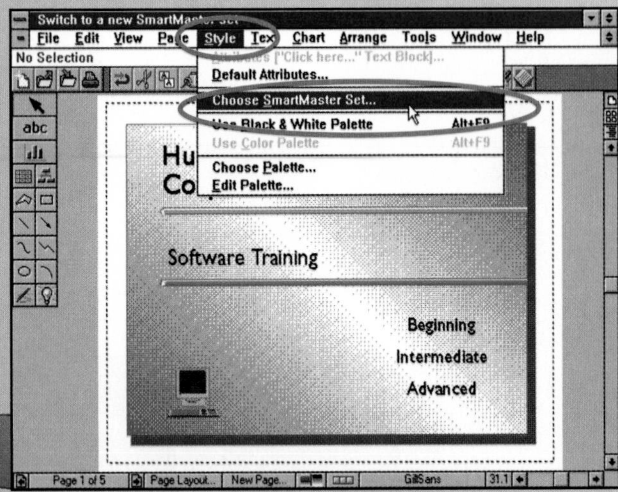

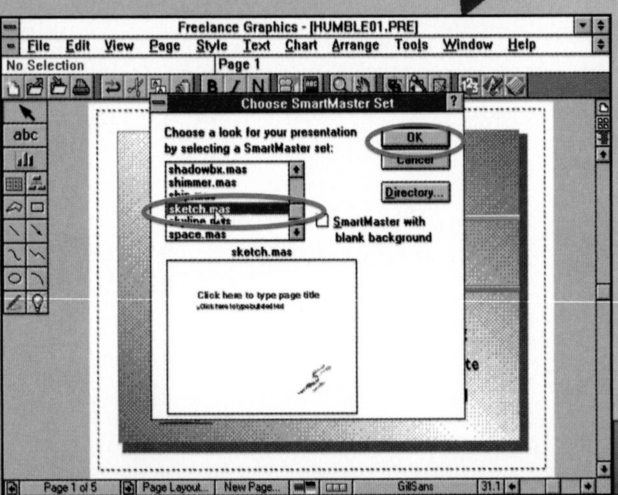

2 In the Choose SmartMaster Set dialog box, choose **sketch.mas**, and then choose **OK**.

NOTE

If you want to add more color, choose Page Background; the Page Background dialog box appears. In Background, choose 1st color and select a color from the palette. Choose OK to view the color change.

3 Click the **Page Sorter** button to show the entire presentation with the sketch.mas SmartMaster set.

WHY WORRY?

If you decide you do not like this set, choose Style Choose SmartMaster Set and select a different set for your presentation's background design.

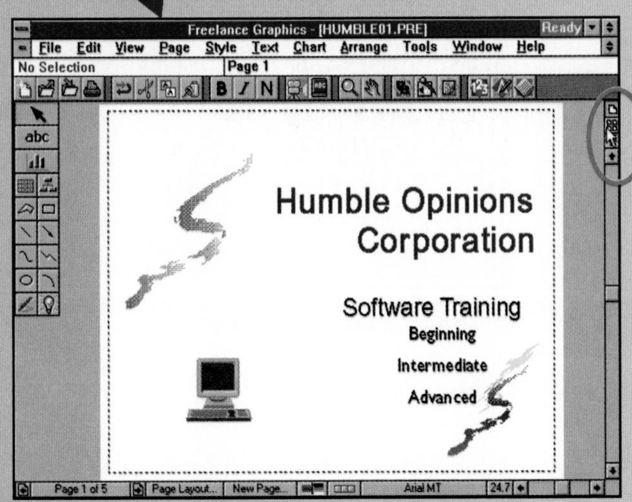

TASK 45

Adding Speaker Notes

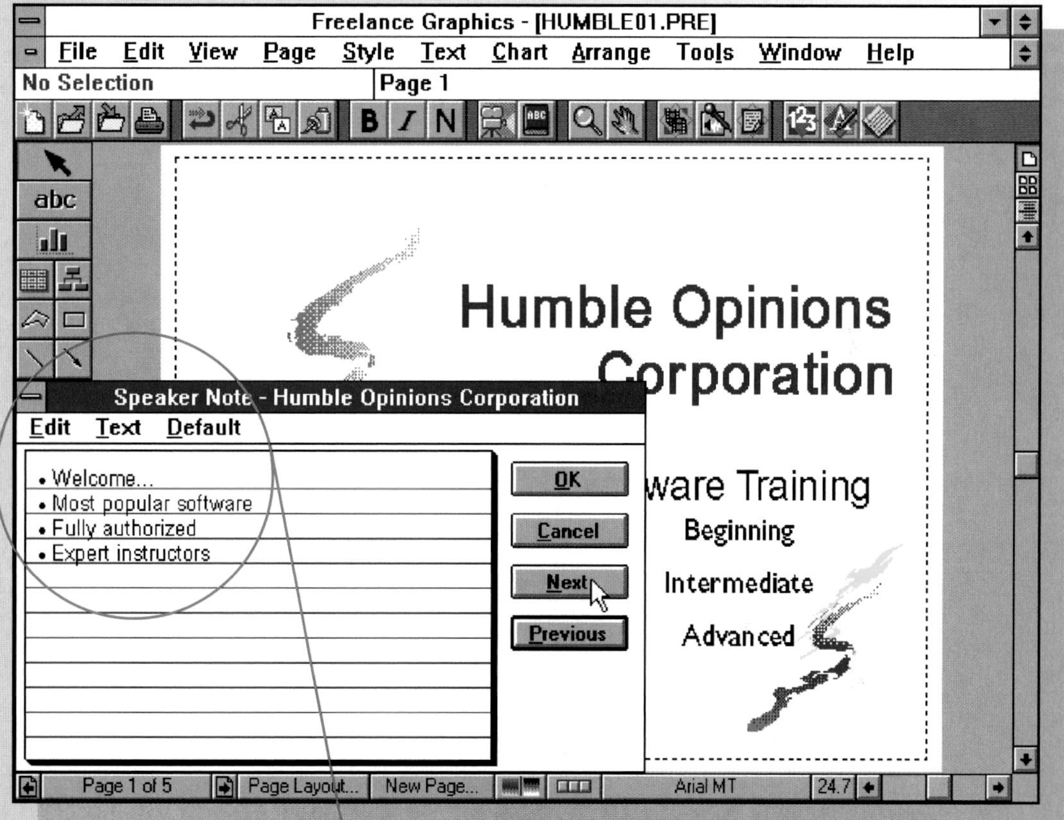

"Why would I do this?"

Speaker notes are annotations you use to spur your memory as you talk about the presentation. You can create speaker notes for your presentation pages and save the notes with your presentation file. Print the notes and use them during a slide show or on-screen presentation like you would use index cards.

When typing your speaker notes, use brief, descriptive phrases you can elaborate on as you speak.

Task 45: Adding Speaker Notes

1 On page one of your presentation in Full Page view, open the **Page** menu and choose **Speaker Notes**. The speaker note for page one appears.

NOTE

You can create one speaker note per page of the presentation.

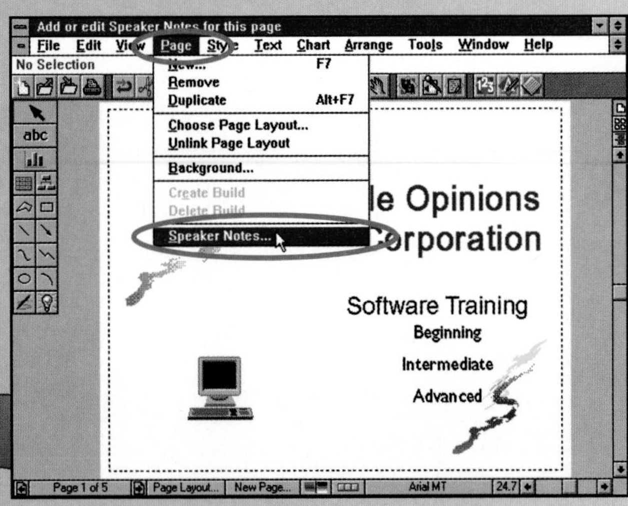

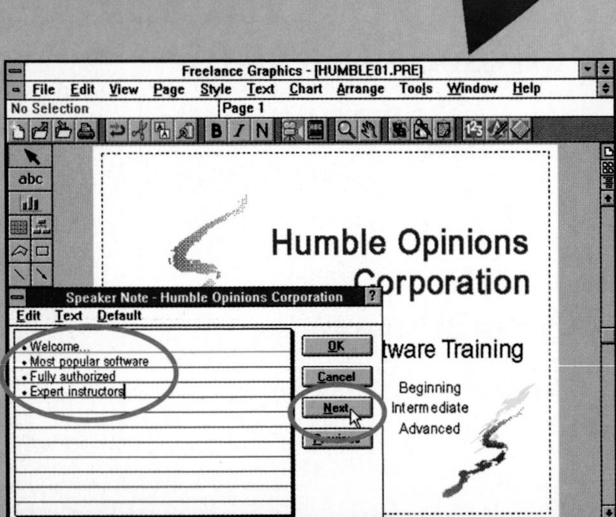

2 On the index card, type **Welcome...** and press **Enter**. On the second line, type **Most popular software** and press **Enter**. On the third line, type **Fully authorized** and press **Enter**; type **Expert instructors**. Click the **Next** command button.

NOTE

You can format the text in a speaker note using the Text menu.

3 On page two, enter the following text: **BA in Education** (**Enter**), **Has educated adults for 16 years**, (**Enter**), **Typesetter**. Choose **OK** to close the dialog box.

NOTE

When you choose the Next or Previous command button in the Speaker Note dialog box, Freelance moves to the next or previous card and page.

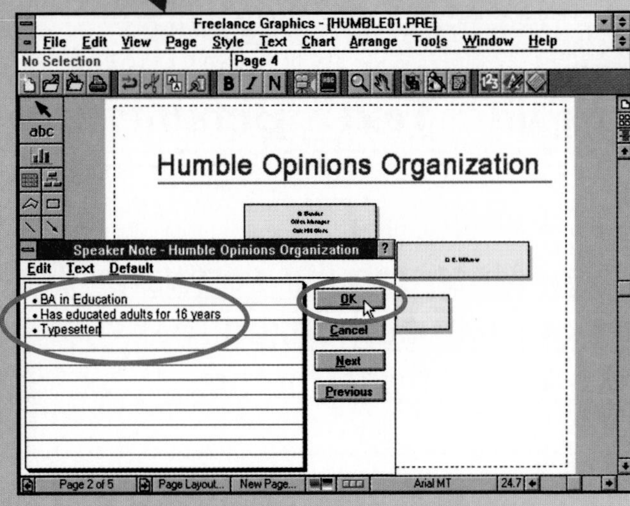

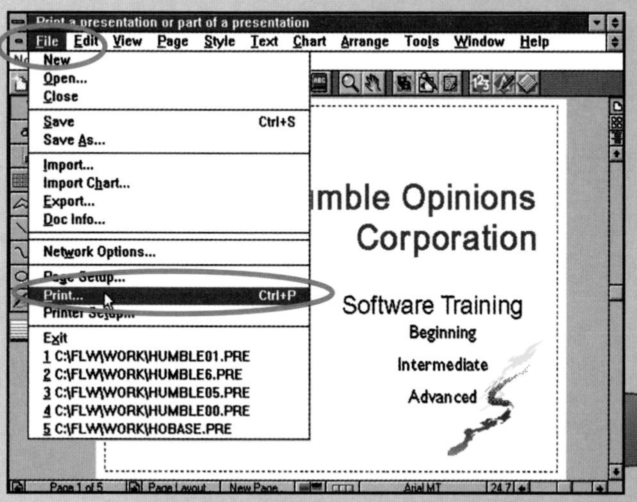

4 To print the speaker notes, open the **File** menu and choose **Print**; or, press **Ctrl+P**. The Print File dialog box appears.

5 In the Format option group, choose **Speaker Notes** and then choose the **Print** command button. Freelance prints the presentation, reducing each page and printing it on the top half of the page and printing the speaker notes on the bottom half of the page.

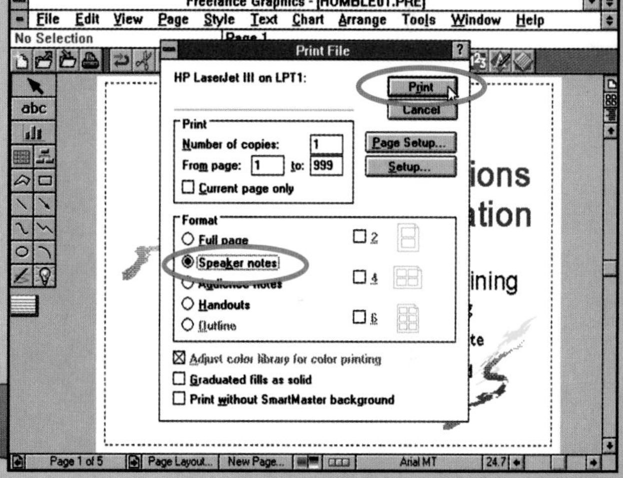

6 You can edit, delete, or add notes at any time by using a shortcut for opening the Speaker Note dialog box. Freelance provides a button that looks like an index card for every presentation page that contains a speaker note. The button is located below the toolbox. Click the **Speaker Notes** button to view or edit the speaker notes.

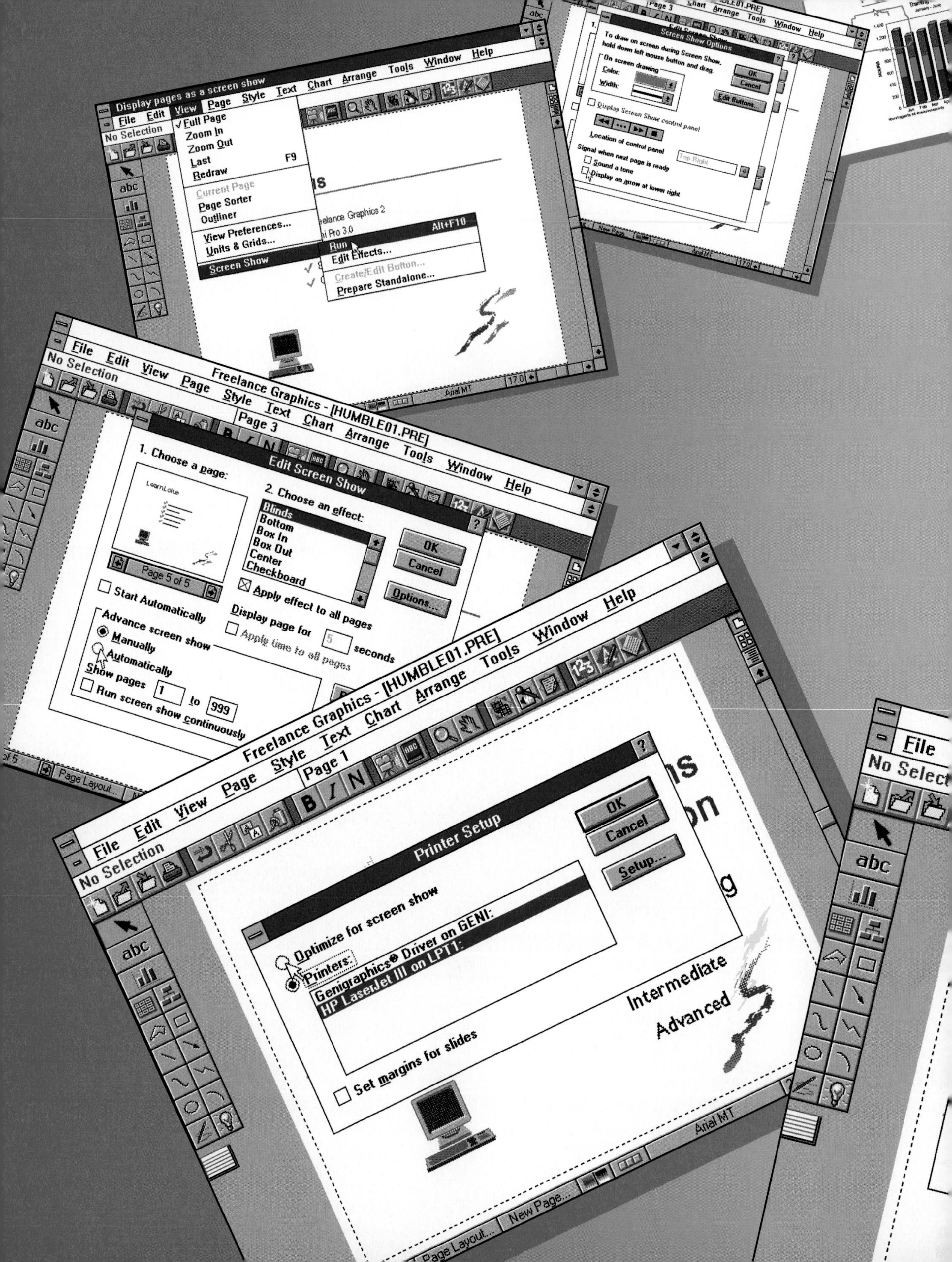

Display pages as a screen show
File Edit View Page Style Text Chart Arrange Tools Window Help
No Selection
✓Full Page
Zoom In
Zoom Out
Last F9
Redraw
Current Page
Page Sorter
Outliner
View Preferences...
Units & Grids...
Screen Show
Run Alt+F10
Edit Effects...
Create/Edit Button...
Prepare Standalone...
Screen Show Options
To draw on screen during Screen Show, hold down left mouse button and drag.
On screen drawing
Color:
Width:
OK
Cancel
Edit Buttons...
Display Screen Show control panel
Location of control panel
Top Right
Signal when next page is ready
Sound a tone
Display an arrow at lower right
Freelance Graphics - [HUMBLE01.PRE]
Page 3
Edit Screen Show
1. Choose a page:
LearnLotus
Page 5 of 5
2. Choose an effect:
Blinds
Bottom
Box In
Box Out
Center
Checkboard
Apply effect to all pages
OK
Cancel
Options...
Start Automatically
Display page for
5
seconds
Apply time to all pages
Advance screen show
Manually
Automatically
Show pages
1
to
999
Run screen show continuously
Page Layout...
Freelance Graphics - [HUMBLE01.PRE]
File Edit View Page Style Text Chart Arrange Tools Window Help
No Selection
Page 1
Printer Setup
OK
Cancel
Setup...
Optimize for screen show
Printers:
Genigraphics® Driver on GENI:
HP LaserJet III on LPT1:
Intermediate
Advanced
Set margins for slides
Arial MT
Page Layout...
New Page...

PART VIII

Creating a Screen Show

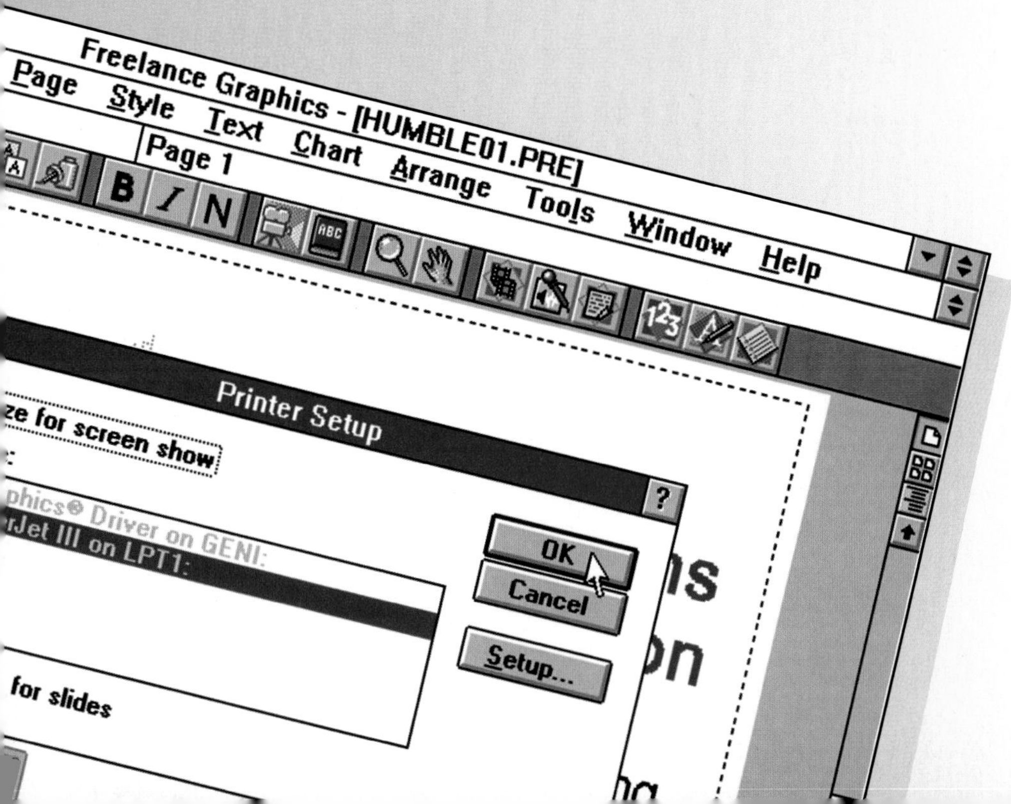

After you complete a presentation, you will want to show it. You can print a presentation to display in a notebook, or print it to transparencies for use with an overhead projector. Or, you can display the presentation on the computer screen. A presentation displayed on the computer screen, called a screen show, is appropriate to use for small groups that can gather around the computer.

One idea for using screen shows is to set up several computers around a display room or other area where customers may frequent. Set the screen shows to start and run automatically. Customers will then see the presentations as they look around your store.

Another use for a screen show is to display it to five or less people at a time. Suppose you invite your clients to your place of business for a tour that concludes with a presentation in your office. After seating the clients and giving them coffee, you start the screen show.

You can display your presentation automatically or manually. If you choose to let Freelance Graphics advance the screens automatically, you can set the time each screen will display. Or, you can manually advance each page so that you can discuss a point or answer questions. When a presentation page displays, all screen elements—including the menu, toolbox, scroll bars, and so on—hide from view so only each presentation page shows.

In addition, you can use the mouse pointer during a screen show to point out various items on the page; all you have to do is move the mouse pointer to the correct position. You also can draw on-screen with the mouse; for example, you can circle especially important items on the page. You can even choose a color and line width with which to draw on-screen.

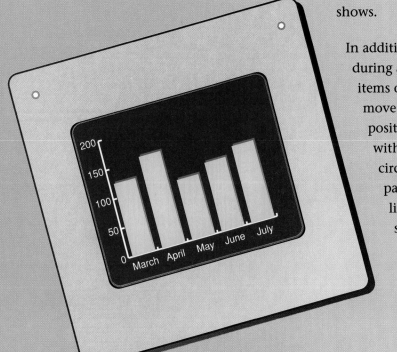

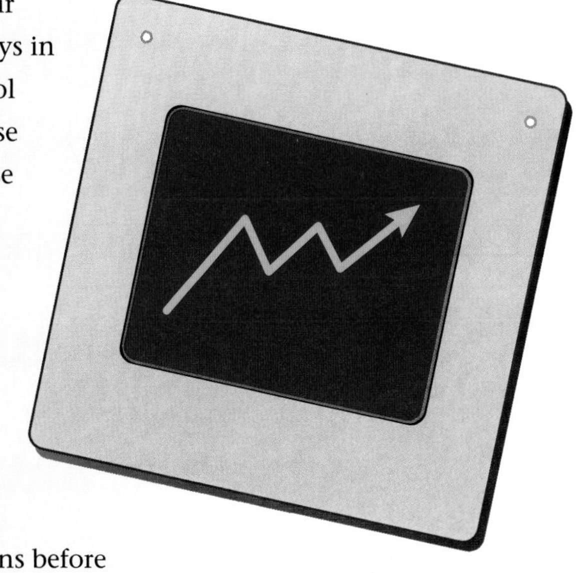

If you like, clients can advance the screen show on their own by using a control panel. The control panel displays in the corner of the show and lets you or the client control which page of the presentation shows. You can even use the control panel to list the slides from which to choose or to end the show.

Another use for the screen show is for proofing purposes. You may want to view the presentation pages to see if they are consistent and check colors, type, and so on. Additionally, you can view the screen show at any time while creating the presentation to make sure you are on the right track. After viewing the show, you can make any modifications before printing the pages or showing it to clients.

Besides showing each presentation page one full screen at a time, you can choose from various effects for changing from page to page. For example, when changing from the first to the second page of the presentation, you can choose for Freelance to fade page one into page two. Freelance provides over thirty effects for changing from one screen to the next, including opening blinds or a curtain to display the new screen, horizontally splitting the screen, using a paint brush, and so on.

Some effects are better than others for specific SmartMaster sets. You will have to experiment to see which effects you like for your presentation. You can even use a different effect for each screen, if you like.

The screen show can be an effective use of your presentation for small groups of people. Freelance lets you show your presentation in a way that best represents you and your company. This part shows you how to create and manage a screen show.

TASK 46

Optimizing for a Screen Show

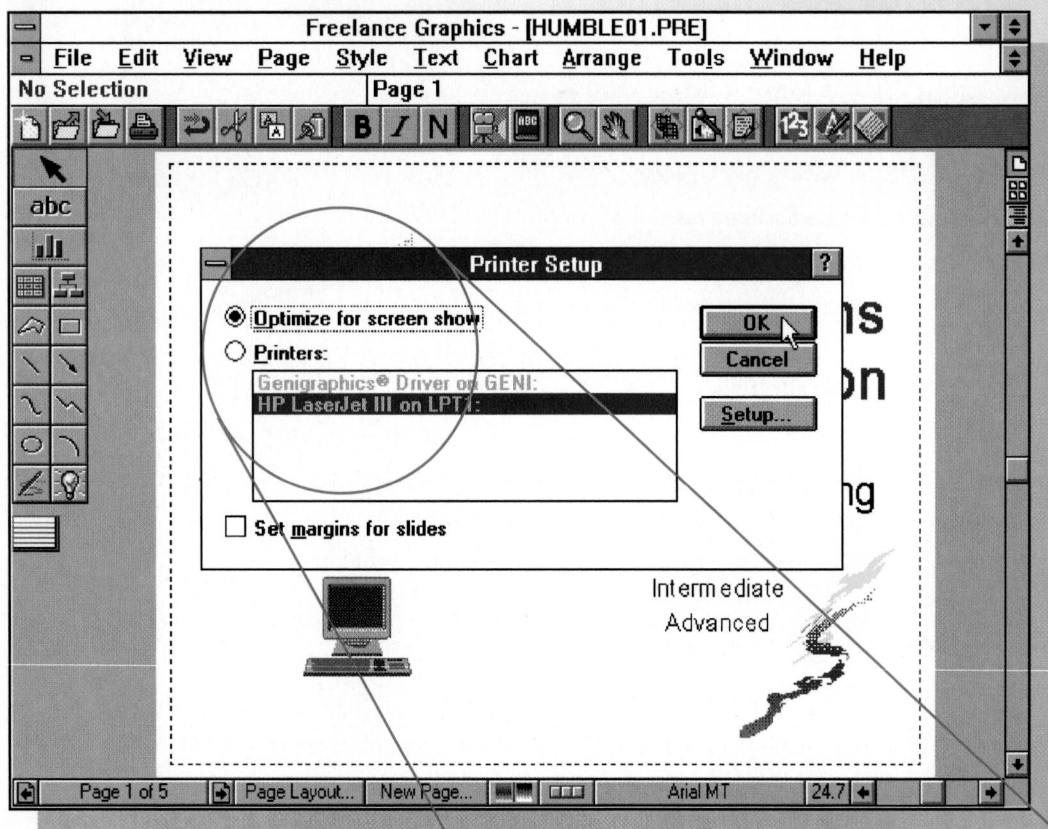

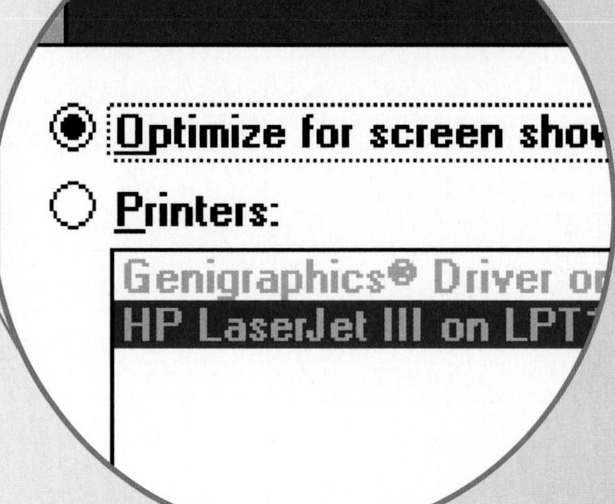

"Why would I do this?"

Choose the Optimize for a Screen Show option so that the height and width of the presentation better fit your screen. This option adjusts the margins, type, graphics, and so on, to better fit your screen.

Because the Optimize for Screen Show option is in the Printer Setup dialog box, you will want to deselect this option before printing a presentation to your printer. This step makes the presentation better suited for the printed page.

Task 46: Optimizing for a Screen Show

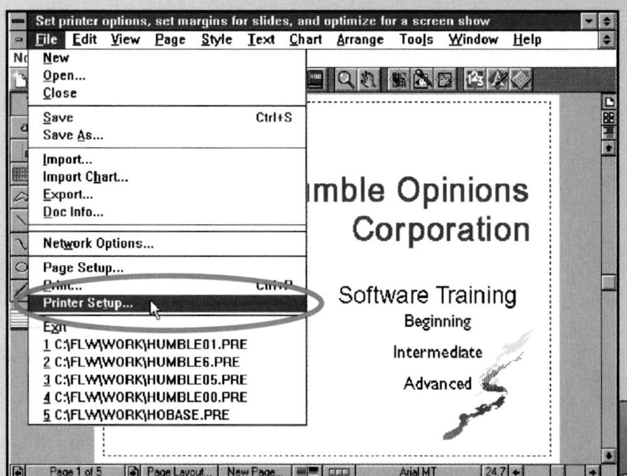

1 To set the optimize option, open the **File** menu and choose **Printer Setup**. The Printer Setup dialog box appears.

NOTE

Make sure you choose the Printers option in the Printer Setup dialog box before printing a presentation. If you do not, Freelance displays the Edit Screen Show dialog box when you choose File Print.

2 Choose the **Optimize for Screen Show** option.

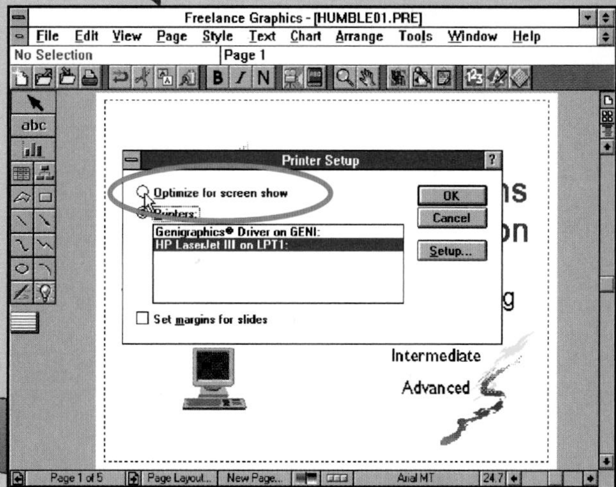

3 Choose **OK**. You cannot tell a difference in the normal view of your pages; however, you can in the screen show. Often, for example, a chart or table will seem distorted if you do not choose the optimize option.

TASK 47

Choosing Screen Effects

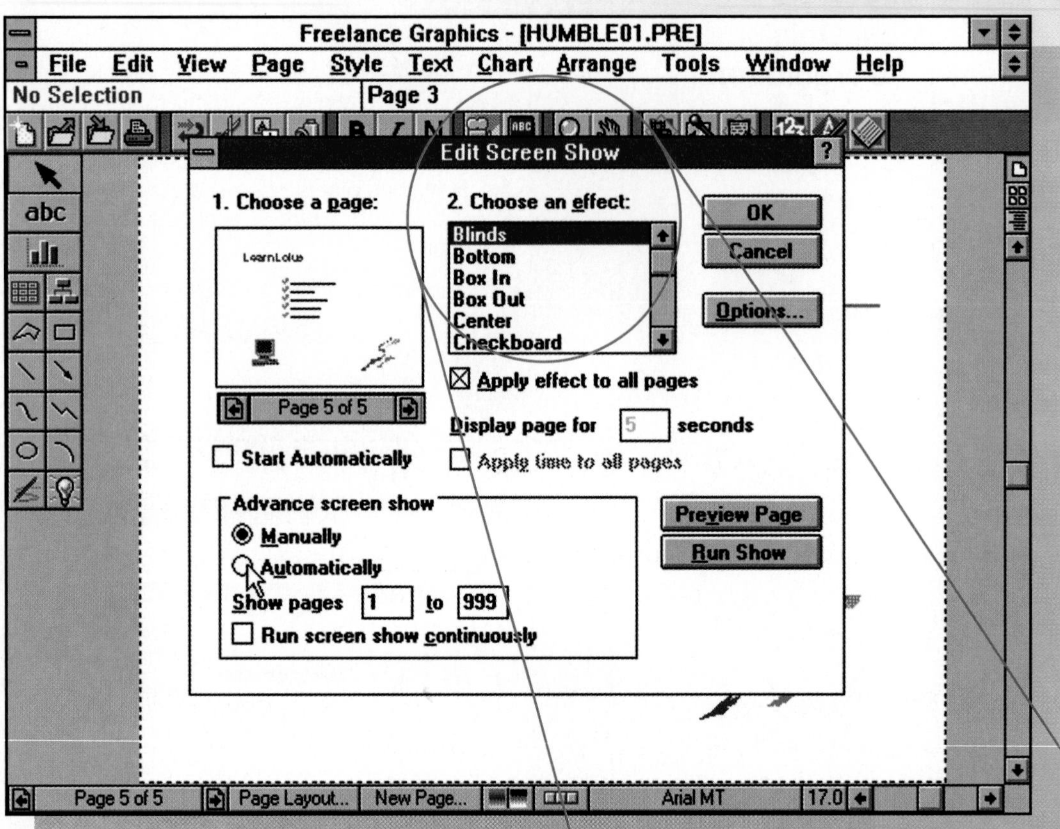

"Why would I do this?"

You can run the screen show using the defaults set by Freelance Graphics. Or, you can add pizzazz to your screen show by editing the way one screen changes to the next. Additionally, you can choose to let the show run automatically and vary the amount of time each screen displays. You also can choose to start the show automatically and run the show continuously, if you want.

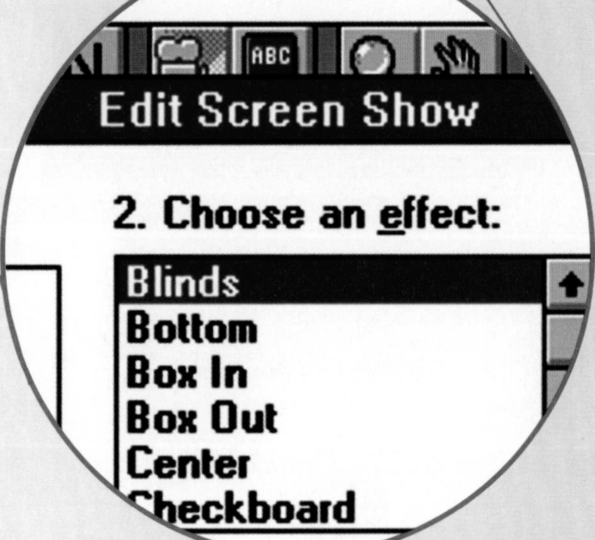

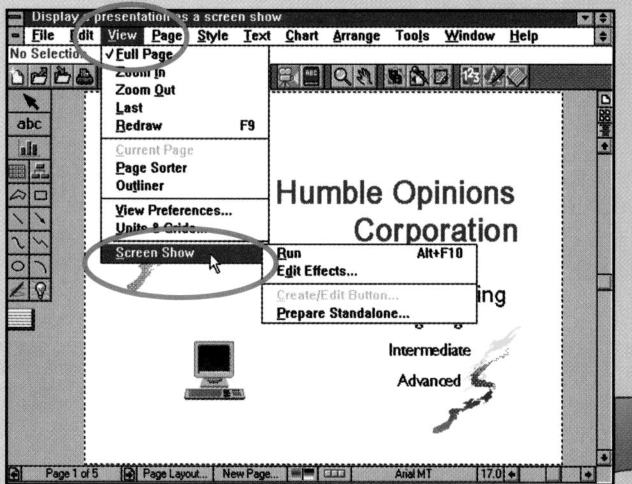

1 Open the **View** menu and choose **Screen Show** to display a secondary, or *cascading*, menu. The secondary menu displays commands that relate to the screen show.

2 From the secondary menu, choose **Edit Effects** to display the Edit Screen Show dialog box.

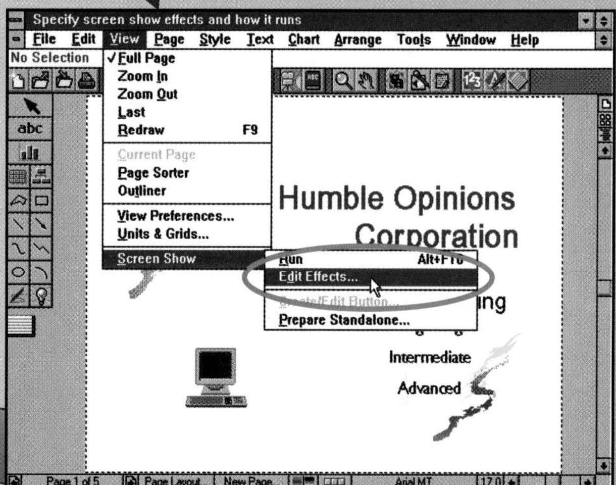

3 In the **Advance Screen Show** option group, choose **Automatically**.

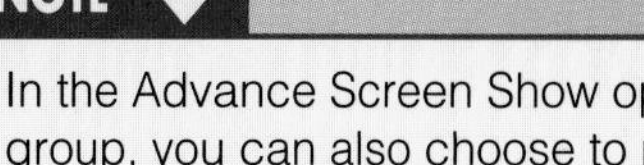

In the Advance Screen Show option group, you can also choose to run the screen show continuously, if you want. The slide show runs in a continuous loop until you press the Esc key. The List Page dialog box appears; choose Quit Show.

Task 47: Choosing Screen Effects

4 In the **Choose a Page** area, make sure **Page 1 of 5** is displayed. This option is particularly important if you plan to use different effects for changing screens; you choose the page you want to apply the effect to in this option group.

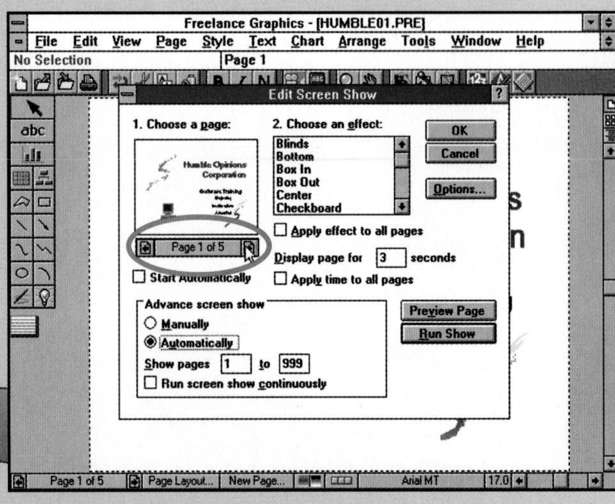

5 In the **Choose an Effect** list box, choose **Blinds**. This effect describes how Freelance will transfer from page one to page two.

6 Select the **Apply Effect to All Pages** check box, which appears below the Choose an Effect list box.

NOTE

The Apply Effect to All Pages option provides consistency; however, you may want to experiment with the effects to see which ones you like best, or choose a different effect for each page change.

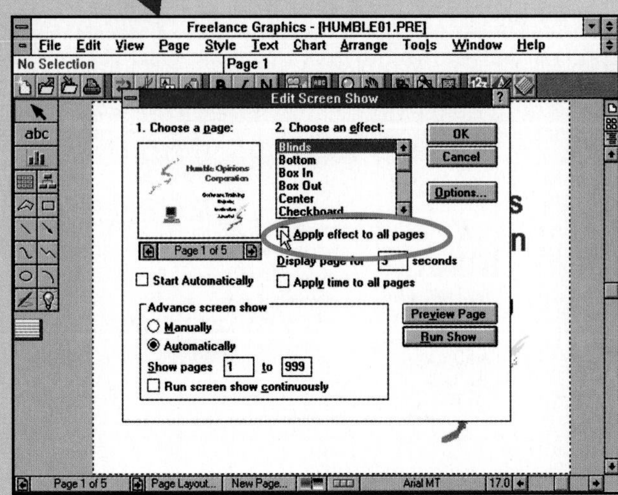

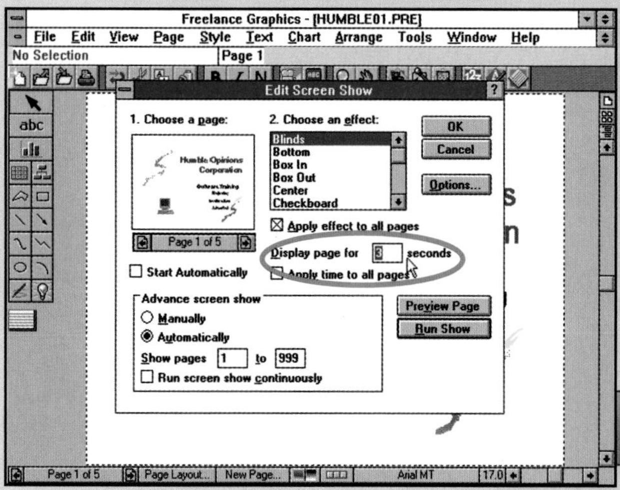

7 In the **Display Page for __ Seconds** text box, delete the 3 and enter **5**.

WHY WORRY?

You may want to display some screens longer if there is a lot of data or text on a particular page.

8 Select the **Apply Time to All Pages** check box.

WHY WORRY?

You can, alternatively, select each page in the first option group, and then apply a different amount of time for each page to display.

NOTE

The settings you create for a screen show are the same settings the next show uses; those settings remain the default until you reset them.

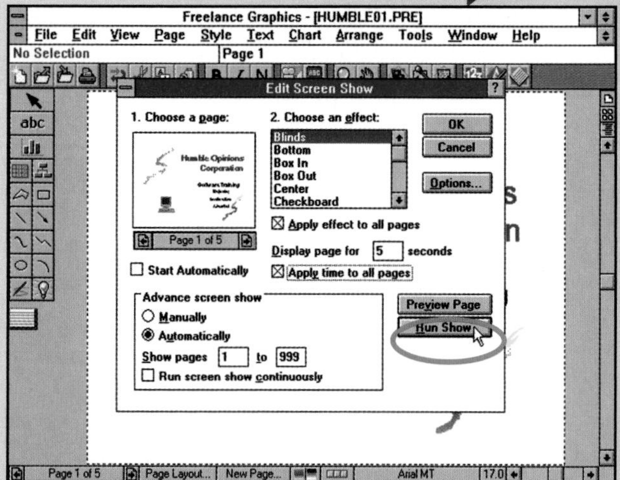

9 Choose the **Run Show** command button to preview the show. When the show is done, Freelance returns to the Full Page view of the presentation and screen elements.

TASK 48

Running the Show

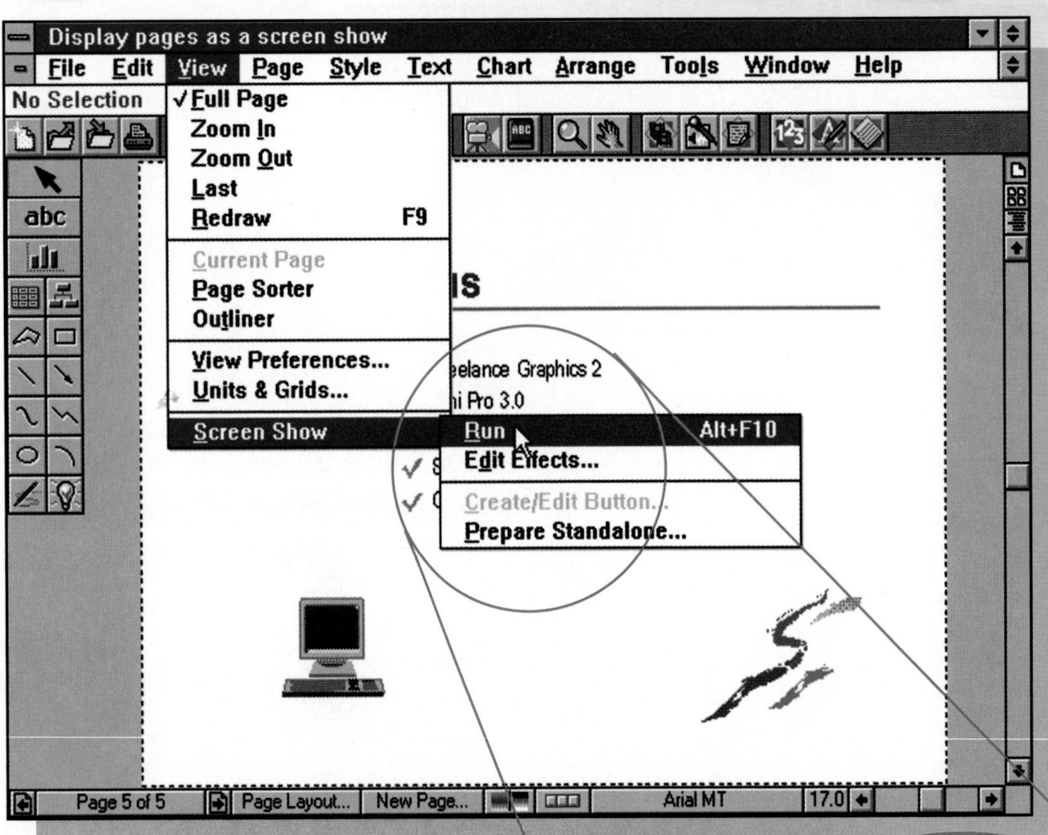

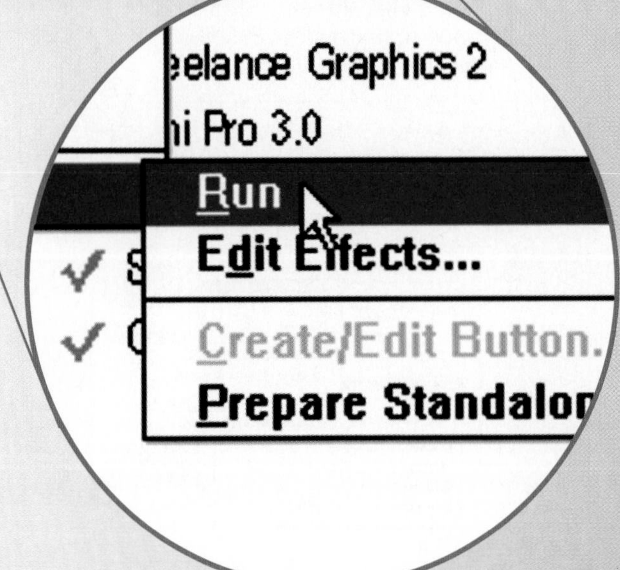

"Why would I do this?"

You can run a screen show on-screen at any time while working on your presentation. You may want to check the consistency, sequence, or look of the presentation during the creation of the pages. In addition, you can run the screen show to exhibit the presentation to your customers, boss, coworkers, or other interested party. This task shows you how to run the screen show.

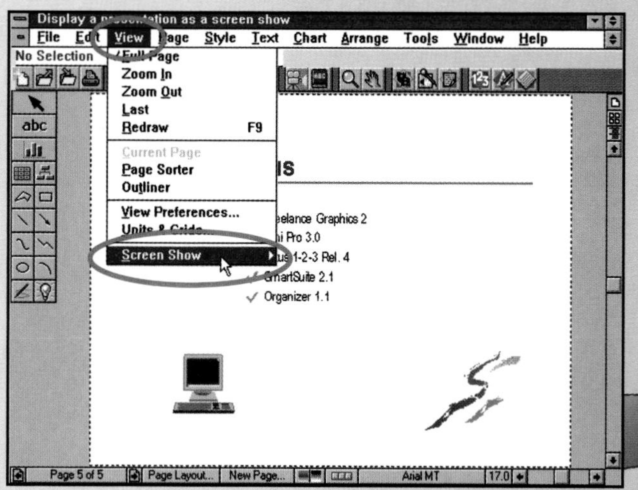

1 Open the **View** menu and choose **Screen Show**. The secondary menu appears.

2 Choose **Run**.

NOTE

You can press Alt+F10 as an alternative to steps one and two.

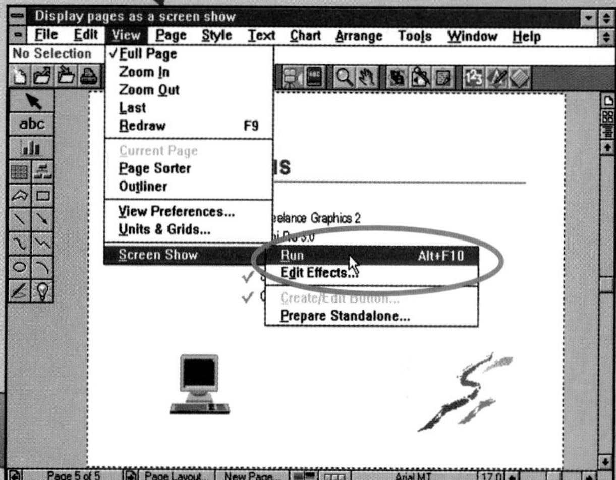

Humble Opinions Corporation

Software Training

Beginning

Intermediate

Advanced

3 Freelance runs the screen show according to the changes you made in the Edit Screen Show dialog box. You can change pages to override the automatic advance by clicking the left mouse button or by pressing the PgDn key.

WHY WORRY?

To pause the screen show when you are using automatic timing, press the space bar. Press the space bar again to continue.

TASK 49

Changing Screen Show Options

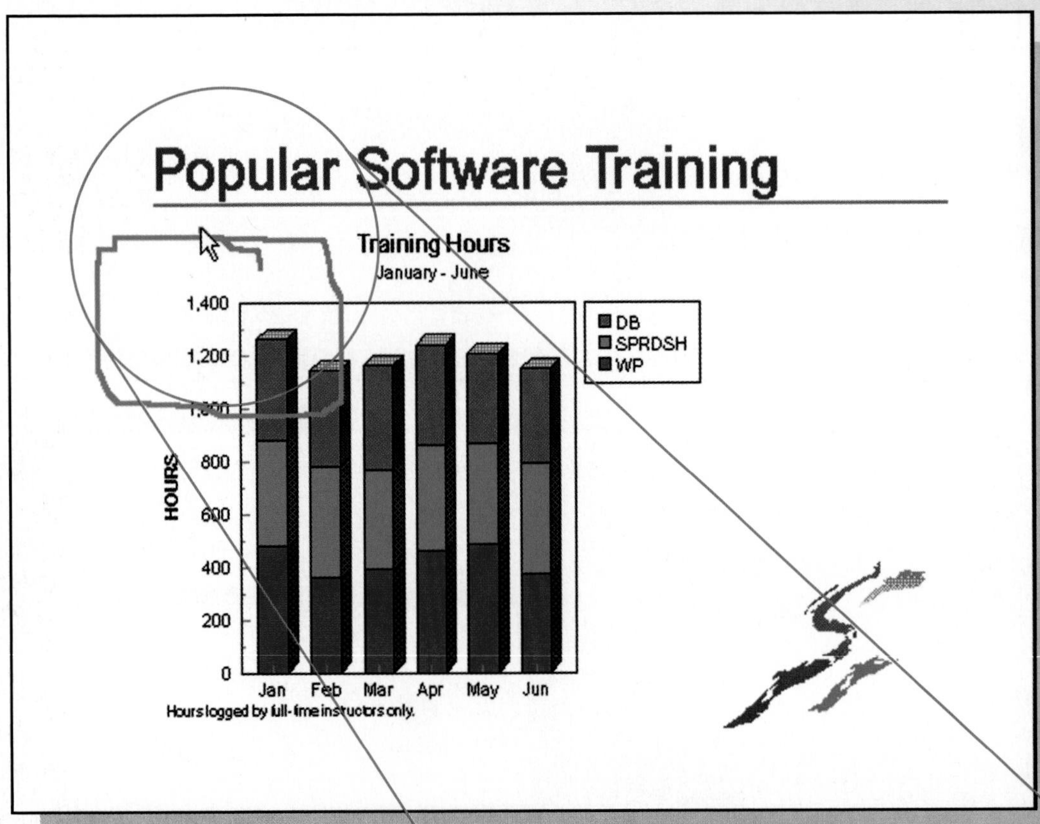

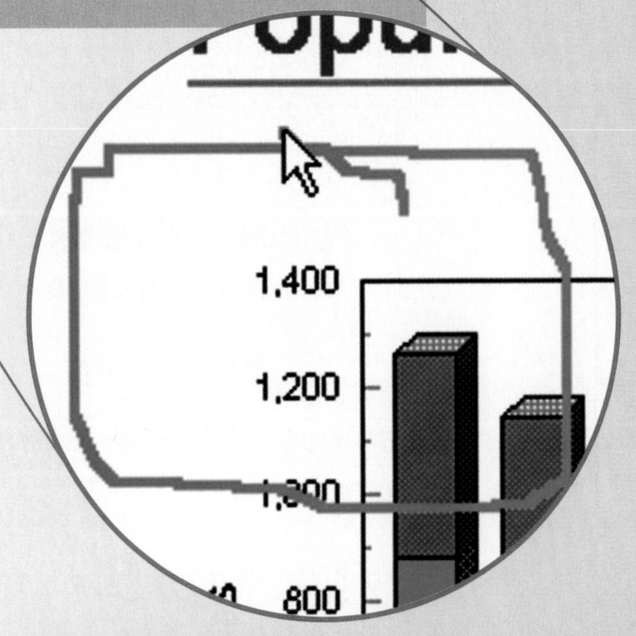

"Why would I do this?"

You can add several features to your screen show to make it more interesting—and easier to show. When you are showing your presentation on-screen, use the mouse to draw on the pages. You can change the color and line width of the lines you draw using the Screen Show Options dialog box. In addition, you can display a control panel to make moving from page to page easier, sound a tone, or display one button to help a client move from page to page.

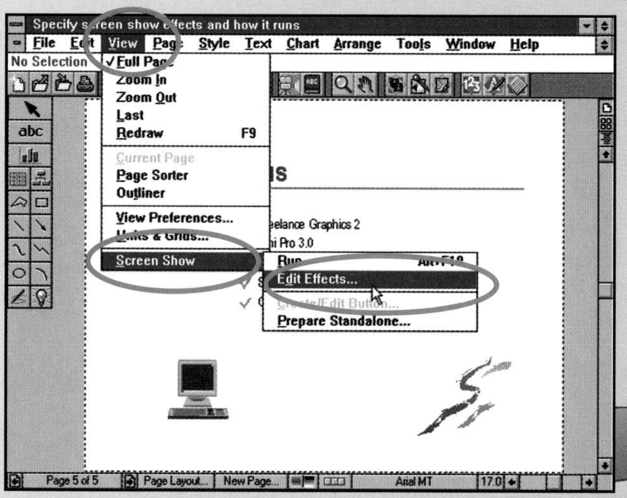

1 To edit screen show options, open the **View** menu and choose **Screen Show**. From the secondary menu, choose **Edit Effects**. The Edit Screen Show dialog box appears.

2 Choose the **Options** command button to display the Screen Show Options dialog box.

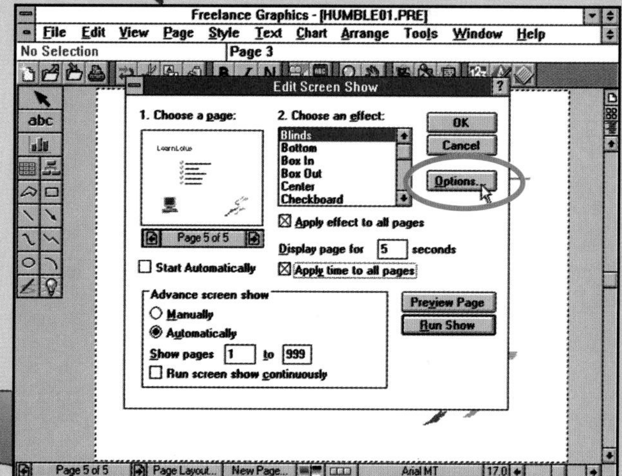

3 In the **On Screen Drawing** area, click the **down arrow** next to **Color** to access the palette and change the line color for on-screen drawing with the mouse.

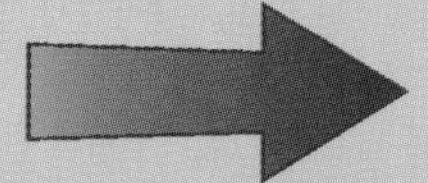

4 From the Palette, choose green, or any color you want. The Palette closes.

NOTE

You can also change the width of the line in the On Screen Drawing area.

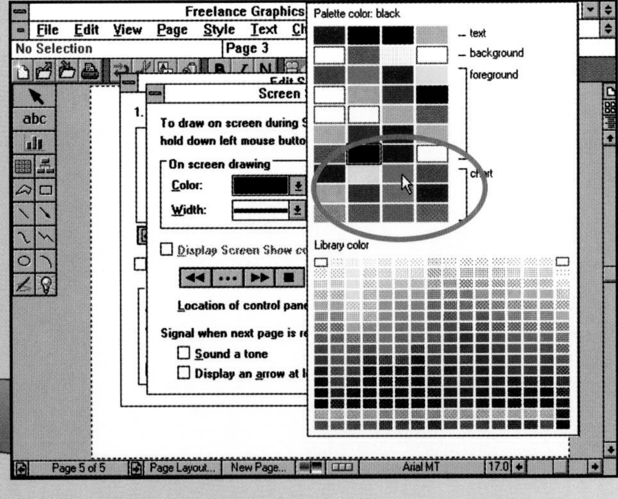

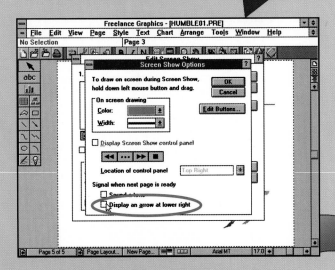

5 In the **Signal When Next Page Is Ready** option group, choose the **Display an Arrow at Lower Right** check box. This option makes an arrow button appear in the corner of each presentation page screen; you can click the button to move to the next page. You can use this button whether the show is automatic or manual.

6 Choose **OK** to close the Screen Show Options dialog box. In the Edit Screen Show dialog box, choose the **Run Show** command button.

NOTE

In the Screen Show Options dialog box, the Display Screen Show control panel option is dimmed. This option is available only when you choose Manually in the Edit Screen Show dialog box.

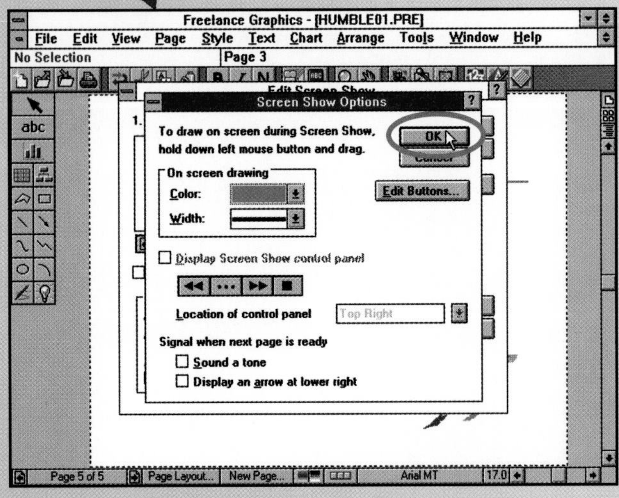

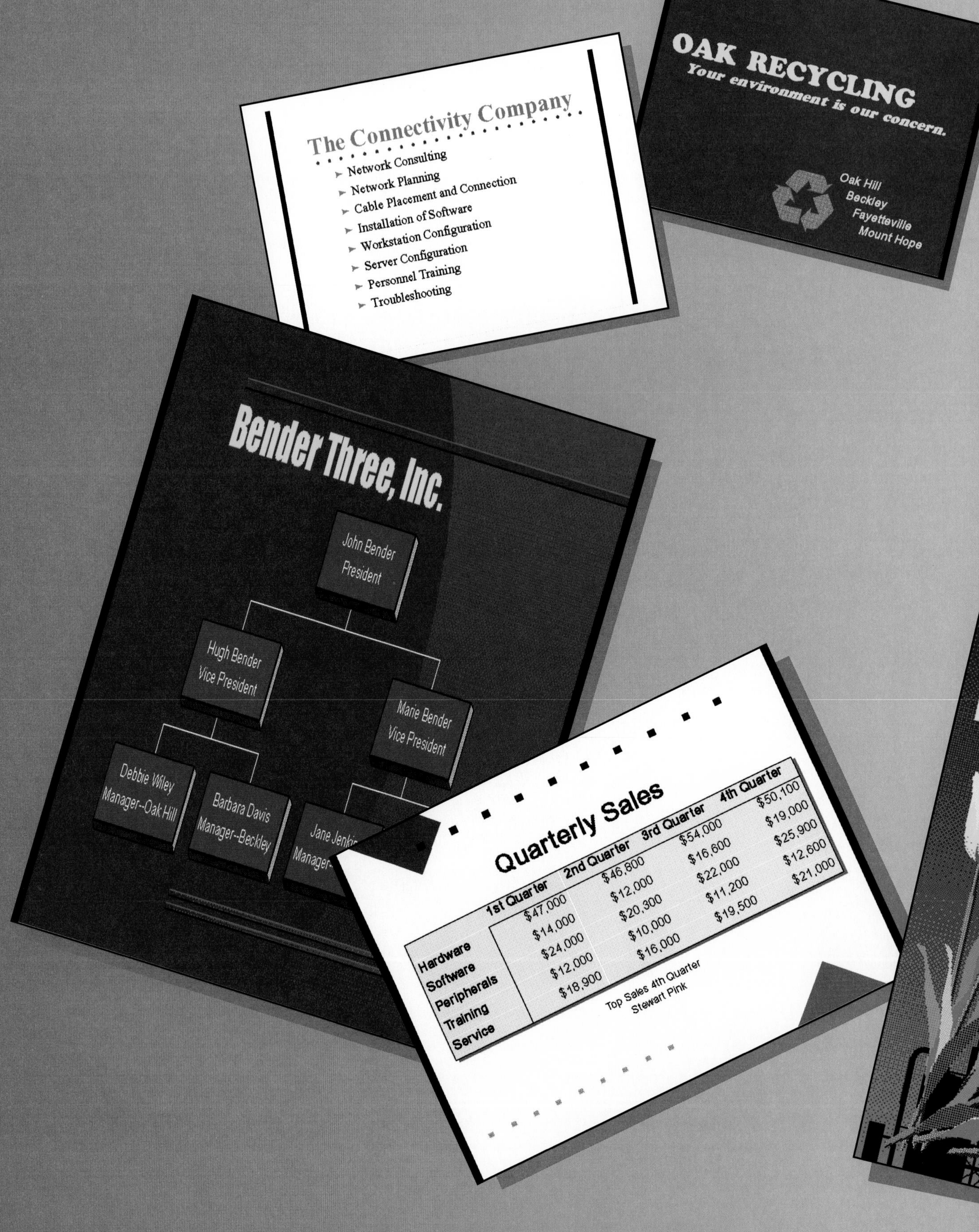
The Connectivity Company
Network Consulting
Network Planning
Cable Placement and Connection
Installation of Software
Workstation Configuration
Server Configuration
Personnel Training
Troubleshooting
OAK RECYCLING
Your environment is our concern.
Oak Hill
Beckley
Fayetteville
Mount Hope
Bender Three, Inc.
John Bender
President
Hugh Bender
Vice President
Marie Bender
Vice President
Debbie Wiley
Manager--Oak Hill
Barbara Davis
Manager--Beckley
Quarterly Sales
1st Quarter
2nd Quarter
3rd Quarter
4th Quarter
Hardware $47,000 $46,800 $54,000 $50,100
Software $14,000 $12,000 $16,600 $19,000
Peripherals $24,000 $20,300 $22,000 $25,900
Training $12,000 $10,000 $11,200 $12,600
Service $18,900 $16,000 $19,500 $21,000
Top Sales 4th Quarter
Stewart Pink

PART IX

Sample Slides

- Create a Title Page
- Create a Bulleted List
- Create an Organization Chart
- Create a Table
- Create a Chart
- Create a Screen Show

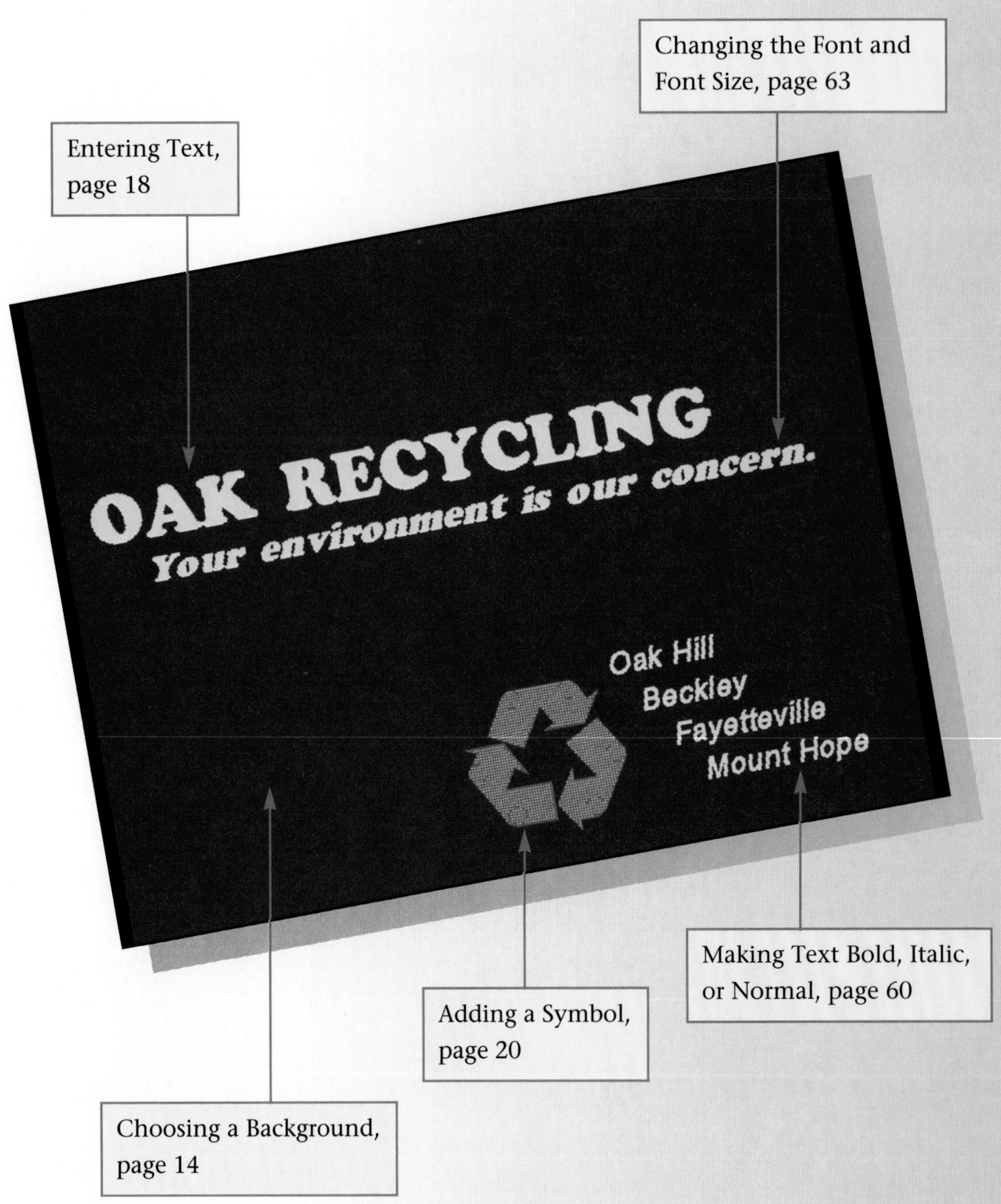
Changing the Font and Font Size, page 63
Entering Text, page 18
OAK RECYCLING
Your environment is our concern.
Oak Hill
Beckley
Fayetteville
Mount Hope
Making Text Bold, Italic, or Normal, page 60
Adding a Symbol, page 20
Choosing a Background, page 14

Create a Title Page

1. Choose a SmartMaster set for the background of the page; you can choose from many colors and symbols. See this task for help on this step:

   Choosing a Background *(page14)*

2. Enter text using the "Click here..." text blocks. The following task can help:

   Entering Text *(page 18)*

3. Change the typeface and type size of text to better suit the information on the page. See this task for more information:

   Changing the Font and Font Size *(page 63)*

4. Add a symbol to the presentation for pizzazz or to illustrate a point. See this task:

   Adding a Symbol *(page 20)*

5. Make some text italic to add interest and emphasis. The following tasks can help:

   Making Text Bold, Italic, or Normal *(page 60)*

   Changing Font Attributes *(page 77)*

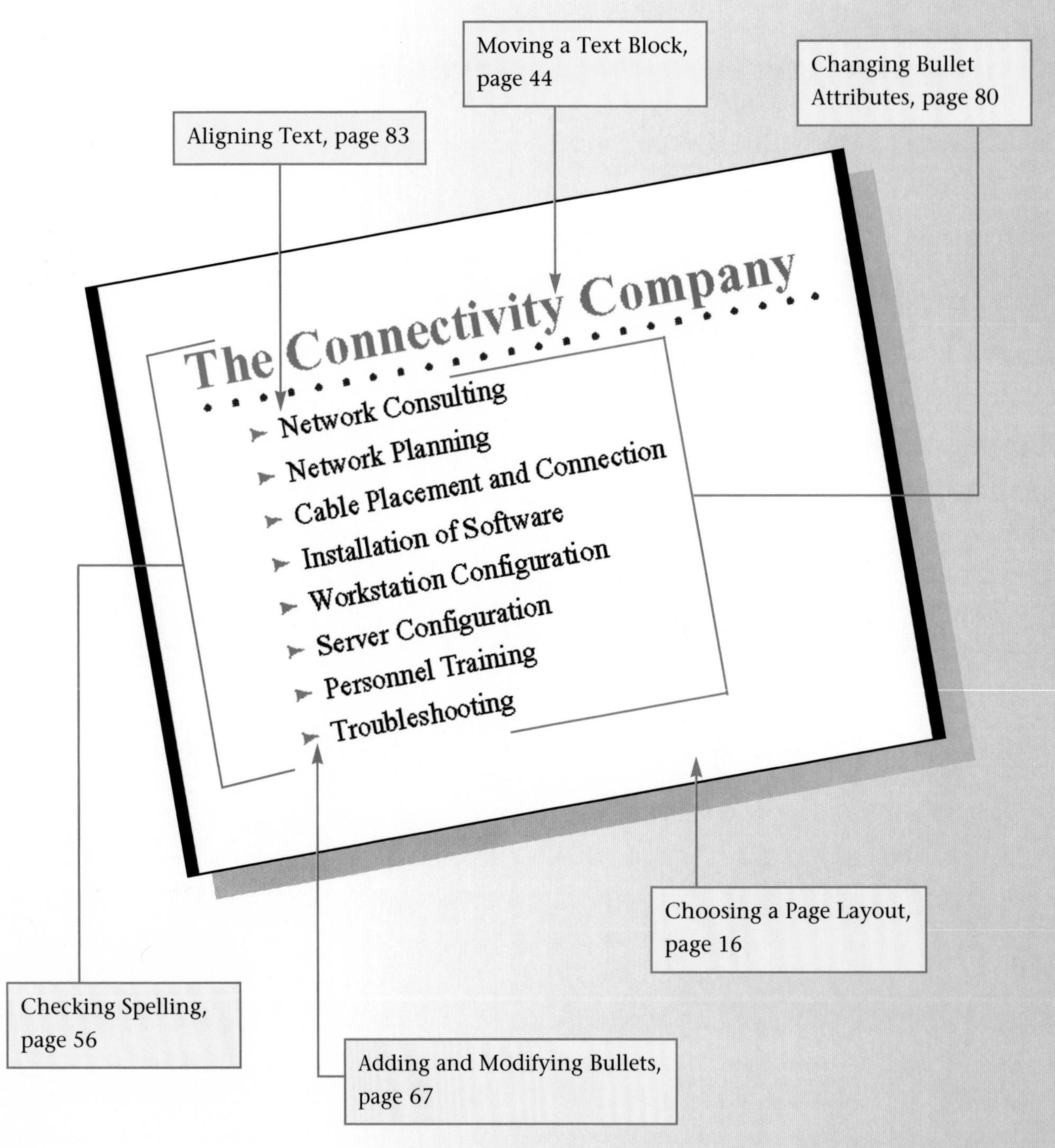
Moving a Text Block, page 44
Changing Bullet Attributes, page 80
Aligning Text, page 83
The Connectivity Company
Network Consulting
Network Planning
Cable Placement and Connection
Installation of Software
Workstation Configuration
Server Configuration
Personnel Training
Troubleshooting
Choosing a Page Layout, page 16
Checking Spelling, page 56
Adding and Modifying Bullets, page 67

Create a Bulleted List

1 Choose the preformatted Bulleted List page layout for quick and easy text formatting. The following task will help:

Choosing a Page Layout *(page 16)*

2 After adding the bulleted text, change the bullet's color, symbol, and spacing. See these tasks:

Adding and Modifying Bullets *(page 67)*

Changing Bullet Attributes *(page 80)*

3 Move a text block to indent text or simply change its location on the page. This task shows you how:

Moving a Text Block *(page 44)*

4 Change the alignment of the title or any text so that the page design better fits the information. See this task:

Aligning Text *(page 83)*

5 Make sure your spelling is correct. This task shows you how:

Checking Spelling *(page 56)*

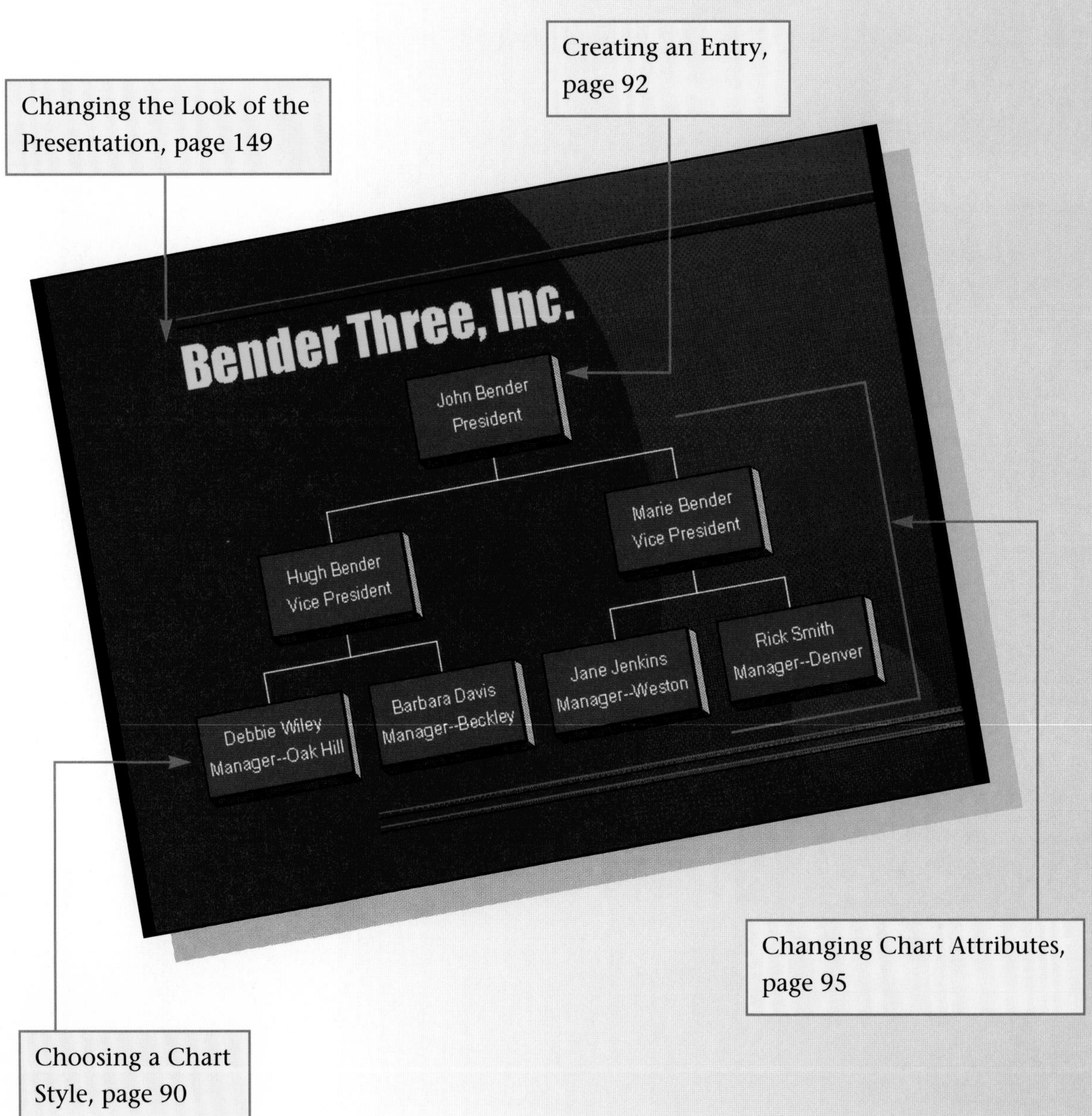
Creating an Entry, page 92
Changing the Look of the Presentation, page 149
Bender Three, Inc.
John Bender
President
Marie Bender
Vice President
Hugh Bender
Vice President
Rick Smith
Manager--Denver
Jane Jenkins
Manager--Weston
Barbara Davis
Manager--Beckley
Debbie Wiley
Manager--Oak Hill
Changing Chart Attributes, page 95
Choosing a Chart Style, page 90

Create an Organization Chart

1 Choose the type of boxes, shadows, and so on, you want to use in your chart. See this task:

Choosing a Chart Style (page 90)

2 Enter names and titles for the organization chart. Promoting superiors and demoting subordinates within the chart organizes the entries. This task will help:

Creating an Entry (page 92)

3 Modify the chart boxes, connecting lines, and text attributes by changing colors, line width, and so on. See this task for help:

Changing Chart Attributes (page 95)

4 Change the SmartMaster background to better suit the contents of the presentation. This task shows how:

Changing the Look of the Presentation (page 149)

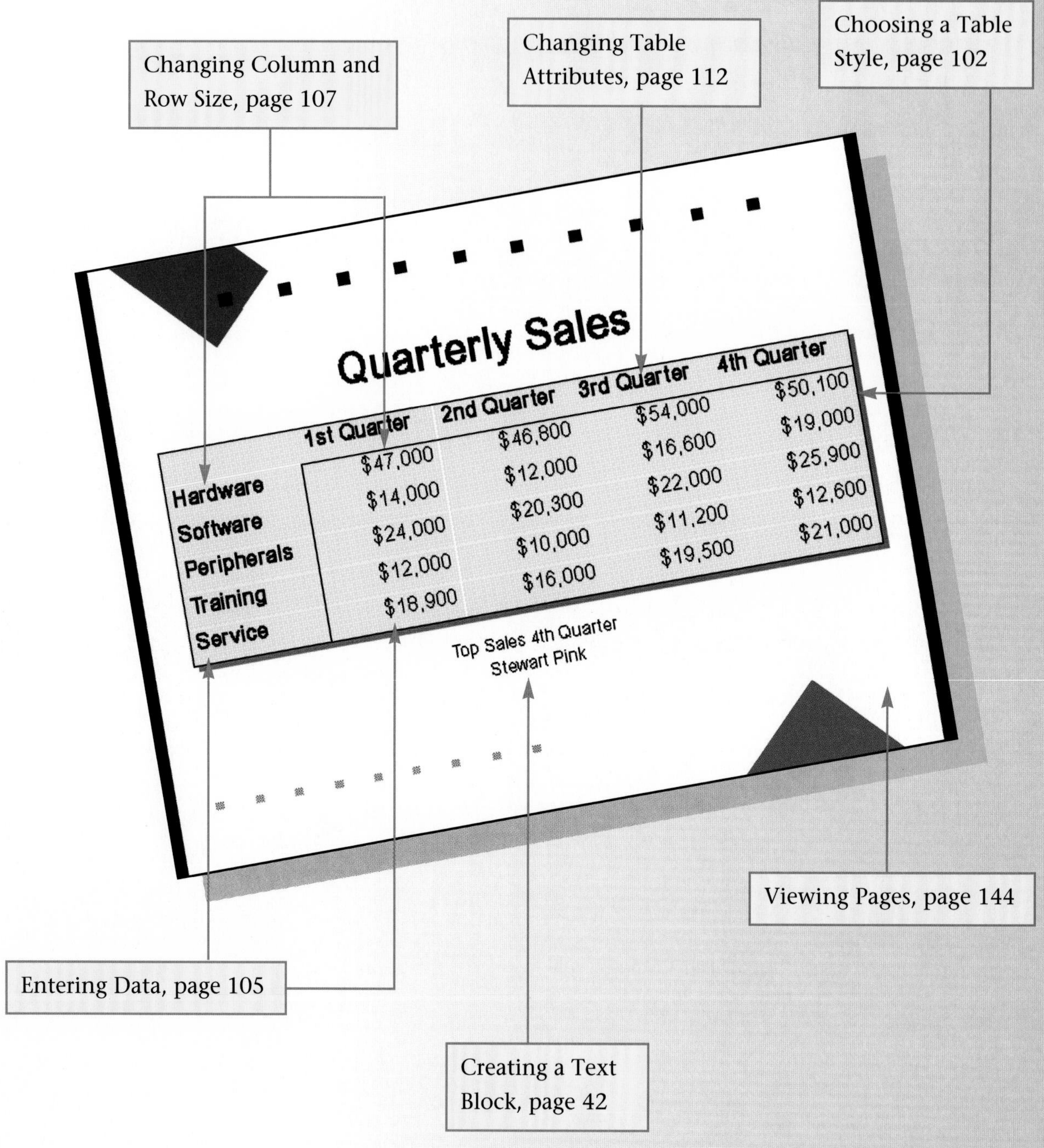
Changing Column and Row Size, page 107
Changing Table Attributes, page 112
Choosing a Table Style, page 102
Quarterly Sales
1st Quarter
2nd Quarter
3rd Quarter
4th Quarter
Hardware $47,000 $46,800 $54,000 $50,100
Software $14,000 $12,000 $16,600 $19,000
Peripherals $24,000 $20,300 $22,000 $25,900
Training $12,000 $10,000 $11,200 $12,600
Service $18,900 $16,000 $19,500 $21,000
Top Sales 4th Quarter
Stewart Pink
Viewing Pages, page 144
Entering Data, page 105
Creating a Text Block, page 42

Create a Table

1 Select any of six table styles to represent your data; you can always switch styles if you change your mind. See this task:

Choosing a Table Style *(page 102)*

2 Type the data in the table, moving around the table with either the mouse or the keyboard. This task will help you:

Entering Data *(page 105)*

3 Adjust the column width and the row height to make the table easier to read and the data more organized. See the following task for help:

Changing Column and Row Size *(page 107)*

4 Change the color of the table, text attributes, lines, or borders to better suit your presentation. See this task for help:

Changing Table Attributes *(page 112)*

5 Add text to the page and then move the text block to any location on the page. See this task for help:

Creating a Text Block *(page 42)*

6 Magnify the page view so you can better see the data in a table. You can also zoom in to a specific area of the page, or reduce the view so you can see the entire page at one time. See this task for help:

Viewing Pages *(page 144)*

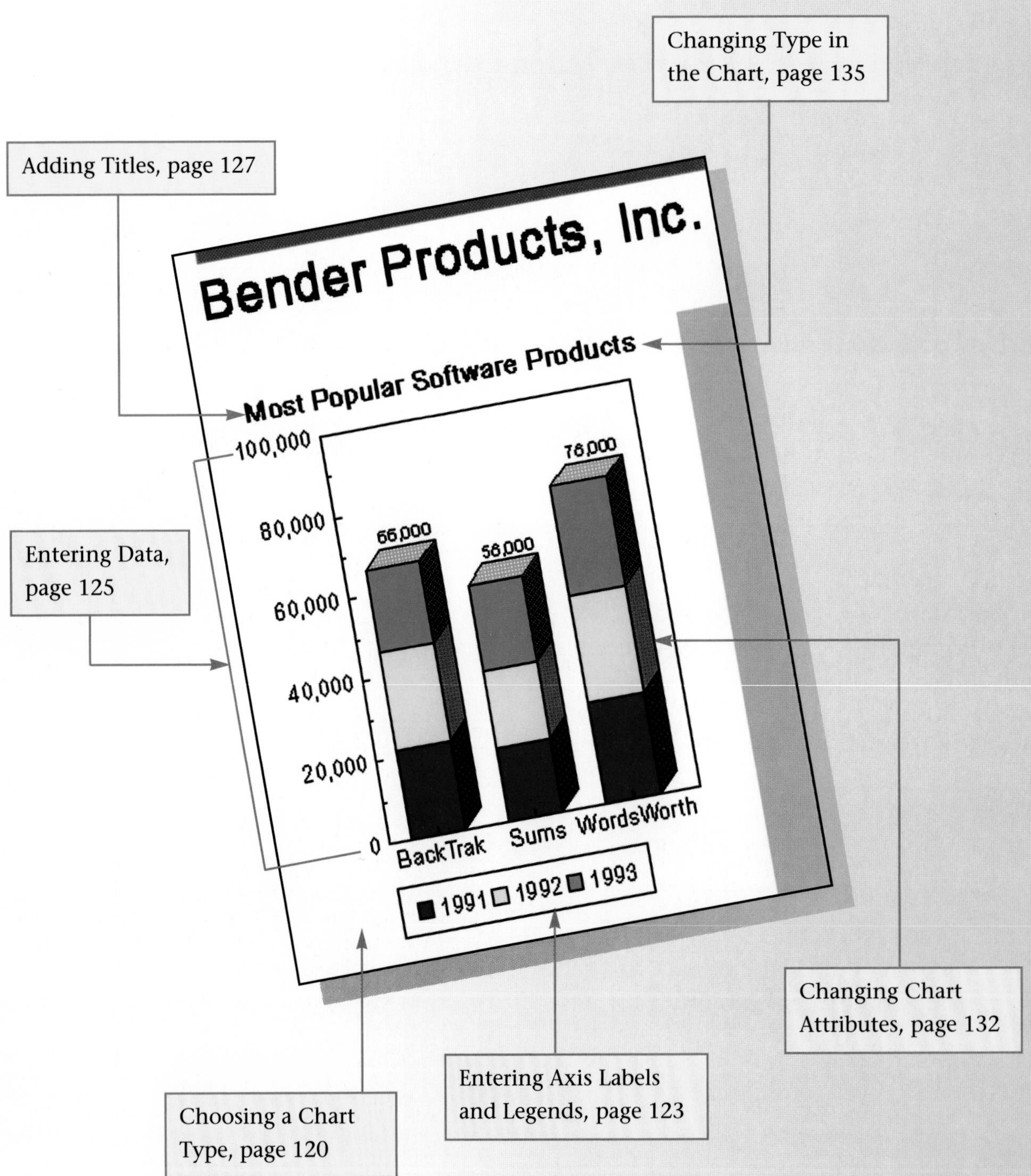
Changing Type in the Chart, page 135
Adding Titles, page 127
Bender Products, Inc.
Most Popular Software Products
100,000
80,000
60,000
40,000
20,000
0
66,000
56,000
76,000
BackTrak
Sums
WordsWorth
1991
1992
1993
Entering Data, page 125
Changing Chart Attributes, page 132
Entering Axis Labels and Legends, page 123
Choosing a Chart Type, page 120

Create a Chart

1 Select the chart type that best represents the data in your presentation. This task will help you:

Choosing a Chart Type (page 120)

2 Enter vertical and horizontal axis labels and legends, if you like, to describe the data represented in the chart. See this task for help:

Entering Axis Labels and Legends (page 123)

3 Type the data in the Chart Data & Titles dialog box before creating the table. See this task for more information:

Entering Data (page 125)

4 Create a title for the chart; the title can contain up to three lines of text. See this task:

Adding Titles (page 127)

5 Modify the colors of the bars or the three-dimensional effects to better suit the presentation design. This task will help:

Changing Chart Attributes (page 132)

6 You can change the text attributes—typeface, type size, alignment, and so on—to better represent the data. This task will help you:

Changing Type in the Chart (page 135)

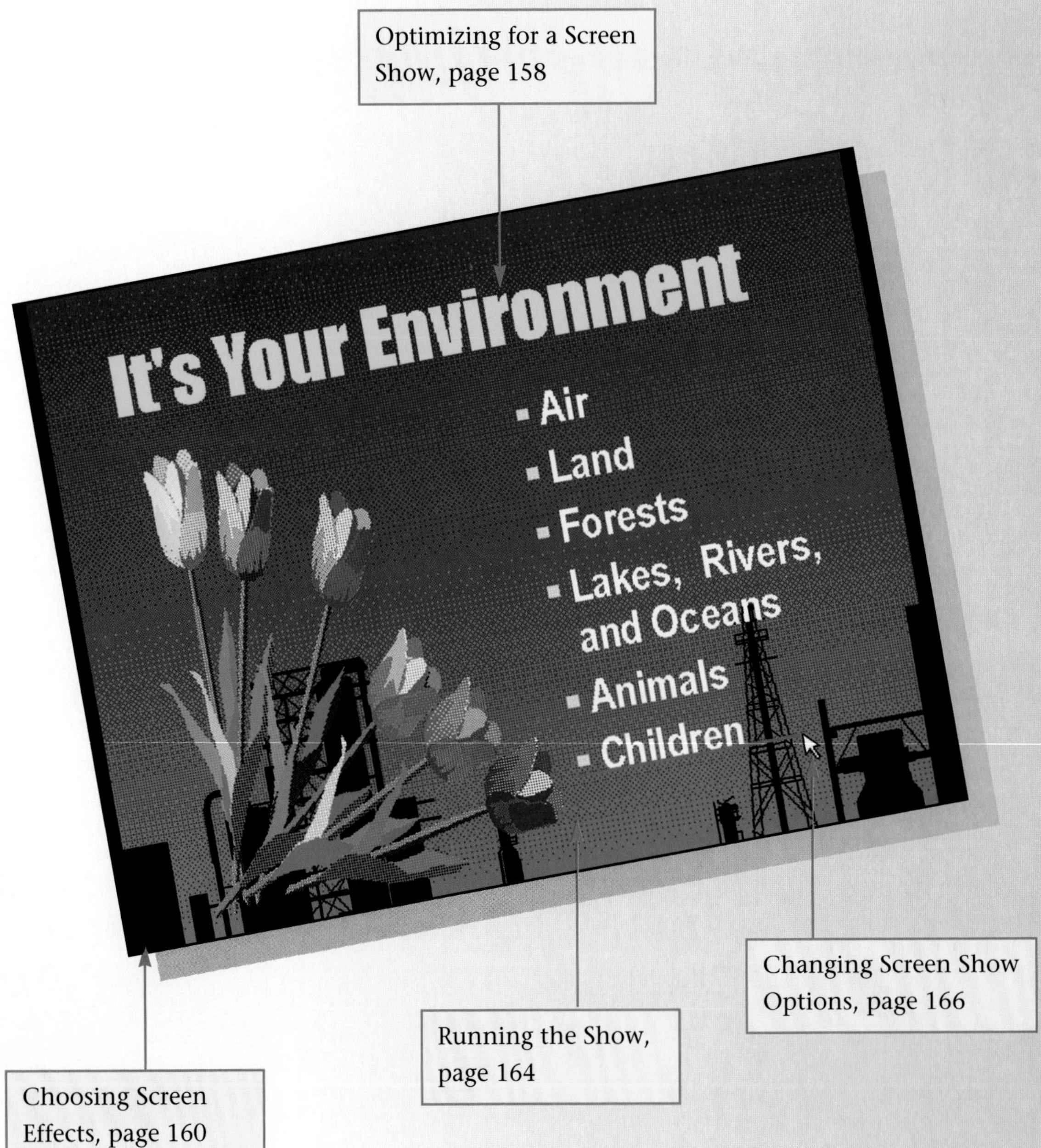
Optimizing for a Screen Show, page 158
It's Your Environment
Air
Land
Forests
Lakes, Rivers, and Oceans
Animals
Children
Changing Screen Show Options, page 166
Running the Show, page 164
Choosing Screen Effects, page 160

Create a Screen Show

1 Make sure you display the screen show so that the text and graphics look their best on your monitor. This task shows you how:

Optimizing for a Screen Show *(page 158)*

2 Set how each screen changes into the next during the screen show presentation; for example, page one could fade into page two, a curtain could raise to reveal page two, and so on. Additionally, set the amount of time for each screen to display. Then, set the screen show to run automatically or manually. See this task for help:

Choosing Screen Effects *(page 160)*

3 Use the mouse to point to various items on the screen; you can even draw on the screen to emphasize points. This task shows you how:

Running the Show *(page 164)*

4 Change the color and width of the line you draw on-screen, sound a tone when it's time to change screens, or display a control panel so the viewer can control the show. See this task for more information:

Changing Screen Show Options *(page 166)*

PART X

Glossary

3D Three-dimensional; used in reference to some chart types—such as bar, stacked bar, and pie charts—to describe shadowed effects added to the chart that make it look as if it has depth.

ABC icon In the toolbox, the icon represents the Text tool. When clicked with the mouse, you can use the tool to draw a text box in which you can type.

Area chart A graph that represents data, usually to show trends or patterns over a period of time.

Arrow pointer In the toolbox, the icon represents the mouse pointer. When selected, you can move, select, delete, copy, and paste text blocks, charts, symbols, and so on, as well as activate the "Click here" boxes.

ATM Adobe Type Manager. Software that ships with Freelance Graphics, commonly used with Windows programs. ATM supplies and manages fonts that display and print in high-quality text of various sizes and styles.

Attribute A quality or characteristic applied to text, charts, tables, and so on. A characteristic of text, such as font, size, and so on; a feature of a chart, such as color, line width, or box shape.

Axes Reference lines in a chart. *See x-axis and y-axis.*

Background Refers to the color or pattern of the area behind the text or graphic. You can change background colors and patterns in a text block, table, chart, and so on.

Bar chart A graph that represents data, usually used to compare similar sets of data over time.

Bullet A symbol, such as a large dot, check mark, or small box, placed at the beginning of each item in a list. A bullet emphasizes the items in the list; each item in a bulleted list is equally important.

Bulleted list One of the Freelance page layouts preformatted to apply a bullet to your text each time you press Enter.

Cell In a table, the box formed when a column intersects a row.

Centered text Text that is aligned on a center point so that half the text extends to the left and the other half extends to the right, creating a ragged-right and ragged-left edge.

Chart An organized, attractive, and easy-to-grasp representation of raw data. Charts can be represented as bar, pie, line, area, scatter, and so on.

Click here Any of many types of boxes—including text, symbols, and chart—built into various page layouts. When you click the mouse on a Click here box, Freelance displays a text editing box in which you can type, a list of symbols from which you can choose, or a gallery of table or chart designs from which you can choose. After creating the text, symbol, or chart, Freelance inserts the result in the presentation page.

Clipboard A Windows feature used with most Windows programs to hold cut or copied items until they can be pasted or replaced with new items.

Column In tables, the vertical division of the text or numbers.

Data Numbers, such as percentages, dollars, and so on, representing the information used to create charts and graphs.

Data set One group of data, such as the sales for one month or products for one year.

Default Any of Freelance's original settings, such as a type size, font, chart color, row height, and so on.

Demote In an organization chart, changing the status of an entry to a subordinate.

Double-click A term used to describe pressing the mouse button twice in rapid succession. Double-clicking selects items in dialog boxes, opens a dialog box relating to a text box, chart, and so on, or performs some other task in Freelance and other Windows programs.

Drawing tools On the toolbox, the fifth through eighth rows of buttons (from the top). These buttons represent drawing tools: Polygon, Rectangle, Line, Arrow, Open Curve, Polyline, Circle, and Arc. Click a tool and drag the tool across the page to create a drawing or callout. *See Freehand tool.*

Format To assign characteristics to text, paragraphs, charts, pages, and so on. Formatting can include making a heading bold and centered as well as changing the color of the background of the entire page.

Freehand tool On the toolbox, the last button on the left. Click the tool and use it to draw freehand lines on the page.

Full Page view Displays one presentation page so that you can see the entire page in the window.

Gallery A dialog box containing various styles of tables, charts, graphs, and so on from which you can choose.

Handles Small black boxes that appear on the corners and sides of selected text blocks, chart boxes, tables, and so on, indicating the object is selected.

Heading The chart title, represented in large, bold, and centered type at the top of the chart box.

Help Press F1 at any time to view a Help screen describing the procedure or task in which you are working.

I-beam A representation of the mouse when it is in a text block or in a table, enabling the entering of text.

Justification Describes the alignment of text in a text block, table, or chart. Text can be left- or right-aligned, centered, or justified.

Justified text Text aligned so that it has flush-left and flush-right edges.

Label Text or numbers that identify points on the axis, such as the year, a value, percentage, and so on.

Layout The way in which a page is designed, or *laid out*; for example, one page may have a layout with a title and a list of bullets, whereas another page may show two charts and a title.

Left-aligned text Text that presents a flush left edge and a ragged right edge.

Legend Text and a sample pattern, symbol, or color to show which data is represented in the chart. Usually contained in a box.

Level In an organization chart, the division of entries by superior, subordinate, and so on.

Line chart A graph that represents data, usually to show trends or patterns over a period of time.

Menu A drop-down list of commands from which you can choose; the File menu, for example, contains related commands such as Open, Close, Exit, and so on.

Menu bar The horizontal strip near the top of the screen that contains available menus.

New Chart tool On the toolbox, the third button from the top. When clicked, the tool displays the New Chart Gallery dialog box with which you can create a new chart.

New Organization Chart tool On the toolbox, the fourth button from the top, on the right side. When clicked, the tool displays the Organization Chart Gallery dialog box so that you can create a new organization chart.

New Table tool On the toolbox, the fourth button from the top, on the left side of the tools. When clicked, this tool displays the Table Gallery dialog box so that you can create a new table.

Note Added text, up to three lines, that describes a condition, qualifiers, or other information about the chart, usually located below the x-axis title.

Organization chart A diagram illustrating the structure of a company, beginning with the president or CEO, for example, and continuing with the vice presidents, managers, and so on. The levels in the chart branch from a superior to a subordinate.

Page layout Any of eleven preformatted page styles in which you enter text, bulleted lists, charts, tables, and so on. The text is formatted and presented in "Click here..." text boxes; other "Click here..." boxes create tables, symbols, or charts. *See Click here.*

Page Sorter view A view in which you can see up to 12 pages of your presentation at a time; the pages are displayed as thumbnails. Use this view to rearrange the pages of the presentation.

Palette A dialog box containing various available colors for text, charts, tables, and so on; located within a style, editing, or other dialog box, and displays when you click the mouse pointer on a color choice.

Paragraph In Freelance, a paragraph can be several sentences, several words, one word, one character, or a blank line, as long as it ends with a paragraph mark created by pressing Enter.

Paragraph Style Attributes Attributes applied to specific styles, such as a Title, Subtitle, Bullet, and so on. You can change these attributes and apply the changes to all text in that same style throughout the presentation.

Paragraph Styles Any of three preformatted styles Freelance supplies for any text block. The bulleted lists, for example, use a second style that indents the text and applies a smaller bullet.

Pie chart A graph that represents data, usually comparing parts of the data (wedges) to the whole.

Presentation A printed or on-screen display of information and data pertinent to a service or product that is attractively formatted for quick and easy reading.

Preview A command button in many dialog boxes that enables you to look at the changes you have made in text, color, formatting, and so on before you accept them.

Promote In an organization chart, moving the status of an entry up, or toward the superior.

Resize To enlarge or reduce a text block, chart, table, and so on by dragging one of the handles with the mouse pointer; the mouse pointer changes to a double-headed arrow when it is in the right position to resize a box.

Right-aligned text Text that has a flush-right edge and a ragged-left edge.

Save Naming a presentation file so that you can use it later. Use Save As (File menu) to save the first time; after you make any changes to the file, use the Save command (File menu) to preserve those changes to the file.

Screen show Displaying the pages of a presentation on the computer screen, one at a time, to create a display for clients, coworkers, and so on.

Scroll bars Gray horizontal and vertical bars appearing on-screen, and sometimes in dialog boxes, that enable you to view those parts of the screen not within the window. Use the scroll bars by clicking the mouse on the arrows or by moving the scroll box.

Scroll box A small, light gray box appearing on a scroll bar. Click and drag the box along the scroll bar to quickly move to a new location.

Selecting To highlight text by dragging the I-beam over the text or by clicking a text block, chart, or other box to display the handles. Selected items can be edited, moved, deleted, copied, and so on.

Sizing Changing the size of a chart, text block, and so on by selecting it and then dragging one of the handles. *See Resize.*

SmartIcons Buttons, usually displayed below the menu bar, that provide shortcuts to such commands as Save, Open, Print, Cut, Paste, and so on.

SmartMaster sets Any of over 50 predesigned page layouts used for presentation backgrounds. Each set contains background colors or scenes and preformatted text in "Click here..." text blocks. *See Click here.*

Sorting Moving and rearranging pages in the presentation.

Speaker notes Notes you can create and print to aid the speaker when presenting the screen show, printed show, or overhead projections of the presentation.

Stacked Bar chart A graph that represents data, usually used to compare similar sets of data over time or to show the relationship of parts to the whole.

Style A preformatted appearance applied to type—such as fonts, indents, alignment, and so on.

Symbol A visual representation of an object, usually simply drawn for impact instead of detailed likeness. Freelance symbols include geometric shapes, animals, people, transportation, and so on.

Symbol tool On the toolbox, the last tool on the right. When clicked, the tool displays the Add Symbol to Page dialog box. Select a symbol to apply anywhere on the page in your presentation.

Table Textual information organized into columns and rows to present the data in a way that is easy to read and understand.

Text block A box in which you can enter and edit text. You can use either Freelance's "Click here..." text blocks or create your own. *See ABC icon.*

Title A preformatted style appearing in several of the page layouts, including the Title page, Bulleted list, 1 Chart, and so on.

Title page One of Freelance's page layout designs in which there are preassigned areas for a title, subtitle, and a symbol. Usually the first page of a presentation.

Toolbox A set of icons, usually located on the left of the screen, that enables you to enter text, create charts, edit tables, and so on. *See the individual tool names.*

Undo A command on the Edit menu that, when selected, reverses the last action you took. Not all actions can be undone. Pressing Ctrl+Z is a shortcut for the command.

x-axis The horizontal reference line in a chart.

y-axis The vertical reference line in a chart.

z-axis When creating a three-dimensional chart, the z-axis represents the reference line going from front to back.

Zoom In/Out view Freelance provides views for magnifying (Zoom In) and reducing (Zoom Out) the view of the page on the View menu.

Index

E

F-G

H-I

J-K

L

M

N

Index

T

U-W

X-Y-Z